CHINA
ENTREPRENEUR

Voices of Experience

FROM

40 INTERNATIONAL
BUSINESS PIONEERS

JUAN ANTONIO FERNANDEZ

LAURIE UNDERWOOD

JOHN WILEY & SONS (ASIA) PTE. LTD.

Other Wiley Editorial Offices
John Wiley & Sons, Inc., 111 River Street, Hoboken, NJ 07030, USA
John Wiley & Sons, Ltd., The Atrium, Southern Gate, Chichester,
    West Sussex P019 8SQ, UK
John Wiley & Sons (Canada), Ltd., 5353 Dundas Street West, Suite 400, Toronto, Ontario
    M9B 6H8, Canada
John Wiley & Sons Australia Ltd., 42 McDougall Street, Milton, Queensland 4064, Australia
Wiley-VCH, Boschstrasse 12, D-69469 Weinheim, Germany

Library of Congress Cataloging-in-Publication Data
ISBN: 978-0470-82321-7

Typeset in 11/13 point, Janson Text Roman by Thomson Digital

Printed in Singapore by Saik Wah Press Pte. Ltd.
10 9 8 7 6 5 4 3 2

To my wife, Wu Hanning and our son, Simon. Also, my deep thanks to China, the country that has given me so much.
—Juan Antonio Fernandez

China Entrepreneur *is dedicated to Madhav Timalsina, Dorothy Staley, Larry Underwood, Sydney and Schafer—the book would not have been possible without your love and support—and to the China Europe International Business School.*
—Laurie Underwood

Contents

Acknowledgments

This book is the result of the cooperation of many people. First, we wish to thank the 40 talented and adventurous China entrepreneurs from 25 countries or territories who so generously shared with us their experiences and hard-learned lessons. Their sole motivation in taking the time to share their insights with us was to help other entrepreneurs be successful in China's vast and vibrant, but maddeningly confusing, business environment. (See pages xx–xxv for a listing of all the interviewees in *China Entrepreneur.*)

We also wish to thank the three experts who offered additional advice for this book, drawn from their years of working in China.

In addition, we are grateful to the nine country representatives whose insightful comments on the key issues facing business managers in China are presented in the appendix to this book.

Finally, we thank the team of researchers who helped us with the interviews: Ms. Linda Song (Song Dongmei), Ms. Cheng Yiting, and Ms. Luyi Bo. We also express our sincere appreciation to the administrators and our colleagues at the China Europe International Business School for their support during the researching and writing of this book. Without CEIBS, neither our first book—*China CEO*—nor *China Entrepreneur* would have been born.

We also wish to thank all those who helped us to make contact with foreign entrepreneurs in China. Finally, we want to add special thanks to Robyn Flemming and Janis Soo for their excellent work.

Foreword

Professor Juan Antonio Fernandez and journalist Laurie Underwood, both members of CEIBS, have come out with another interesting book when we are still rereading their excellent text on successful chief executives in China. In the three years since their first book's publication, I have often seen *China CEO* being read by business class passengers during my frequent flights to China. With the world even more focused on China in 2009 than it was in 2006, I fully expect *China Entrepreneur* to be even more widely read by international business executives than its predecessor.

For their second joint book, Laurie Underwood and Juan Antonio Fernandez have turned their focus toward entrepreneurship—my field of interest as an academic. The authors have continued with their methodology of basing their book on interviews, in this case capturing the insights, anecdotes, and knowledge of 40 successful, China-based entrepreneurs, three China-based experts on different areas, and nine country representatives. Going out into the real world, using academic skills to raise relevant questions, and then using journalistic principles to present the interviewees' responses in an accessible manner, is an extraordinary task; and the results are useful, practical, and educational. The rigorous academic research and the authors' combined total of 24 years of working and living in greater China has created another richly information, carefully developed, but easy-to-read work.

Entrepreneurship is the art of spotting an opportunity and transforming it into business returns. It is the art of fast creation of value. How do entrepreneurs identify opportunities in China? How do they go about transforming a promising possibility into real business activity? Specifically, what are the best ways to handle the serious challenges in hiring, organizing, financing, and selling the new business?

In answering these questions, seasoned entrepreneurs and academics will likely agree that the basics are global. Even so, no one would dispute the fact that surviving in the complex and vast China market requires unique skills. This book, delivering the richness of 52 first-hand perspectives, provides readers with many reference points for understanding—and even practicing—entrepreneurship in China. For any international businessperson working in or with China, I have every confidence that this book will bring you closer to realizing your China dreams.

Pedro Nueno
Professor of Entrepreneurship
Executive President
China Europe International Business School

Introduction

"We had a couple of crazy experiences that tested my commitment
to starting my company in China. Our first customer was also a
potential competitor, a well connected local company. They had
a very large deal with us (but later) . . . I guess they felt
threatened that we would take away their customer. That wasn't
my intention, but they still felt threatened.

They knew we hadn't got our business license yet, and that we
were very poorly funded, so they decided to attack us. Their
intention was to try to scare me out of China, and force my staff
to join them. What they did was tell the police in Hangzhou that
we had placed an espionage code into the telecom system. That is
a very serious offense in China. It wasn't true, but who knows
whether truth is the deciding factor in these cases in China?

So, one Friday afternoon, at 5.30, the police showed up at our
office. It was a very dangerous situation because I didn't have a
business license, so I didn't have any ground to stand on. I didn't
have a lawyer either, as I'd never really needed a lawyer before.
The police locked our door and put a seal across it. I thought I was
going to be arrested for espionage!"

Interviewee, China Entrepreneur

Why Read *China Entrepreneur?*

Have you ever dreamed of launching a business venture in the world's largest, fastest growing, and most dynamic consumer market? Many adventurous businesspeople from around the world have dreamt this dream, and more are joining them as China matures, opens, and internationalizes.

But as the anecdote in previous page shows, launching an enterprise in China can be fraught with more perils than even the most adventurous businessperson might anticipate. (For the full story of the fake espionage case, see the case study titled "The Price of weak *Guanxi*" on pages 154–155.)

It was the stories which foreign entrepreneurs in China shared with us of their "big China dreams"—as well as their "China nightmares"—that inspired us to embark on writing *China Entrepreneur: Voices of Experience from 40 International Business Pioneers.*

In the year following the release of our first book, *China CEO: Voices of Experience from 20 International Business Leaders* (John Wiley & Sons, 2006), the reception from readers worldwide was far beyond our expectations. Within 18 months, the book had sold 25,000 copies in English and had been translated into Chinese (both traditional and simplified characters), Vietnamese, Indonesian, and Korean.

Since the first book's launch, we authors have spoken to thousands of businesspeople in Asia, Europe, and America, all of whom share an interest in doing business in China. Most satisfying have been the numerous times we have spoken with business executives working in China, who have commented: "This is exactly what I went through when I got here. I'm going to give this book to my new directors coming into China from Europe (or the U.S., or Australia, or India . . .)."

But another message we heard quite often, whether we were speaking to business associations, chambers of commerce, trade delegations, or business school students, was this: *What about small business owners entering China?* As one Australian businesswoman said during a book talk: "I'm not GE. I'm just me. I don't have an army of people helping me deal with the government here. What advice do you have for *me*?"

So, in 2008, we again ventured into the China market with our digital recorders in hand to collect first-hand accounts of foreign (non-Chinese) businesspeople who had succeeded in launching their own businesses in the China market. Using our differing strengths in academia and business journalism, we aimed to produce a meticulously researched, yet easy-to-read guide to starting and managing a successful small business in China. As with *China CEO*, we sought to draw upon our strong points— Dr. Juan Antonio Fernandez's strengths as a professor of Management at the China Europe International Business School, where he has taught since 1999, and Ms. Laurie Underwood's 15 years of business journalism expertise in greater China (before joining CEIBS as Director of External Communications and Development).

More "Blood, Sweat, and Tears"

In crafting *China Entrepreneur*, we began by interviewing a select profile of business pioneers—expatriates who had successfully launched a business of their own in China, rather than executives who had been sent to China with the backing of a well-established multinational corporation. Although we had originally planned to interview the founders of 20 successful startups, we ended up talking with twice that number. Each interview seemed to lead to yet another pioneer with another fascinating tale of having triumphed over the business challenges that the entrepreneur faces in China. Several weeks into the project, we knew we were gathering valuable material for a second book. As one of our draft manuscript readers, Shanghai-based entrepreneur John Van Fleet, put it: "There is a lot of blood, sweat, and tears in these interviews."

Who is in This Book?

By the time we had finished interviewing for *China Entrepreneur*, we had painstakingly tape-recorded, videotaped, and transcribed detailed interviews with 52 experts on China, each offering a wealth of insights into their experiences in this unique—and uniquely challenging—market.

Our interviewees are composed of three types of experts:

1. *Entrepreneurs (40):* Hailing from 25 nations and working in different industries (see Tables 1 and 2), these 40 daring pioneers successfully started businesses in China, and lived to share their experiences with us. While this group works across a wide range of industries—from software to real estate, restaurants to fashion retailing—it also includes seven consultant entrepreneurs who not only share their own first-hand information on launching their companies but also draw upon the insights formed through working with hundreds of clients.

2. *Experts/advisors (3):* These professional China hands (see Table 3) offer insights into their areas of expertise, including Chinese law, negotiation, and entrepreneurship.

3. *Country representatives (9):* We interviewed a series of China-based commercial officers, directors of chambers of commerce, and business associations representing key trade nations (see Table 4). These country representatives represent Africa (South Africa and Nigeria), the Americas (the United States, Mexico, and Brazil), Asia (India and Japan), Australia, and the European Union. The interviews, included in Q&A format in the appendix to the book, give readers an understanding of the specific challenges and opportunities that exist in China for businesspeople from different nations. They also offer insightful comments on how China is perceived by the business community in their countries, on trade and investment trends, on the sectors they consider most promising for business in China, and on the experiences of companies that are already established in China.

Profile of the Entrepreneur Interviewees

While our pioneers hail from 25 countries and provinces, they have certain shared characteristics. The average interviewee is aged 47, has an MBA, is married, has been in China for 12 years, speaks basic-or-above Chinese, and has been operating his or her current business for nine years. Among the 40 interviewees, 33 are men, and seven are women. (In *China CEO*, all 20 of the CEOs we interviewed were men, as we were unsuccessful in finding women CEOs to interview.)

China Entrepreneur interviewees' countries/provinces of origin are as follows:

- North America: 10 (United States, 9, Canada, 1)
- Latin America: 2 (Brazil, 1, Mexico, 1)
- Europe: 13 (Belgium, Denmark, France, Netherlands (3), Ireland, Italy, Macedonia, Spain, Switzerland, U.K. (England, Scotland))
- Middle East: 4 (Iran, Israel (2), Turkey)
- Asia: 8 (India, Japan (2), Korea, Taiwan (3), Singapore)
- Australia: 1
- Africa: 2 (Morocco, South Africa)

Their places of origin are indicated on the map.

The composite profile of the China entrepreneurs we interviewed would be a 47-year-old who has lived and worked in China for 12 years, speaks Chinese well, has an MBA, is married, and started his or her own business nine years ago."

The Authors, China Entrepreneur

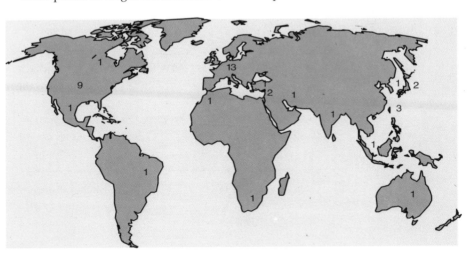

In total, our 40 entrepreneurs have a combined 500 years of experience in China.

In terms of education, the most popular degree among our interviewees was MBA (17), followed by Bachelor of Arts (13), while five had advanced degrees (three master's degrees and two PhDs). Concerning Chinese language ability, aside from our four native Chinese speakers (who held non-Chinese passports), most had achieved an intermediate (15) or advanced (11) level of Chinese. Only three interviewees said they had a "less-than-basic" ability in Chinese. Most were married (30). In 12 of these cases, their spouses were from greater China (including Taiwan).

Our interviewees represent a full range of business sectors. In addition, our featured entrepreneurs run the gamut of business operations. In terms of their China operations, 22 of the interviewees operated a foreign invested enterprise (FIE), while 14 ran an offshore entity or a representative office, and seven operate as Chinese-owned companies (via a Chinese partner). In total, our 40 entrepreneurs have a combined 500 years of experience in China.

The following tables introduce our interviewees in more detail. Table 1 identifies the entrepreneur interviewees.

TABLE 1

Entrepreneur Interviewees

Name	Country of Origin	Company	Primary Business	Website
Bernstein, Jeffrey	USA	Emerge Logistics Shanghai Co.	Import/export logistics, market entry consulting, sales & distribution	www.emergelogistics.com www.emergechina.com
Branham, Phillip E.	USA	B & L Group, Inc.	Project management, construction management & procurement	www.blgroupinc.com
Carroll, Ken	Ireland	Kai En English Training Center, Praxis Language, On Demand Training	Education/ training	www.ken-carroll.com

Name	Country of Origin	Company	Primary Business	Website
Chu, David	USA	Shanghai Venture Partners	Capital raising & financial advisory services	www.shanghaivp.com
Chun In Kyu	Korea	Shanghai Asset Inc.	Financial investments advisor	NA
Di Rollo, Jonathan	UK, Scotland	Career Development China (HK) Co. Ltd.	Consulting education	www.propathchina.com
Firoozi, Shah	USA/Iran	The PAC Group	Project management, product development, vehicle management development	www.pacgroup.com
Heffernan, Susan	Australia	Soozar	Industrial design, high-end retail displays and furnishings	www.soozar.com
Hsui, Jenny	Singapore	ChinaVest	Merchant bank, M&A, private placement, financial advisor	www.Chinavest.com
Lichtenberg, Simon	Denmark	Trayton Group	Furniture: design, manufacturing, distribution, retailing	www.trayton.com
Ling, Winston	Brazil	1. Fully Strong Ltd. (HK) 2. Yi Cai He Exciting Ventures International Ltd.	Import, export, & distribution	www.madeinbrazil.com.cn

Name	Country of Origin	Company	Primary Business	Website
Litjens, Olaf	Netherlands	Unisono Fieldmarketing (Shanghai) Co.	Field marketing, brand activation	www.unisonofieldmarketing.com
Martinez, Juan	Mexico	Solis Holdings Import & Export (SOLHIX)	Trading	www.solhix.com www.aquienchina.com
Menon, Prakash[1]	India	NIIT (China)	IT education & training	www.niit.com
Mrabet, Aziz	Morocco	Impact Promotional Items	Export	www.impact-promo-items.com
Oztunali, Onder Bogac	Turkey	Globe Stone Corp.	Building materials— natural stone products	www.globestonestudio.com
Pannekeet, Nic	Netherlands	CHC Business Development	Export of cleaning products, industrial accessories	NA
Petroski, Oto	Macedonia	Trading company	Exporting	NA
Pummell, Mark	UK, England	1. Sinapse 2. ChinArt 3. Music Pavilion	1. Psycho-therapy 2. Fine art export/import 3. Musical instruments, recording studio	www.sinapse.com.cn www.chinart.co.uk www.doublebass.com.cn
Robertson, Bruce	USA	Asia Pacific Real Estate Ltd	Property development	brucerobertson65@hotmail.com
Rongley, Eric	USA	Bleum	Offshore software outsourcing	www.bleum.com

Name	Country of Origin	Company	Primary Business	Website
Secchia, Mark	USA	Sherpa's	Call center & courier services	www.sherpa.com.cn
Suzuki, Fumito	Japan	AOI Business Consultant	Accounting services	NA
Tai, Wendy	Taiwan (China)	Haus658	Interior decorative items	www.haus658.com
Theleen, Robert	USA	ChinaVest	Merchant bank, M&A, private placement, financial advisor	www.Chinavest.com
Touya, Valerie	France	Curiosity Fashion Store	Fashion distribution	valerietouya@yahoo.fr
Van der Chijs, Marc	Netherlands	Tudou	Website	www.tudou.com
Woo, Marjorie	USA	Management International (China)	Leadership development training	www.lmi-china.com
Wu, Chee-Chin	Canada	Novalis International	Luxury floor tiles	www.novalis-intl.com
Yang, Michael	Taiwan (China)	East West Restaurant	Restaurants	NA
Yu, Maggie	Taiwan (China)	Asian BizCenter & Consulting Co. Ltd.	Serviced offices, China market entry consulting, business registration, bookkeeping & tax services	www.asianbizcenter.com

Name	Country of Origin	Company	Primary Business	Website
Zilber, Aviel	Israel	Sheng Enterprises	Business development & investment	www.sheng-cn.com
Zilber, Jordan	Israel	Sheng Enterprises	Business development & investment	www.sheng-cn.com

[1] While not the founder of NIIT (India), Mr. Menon started the operations of the company in China from scratch and went through the same process as the other entrepreneurs.

The seven consultants listed in Table 2 contributed to this book in terms of both their experience as China-based entrepreneurs and their expertise as consultants to hundreds of clients in China.

TABLE 2

Consultant-Entrepreneur Interviewees

Name	Country of Origin	Company	Primary Business	Website
Borgonjon, Jan	Belgium	InterChina Consulting	Consulting	www.interchinaconsulting.com
Ganster, Steven H.	USA	Technomic Asia	Management consulting	www.technomicasia.com
Giro, Josep	Spain	SBC & Associates Co. Ltd.	Consulting	NA
Jenna, Ruggero	Italy	Value Partners	Management consulting	ruggero.jenna@valuepartners.com www.valuepartners.com
Musy, Nicolas	Switzerland	CH-ina (Shanghai) Co. Ltd.	Integrated China entry solutions & operations	www.ch-ina.com
Shoda, Hiroshi	Japan	Shoda & Partners Co.	Consulting	hiroshishoda@tcn-catv.ne.jp
Van der Wath, Kobus	South Africa	The Beijing Axis	Business bridge for MNCs going into China and Chinese going international	www.thebeijingaxis.com

The three expert advisors listed in Table 3 added their experience in the fields of entrepreneurship, negotiation, and law in China.

Name	Country of Origin	Title	Organization	Website
Ge, Dingkun	China	Prof. of Strategy and Entrepreneurship	CEIBS	www.ceibs.edu
Slusiewicz, Gene	USA	Negotiation expert	The PAC Group	www.PACgroup.com gene.slusiewicz@pacgroup.com
Sunyer, Lluis	Spain	Consultant & lawyer	Guangsheng & Partners	www.shslaw.com luis.sunyer@shslaw.com

TABLE 3

Expert Advisor Interviewees

Finally, the nine country representatives listed in Table 4 added insights on doing business in China from the perspective of the countries they represent. These interviews appear as an appendix at the end of the book.

Name	Country	Organization	Website
Wright, Christopher	Australia	Senior Trade Commissioner and Australian Deputy Consul General, in Shanghai	www.austrade.gov.au
Primo Portugal, Ricardo	Brazil	Deputy Consul General, Brazilian Consulate in Shanghai	www.brazil.org.cn
Ceballos Baron, Miguel	European Union	EU Counselor, Trade & Investment, Beijing Office	www.delchn.ec.europa.eu
Sharma, Madhav	India	Chief Representative, Confederation of Indian Industry	www.ciionline.org
Takahara, Masaki	Japan	Vice President, (China) Japan External Trade Organization (JETRO)	www.jetro.go.jp/china/shanghai/

TABLE 4

Country Representative Interviewees (country by alphabetical order)

I think people should talk to other entrepreneurs. Recently, I was involved in a young entrepreneur organization. I realized that I should have been involved in it at the very beginning, because people here tell you the real stories. You hear real stories from people who have been through it before."

Susan Heffernan
(Australia), Founder and Managing Director, Soozar

Name	Country	Organization	Website
Valdez Mingramm, Rafael	Mexico (& Latin America)	Co-founder, Latinoamericanos EnChina.com VP Latin America, ChinaVest	www.chinavest.com www.latinoamericanosenchina.com
Abikoye, Badeji A.	Nigeria	Trade Commissioner, Nigerian Trade Office in Shanghai	www.nigeriaembassy.cn
Khumalo, Vika M.	South Africa	Consul General, South African Consulate in Shanghai	NA
Foster, Brenda L.	USA	President, American Chamber of Commerce in Shanghai	www.amcham-shanghai.org

What We Cover

The goal of *China Entrepreneur* is simply this: to help non-Chinese businesspeople who are interested in doing business in the Middle Kingdom to clearly understand the challenges, risks, and opportunities. Our focus on small businesses and startups helps to outline the challenges faced by pioneers who launch and operate their own ventures, rather than beginning in China with the backing of a global company. As one of our entrepreneurs told us, "I think people should talk to other entrepreneurs. Recently, I was involved in a young entrepreneur organization. I realized that I should have been involved in it at the very beginning, because people here tell you the *real* stories. You hear real stories from people who have been through it before."

The purpose of our book is to collect and share those "real stories" and real advice from real China entrepreneurs.

Chapter 1
Getting Started

Understanding the Business Environment and Dealing with the Chinese Government

THEN: "I came to China in 1976 as a young banker. . . . We had friends doing business in China in those years who were thrown in jail for the slightest little infraction. If I had to choose one word to define that era in China, it is 'courage.' It was courage that drove those men and women who had no guidelines for what they were doing."

Robert Theleen (USA), Chairman, ChinaVest

NOW: "The opening of China—the access to the WTO trading culture, and especially the influence of American and European companies—has created new role models and icons in China. In the past, role models were national heroes like Lei Feng. Now, it is Bill Gates, Michael Dell; they are the role models, with their rags-to-riches stories."

Ge Dingkun (China), Professor of Strategy and Entrepreneurship, CEIBS

Introduction

In order to appreciate the complexity of the environment in China for international entrepreneurs, it is useful first to look backward and review the realities of the past. Only then can you gauge how great a transformation has been necessary to create the realities of the present. In this chapter, we start by looking back to when China first began to open up to the outside world. We draw upon the first-hand experiences of two of the first non-Chinese businesspeople to work in China during that era—American banker Robert Theleen and his Singaporean wife Jenny Hsui, who were invited to China as advisors to the central government in the late 1970s. Theleen and Hsui, who now operate ChinaVest, a successful investment bank, paint a detailed picture of China at its opening, in order to remind newcomers of just how far the nation has come in the past 30 years. From there, several other "not quite so experienced" China hands take the reader through the past two decades, leading to the dynamic business environment of today, while also giving expert advice on how to deal with the Chinese government.

This chapter covers six main topics:

1. The past: China opens its doors
2. The transition: China in the 1990s
3. The present: "Better for entrepreneurs than Silicon Valley"
4. Dealing with the Chinese government
5. Bureaucratic challenges for entrepreneurs
6. Strategies for successful government relations

The Past: China Opens its Doors

Operating effectively in China's evolving business environment, especially for international entrepreneurs, first requires an appreciation for the fact that the nation's "open for business" status is still quite new.

Several of our interviewees offered a first-hand perspective on the transformation of the past 20 or even 30 years. American finance expert and businessman Robert Theleen describes his arrival in China in 1976 as a rare foreign guest of the central government, invited to give a lecture at the Ministry of Petroleum. At that time, he worked as petroleum banker for a Texas bank specializing in offshore petroleum finance. Here is his account of his first official visit to pre-reform China:

Petroleum was the very first major foreign industry to enter China back in that period. [The Chinese government] was very interested. I had an invitation to speak to a delegation, but how that happened was an oddity. I received a note at Peking Hotel that said, "Be outside the hotel on the corner of Wangfujing at 7 o'clock at night." I went out of the hotel to the designated place at the designated time. It was a spooky environment out in the street in 1976. There was an old Hongqiao limo waiting outside, China's imitation of a Rolls-Royce. A man opened the door and told me to get into the car. I didn't know what I was getting into—it was right out of a *James Bond* movie.

We drove to a remote site far away from the eyes of any other foreigners. I entered a kind of conference room. There were about 40 people sitting there, stone-faced. There was an interpreter who told me in English, "Thank you for coming. This is a delegation from the Ministry of Petroleum and they are here to listen to your remarks." Wow! Only then did I know what I was doing!

They asked me to talk about financing petroleum. We talked about every aspect of the petroleum industry: exploration, production, equipment financing, rigs drilling—you know, the whole industry. So, I talked about it. It went on and on until the [cigarette] smoke filled the room. At the end, one member of the group told me, "You must come back. We need to learn about this industry." So, I went back and forth to China from that time on. I would meet government officials in one place or another. Then I started to think about China as a place to do business.

"

I saw a nation that had no hope, but it had a strong desire to improve, to get out of the bottom. The rapid changes that took place afterwards can only be explained by seeing what China was then."

Robert Theleen, (USA), Founder and Chairman, ChinaVest, speaking on China in the 1970s.

Such was the hair-raising start to Theleen's career in China, which has so far spanned three decades. Through the mid- and late 1970s, he traveled regularly to China. It was a time he describes as "like going into a black-and-white movie in the 1930s or 1940s—everything was black and white, or should I say green and blue?" (Theleen is referring to the government-issued, coarsely made blue or green pants and "Mao jackets" that both men and women wore during those years.)

Theleen says that seeing China during the years before the economic reforms of the 1980s was "a privilege, because it helps me to understand the changes the nation went through." He describes China 30 years ago as being "absolutely at the bottom" in terms of national spirit and pride. "I saw a nation that had no hope, but it had a strong desire to improve, to get out of the bottom. The rapid changes that took place afterwards can only be explained by seeing what China was then."

Theleen recalls another of those early groundbreaking meetings. "We were invited to Beijing to give the first seminar on venture capital ever given in China. I'll never forget that. The institution was the newly created China Development Bank." As he was addressing the participants, Theleen realized that they included the vice governor of the Development Bank, who went on to become the chairman of the China Banking and Regulatory Commission, one of the most powerful positions in the government today. At the end of the seminar, the vice governor said to him: "No one has ever spoken to us about this. We had no knowledge of this."

During those years, Theleen says, it took courage for businesspeople to be pioneers in the Chinese market, and for government officials to support the efforts to open and internationalize China. "You can use different words to describe China's change, but I think the best way to describe it was as an act of national courage. Everything else is the consequence of that; everything you can say about *development*, *decision-making*, and the *Four Modernizations*. Those are all rather flat words. It was about *courage*."

Together with his wife and partner Jenny Hsui, Theleen launched ChinaVest, one of the first venture capital funds, in

1981. Hsui recalls how playing the role of foreign "educator" could still be a dangerous mission even then: "When we first brought up the subject of venture capital at the central government level, the [officials] didn't understand," Hsui says. "We actually used the word 'risk capital' at a meeting with the Planning Commission of the Bureau of Financial State Funds, and [the top official] stopped us—I mean *loudly* stopped us. He said: 'In China, there is no risk. There is no such thing as risk. You do not have any risk when you invest in China.' So, we changed the term to 'enterprise capital.'"

Another anecdote recalls the atmosphere of austerity and caution that permeated Chinese society at the time. Theleen tells of the first time he was invited to meet alone with a senior official. "It was a demonstration of real trust. [The official] said, 'I want to continue this conversation. Instead of having a formal lunch somewhere, why don't we go someplace very close to here, somewhere very casual.' . . . So, we arrived at this little restaurant. It was a hot summer day and he said, 'Do you mind if we take off our jackets?' I had never seen an official without his Mao jacket on; it was unheard of. Under his Mao jacket, he was wearing a beautiful shirt with gold cufflinks. I was stunned. He smiled when he saw my face. He told me about the shop in Hong Kong where he had bought the shirt. 'In the West,' he said, 'you can express yourself on the outside, wearing beautiful things. In China, we have to wear them on the inside.'"

Beyond the government offices, the mindset of the general public was even more closed and cautious. Says Theleen: "The country was a blank palette. You remember Mao's famous quote: 'The Chinese peasant is poor and blank.' *Everyone* in China was poor and blank then. 'Blank' was the right word; it was the effect of the Cultural Revolution. The Revolution simply erased everything, the entire society. There was nothing to build on."

Still struggling to regain its footing after the Cultural Revolution, China was a nation unsure about which direction to take, says Theleen. The country was in a state of turmoil politically, socially, and economically. Anyone wishing to venture into the business areas that were beginning to open up faced real personal dangers. Although Theleen and Hsui went through all the proper legal channels to establish their company, only the bravest Chinese dared to interact or do business with them. The political and social environment was one of such upheaval that Chinese citizens generally felt extremely insecure. Theleen says of his first employee: "She was very nervous when she came to work for the first time. I said, 'Why you are so nervous?' and she said, 'Because when I go to work for you, you have to understand that I cut myself off from my entire life. I have no support from the state, I have no health-care, I have nothing. . . . I am throwing myself into the bitter sea.'" While this phrase would make a modern Chinese employee laugh, Theleen says that, back then, it was a real act of courage to choose to work for a foreign company.

Beijing Disco Scene, circa 1976

Robert Theleen relates this telling anecdote about the culture clash that existed between China and the West in the mid-1970s. He was on his first visit to China, with a group of foreign tourists. "One of the persons on this tour was a fantastic Venezuelan businessman named George. He was my image of a debonair South American businessman—witty, smart, elegant. We had a lot of fun together despite China being so communist, so rigid. The tour guides were like Red Guards: everyone had to be up at 5 am, breakfast at 6 am, and so on."

When the tour reached Beijing, the group stayed in Friendship Hotel, which Theleen describes as "Russian-designed, drab, grim, gray . . . like a prison." But inside, the managers had an idea. "It was a cold winter day. The hotel management thought, 'Maybe we could make a few coins out of these foreigners!' So, they hung a little hand-painted sign in funny English saying: 'The opening of our new disco tonight.' George, being a good Latino, insisted on going to the disco, which entailed an entrance fee of 5 yuan in Foreign Exchange Currency [a special currency for foreigners, used in the 1970s and 1980s]."

Inside, the two found "a sad room, with huge sad Christmas tree lights on the ceiling and an ancient record player playing ancient music." Theleen describes what happened:

After a few beers, George became agitated. "This is not right," he says. "In my country, in a discothèque, you have men and women. Do you see any women

Foreign business pioneers in China—including Theleen and Hsui—also needed a fair amount of chutzpah. As the chapter-opening quote describes, Chinese friends of Theleen were thrown in jail "for the slightest little infraction." A Chinese citizen who moved quickly to take advantage of the new business opportunities—for example, if he or she took a job with a foreign company, or began trading with foreigners, or befriended a foreigner—ran the risk of being criticized if the Communist Party line were to shift away suddenly from opening up China to the world. In those early years, when the ground was uncharted

here, Roberto?" Then he goes up to the manager and says: "This is wrong. Disco means a place with men and women and dancing. Where are the women?" He says this to the guy like 10 times, and the guy was stone-faced. I said, "George, I don't want to get thrown in jail for this. Come on. . . ." And he says, "I don't care. In my country. . ." and so on.

We sit there drinking a few more beers and I forgot about the incident. An hour later, 10 women from the People's Liberation Army march into the room! This is true. They were dressed in uniform, very serious—boots, PLA uniform. One woman—I think she was the designated speaker, because she could speak a little English—comes up to me with this very serious face and asks me, very mechanically: "Hello, my name is Mei Lin. Do you wish to dance with me?"

Ah! George was so happy! "I *told* you, I *told* you!" he said. "The problem is you are too American; you have to be more Latino!"

We danced with each of these women. Within half an hour, George was leading a conga line around the room. Here I was, dancing with the leader of the third division of the first army of the People's Liberation Army women's attachment. Within five minutes, these women's hearts just melted and they were having fun. They were also frightened that they were actually having a nice time with these two crazy foreign guys—that's how totally isolated they were at the time. But when they started dancing, how quickly their eyes changed!

and there were few business regulations or useful precedents, any misstep could easily backfire and be deemed illegal.

Theleen himself received threats after setting up business in China. "In the early years, a government official once put a note under our door. In Chinese, it said: 'If you cheat us, you could go to jail.' That meant, you know, jail forever. We could have been killed."

The Transition: China in the 1990s

A small but diverse group of foreign businesspeople had been allowed into China when the country started opening up during the early 1980s. Theleen describes an extremely close-knit expatriate community in China during those years, completely different from today's competitive environment. "In those years, the [government] put all foreigners in two hotels [in Beijing]: Peking Hotel and Friendship Hotel. They wanted to keep us isolated, but they didn't realize that this was good for us. By keeping all the foreigners in one place, they created the greatest intelligence network you could have imagined. All of us shared information. We'd visit each other's rooms and ask, 'What deal did you cut?' or 'Did you hear about that Mr. Wang? Avoid that guy.' The networking was incredible. It didn't matter if you were American or German or Bulgarian. . . . We shared information with other foreigners whatever their nationalities were."

From an atmosphere of fear and uncertainty in the early 1980s, China's economic reforms began to take root, and then to mushroom, during the mid- and latter part of the decade, especially after Deng Xiaoping's famous tour of Southern China, during which he declared, "To get rich is glorious." Theleen describes the late 1980s: "The country went fast forward, and some important economic decisions were starting to be made. Some decisions were awkward and used to drive everyone crazy, but China made some very interesting decisions almost by accident."

Several of our interviewees began their China business dealings in the 1990s and describe a period of optimism, along with chaos and uncertainty. There was less fear and more frustration, but also, ultimately, greater chances of success.

Danish furniture entrepreneur Simon Lichtenberg describes the chaotic but vibrant environment in China when he arrived in 1993. "At that time, so many things were so new. It was a mess. The concept of having a business license was new at the time. So, there were lots of people doing business without having a company—I'm talking cash business. I spoke Chinese and I could get myself around Shanghai, so I could get around things, but it was a mess."

American real estate entrepreneur Bruce Robertson describes the mood of promise and potential that lured him to China from Hong Kong and Singapore in 1994: "There were all kinds of crazy, crazy things going on in the early nineties. But it was clear to me that there were business opportunities, especially as an entrepreneur. I saw that immediately. I also saw that my business wasn't really required in Singapore and in Hong Kong. The opportunity was going to be in China."

Robertson describes an overriding optimism among businesspeople then: "I had this vision that China was going to be an enormous, rising economy that would float all the boats—even if you were in trouble, you were still going to rise."

Once he began doing business in China, Robertson quickly recognized the newness and instability of the business environment. "In 1994, and for the following few years, China was in a transitional state. Sometimes, it was very difficult to tell whether it was a free enterprise system, or whether the government was still calling all the shots."

Other long-timers agree that China was an easier market to crack back in the late 1980s and early 1990s, especially if your company had good relations and contacts. Says Swiss consultant Nicolas Musy: "Everything was much easier then. Fifteen years ago, it was stricter in terms of restrictions on the type of business you could do, but actually operating was much easier. At that time, there was always a way to do anything through your contacts."

On the positive side, says Belgian consultant Jan Borgonjon, the regulations may be stricter now, but they are also generally clearer and more transparently applied. "In the late 1990s, even until a few years ago, the environment had no clear rules. You had to be very, very careful. Now, it has improved, but it's still not easy."

Danish entrepreneur Simon Lichtenberg agrees with Borgonjon that cheating is still a danger in China, as the case study below illustrates.

CASE STUDY

COWBOY TIME

Simon Lichtenberg, one of the early foreign pioneers doing business in China, first stayed in the country as a Chinese student in 1987, and has lived there permanently since 1993. He describes an incident that occurred when he started doing business in China in the early 1990s:

We sold 10,000 tons of Ukrainian steel wire coil to the largest import–export company in Shanghai. (This was before I did any furniture business.) It happened that there was no steel. The Ukrainian supplier was a crook, but we didn't know this. So, the Shanghai trader had opened a US$1.6 million letter of credit to the Ukrainian, but there was no steel. The Shanghai importer had already resold the steel to a company in Ningbo that was actually owned by the police department. This would never happen today—a company being owned by the police department. Those policemen had taken out a high-interest loan to buy the steel. So, when the steel didn't come, the Ningbo police bureau was in trouble.

We weren't responsible for the mess and, besides, the US$1.6 million hadn't disappeared because the letter of credit was still standing. The Shanghai importer then canceled the letter of credit and everything was settled, *except* the Ningbo police were in trouble because they owed big money to the loan shark.

The Present: "Better for Entrepreneurs than Silicon Valley"

Given the strict anti-entrepreneurial environment of 30 years ago, and the chaotic transition since then, just how welcoming is China today for international businesspeople interested in starting a venture?

Consider the following assessment of the current environment by Ge Dingkun, Professor of Strategy and Entrepreneurship at the China Europe International Business School (CEIBS) in Shanghai. Professor Ge describes China's current environment

There was only one guy for the Ningbo police to go after—me. So, one day, the Shanghai importer told me I needed to come to his office to discuss this steel case. I went to his office on the sixth floor in the beautiful but worn-down 27 on the Bund, next to the Bank of China. I arrived there and met the Ningbo police guys. Only at that point did I learn that the steel had been resold-on to black market police crooks! There were six of them, driving Mercedes S600s—black suits and shades, and probably guns in the trunks. Seriously. It was a different China, I tell you. They locked the door. Those guys were very, very powerful and not subject to the law; no one could touch them. They told me, "You either give us the steel or US$200,000 now, or you are not going to leave this room."

I had no money. I told them, "You can throw me into the Huangpu River or whatever, but you won't get any money out of me because I have no money. You can kill me, or break my arms, but you can't get any money."

I was there for eight hours. It was like a bad movie—a very different China, for sure. Finally, when they really realized I had no money to give them, they let me go.

"Today, this could still happen in Sichuan, or in Guangxi or Gansu," Lichtenberg says, "but not in Shanghai."

for entrepreneurs as "more welcoming" than California's Silicon Valley, the world-famous entrepreneurial hot spot where he studied, worked, and taught for four years before returning to his native China. China today is "a really good place to start a company," he says, with all the elements that startups need in order to take root and thrive.

First and foremost, Ge says, is high demand. "Demand is much more pronounced in a high-growth economy like China than in a developed nation. There is a huge market demand for products and services here. If you simply modify existing products slightly to improve them, someone will buy them." In developed markets, by contrast, entrepreneurs generally must work much harder to improve upon existing products and attract consumers, Ge says. "On the one hand, China's traditional state-owned enterprises, and many former SOEs, are not efficient. On the other hand, demand is strong. So there is asymmetry — low supply and high demand." Given this environment, Ge says, entrepreneurs in China can succeed by offering a product or service that is slightly better, faster, or cheaper than existing suppliers. "In China, many people are seeking better products, but there are still not many choices."

Government support is the second key ingredient in China's currently welcoming environment for entrepreneurs, according to Ge. "Basically, the Chinese government is very favorable to entrepreneurs." He points out that, especially for startups in the high-value-added fields that the Chinese government is seeking to promote, such as R&D and biotech, businesspeople can receive licenses and approvals in a matter of weeks, whereas such applications took a year to process in the past. "China can now be one of the world's most efficient countries for starting a business. Depending on where your new business is registered, it may take from two weeks to two months," says Ge. "It is up to the entrepreneur to search and find the right place to establish the company." (Note that not all of our entrepreneurs experienced this world-class efficiency, as will be apparent later in this chapter.)

Ge does cite one disadvantage of China, as compared to the United States: the lack of developed government agencies or banks offering startup funding. While venture capital money is pouring into China, many venture capitalists prefer to fund ventures that are already up and running, Ge says. Thus, finding seed money in China can be extremely challenging (see Chapter 3).

Overall, though, Ge believes that China is the right place at the right time for many types of entrepreneurs, even international ones. "I tell my students, 'If you want to start a company [in China], start now. Ten years from now, competitors will all be here.' Many, many industries are consolidating already. In the future, the entry barriers in many industries will be huge."

Dealing with the Chinese Government

Our international entrepreneurs' experiences with government entities in China varied widely across companies and industries. Indeed, some of our interviewees had as "rosy" a view as Professor Ge. Iranian-born American entrepreneur Shah Firoozi expresses a typical cautious optimism, explaining that there are many promising opportunities in China, but that they are not easy to find: "China is very complicated. There is no single rule that applies to the whole country." Firoozi says that operating in China requires constantly researching evolving rules and regulations nationwide, so as to keep up with the shifting situation. "If you miss out on a new perk—such as tax breaks in Western China or new incentives for those in the IT field—your competitors may find it before you. You really have to be on your toes in this country; you have to really be in touch. It's very difficult for foreigners to do that. There is so much information, that you will never know it all—and it is even worse if you don't speak the language."

For American real estate entrepreneur Bruce Robertson, setting up his business venture in China was a quick and painless process. One of his earliest projects even came together far faster

I tell my students, 'If you want to start a company [in China], start now. Ten years from now, competitors will all be here.' Many, many industries are consolidating already. In the future, the entry barriers in many industries will be huge."

Ge Dingkun, Professor of Strategy and Entrepreneurship, China Europe International Business School in China than it could have in his native U.S., he says. "With my first [construction] project in China, the time from when I signed my initial commitment letter to do the project, to when I finished my construction work, was 10 months. No one challenged our project or caused us any trouble. It's interesting; in a country with a communist system, you would think the government would be all over you. In fact, it was clear sailing right through the project." But it hasn't *all* been smooth sailing; Robertson's 14 years in China have also brought periods of frustration, delay, and near disaster. (See the case study "The Trouble with Facing South," later in this chapter.)

Dutch internet entrepreneur Marc van der Chijs cites the stresses of doing business in China when the government unexpectedly changes the rules. "You may be out of business if they change the rules. Rules can be changed at any time. So, if it's your first time doing business in China, you take high risks."

It is accurate to say that each of our 40 entrepreneurs has, at some time, suffered at least some degree of setback and frustration while working with the Chinese government; however, they have all negotiated well enough with the official entities to successfully launch and operate their companies. In the remainder of this chapter, our entrepreneurs share their views on working with Chinese government officials to launch, operate, and expand their business.

Entering the Gray Zone

If the colors that typified China before its reopening to the world in the mid-1980s were "green and blue" (as described earlier by China veteran Robert Theleen), then the color of post-opening China is "gray." Not because the country itself is drab (it is anything but!), but because the business landscape is confusing and unclear. The nation's evolving legal structure and incomplete business regulations leave in limbo many aspects of doing business there. Thus, entrepreneurs find themselves encountering laws, regulations, and procedures for which the details are not black-and-white but confusing shades of gray.

British businessman Mark Pummell, whose diverse China ventures include an art gallery/teahouse, a professional-level musical instrument export business, a recording studio, and psychotherapy services, describes the situation this way: "If you literally follow every [Chinese] regulation, you will never move forward, and you will be drawn into the bureaucracy. You should evaluate your risks and make yourself as safe as you can within the legal framework, but sometimes you have to move a little bit forward into gray areas of business."

One of the first challenges described by China-based business-people is that the laws and regulations are vague, incomplete, or inconsistently implemented, and may be frequently (and suddenly) changed. This leaves companies operating in a no-man's land where they are never 100% sure that they are following the appropriate laws and regulations correctly. Real estate developer Bruce Robertson's reaction is typical of our interviewees: "We've had some big-time trouble with changes in government regulations. I would consider it the single biggest risk in doing business in China. It affects everybody."

The good news is that all foreign enterprises—and even Chinese companies, to some extent—are sailing across the same foggy sea.

> *If you literally follow every [Chinese] regulation, you will never move forward, and you will be drawn into the bureaucracy. You should evaluate your risks and make yourself as safe as you can within the legal framework, but sometimes you have to move a little bit forward into gray areas of business."*
>
> **Mark Pummell** (UK), Founder and CEO, ChinArt, Sinapse, and Music Pavilion

Same Law + New City = Different Interpretation

Making the voyage into China particularly challenging, our interviewees said, is the fact that implementation of regulations can vary widely throughout the country. For international businesspeople, this causes serious difficulties in planning a nationwide business strategy, as the business plan and operations may need to vary from region to region. Japanese accounting services business founder Fumito Suzuki explains: "The main obstacle in China is the absence of unified regulations and rules. For Japanese businesses in China, their fundamental desire today is to have more freedom in operating in China. There are so many regulations, old and new, and sometimes they contradict each other." Suzuki has also experienced laws

Take calculated risks in China. Sometimes, you may need to act in the gray zone.

being applied differently in different cities. "One of the biggest issues is in interpretation. The interpretation in Beijing is different than in Shanghai or in Guangzhou."

In other instances, the local government and the central government may interpret the same regulations differently, Suzuki says. "There are cases where a company had the approval of the Guangzhou government to open a store, but the central government says, 'No, you can't do it.' Each city is different. Regulations change from location to location."

How can business owners manage in such a confusing environment? Where central and local government implementation differs, consultant Hiroshi Shoda advises clients to seek a final answer from the highest-possible government body. He has asked for interpretation from the central government Ministry of Commerce, on behalf of his clients. In one instance,

Working in a "Transitioning" Business Environment

Macedonia vs. China

Importer–exporter Oto Petroski, who was raised under a communist system in his native Macedonia, says the experience of watching the transformation to a market-based economy in his own country helps him to navigate the transition currently under way in China. "A few years after I graduated [from university], communism disappeared and there was a new system. I am glad I had that experience," he says, "as now, I can understand how China is changing. China is in the same position as my country was in, in the late 1960s and early 1970s, when everything was growing extremely quickly, and people's living standards and quality of life were improving day by day. In China, it's like I always have déjà vu. I see Yugoslavia 30 years ago. Everything is the same."

While Petroski says that some things are quite different—for example, China's economic development is based on exports, while Macedonia's was based more on

Shoda says, the Shanghai government turned down an application made on behalf of Sony. When he raised the matter with the central government, the Ministry of Commerce in Beijing intervened. "A couple of days later, the Ministry of Commerce called the Shanghai Bureau and asked them to explain why they had said no." In the end, Sony moved the application forward.

Bureaucratic Challenges for Entrepreneurs

Our 40 international entrepreneurs shared with us their views on the two main difficulties they face in working with the Chinese government: winning the support and cooperation of

internal growth supported by Western bank loans—the scenario of growth and a changing government mindset is familiar in China, just faster. "What is interesting for me personally is that whatever happened in my country in five years, it happens in China in two years. Here, it is happening fast, fast, fast."

The changes may be happening *too* quickly, Petroski warns. "In China, at this moment, thousands of people are making huge amounts of profit. Sooner or later, they will start thinking about having political power. This will bring about some kind of earthquake in the society and economy of this country." He believes that China's runaway economy may lead to social and political upheaval. "It is very easy to control a country that is in misery and has a low level of economic development. From the moment private people become richer than the national banks, then the central government cannot tell these people what to do. In the last few years, some very rich people have emerged but the Chinese government can still find something in their background to expose them, and then remove them from the page [meaning: stop them from causing trouble by threatening to expose a scandal]. During the next few years, the Chinese government can still manage to do this—but in the future, they will no longer be able to."

individual officials, and fighting a bias against young, small, foreign-invested firms.

Winning-Over Officials

Negotiating successfully with the government requires winning over individual officials, our interviewees explained, which can be tricky. However, most of the long-time China investors we interviewed commented that the attitude of officials toward foreign investors generally has improved markedly over the past 20 years. Taiwan-born interior decoration manufacturer Wendy Tai describes working with officials from Xiamen, in Fujian Province, where some of her largest operations are located, as "quite positive. . . . The local government in Xiamen encourages people to start foreign companies in order to contribute to the growth of their economy. They tried their best to help us with both the license and the legal papers. We didn't use any lawyers; we finally finalized the legal steps with the help of our employees."

However, Tai hasn't always found the official attitude so welcoming. She recalls her first meeting with Xiamen officials in 1989: "At that time, the people who worked in the government were far from efficient. Sometimes, you saw them just drinking tea and reading newspapers, but if you asked them to help you, they would become annoyed. 'Can't you see I'm busy?', they would say. Nowadays, the situation has been greatly changed and improved."

Even though official attitudes have improved, working with the government remains both challenging and critically important for incoming entrepreneurs. Fellow Taiwanese business founder Maggie Yu says that one of the main reasons she was able to found her company in a brand-new sector—serviced office facilities—was her emphasis on establishing good relations with the government. Yu's business strategy boiled down to establishing good *guanxi* with district governments throughout Shanghai, and then locating her facilities in the districts where her company had the best relationships. "Luckily, we have a very good relationship with the Jing'an government [a district in eastern Shanghai] now, and they've been very supportive of us. So, we set up a new company there, and this is going to be our headquarters in the future."

The trick, Yu says, is to determine which local government most favors your type of business. In her case, she sought a Shanghai district that was particularly interested in attracting the type of international clients who lease Yu's serviced offices. "We are an authorized agent to attract foreign investment to Shanghai, and especially to the Jing'an area," she says. Thus, her company directly helps the local government to attract investment, and increase tax revenue.

Yu's second piece of advice, which she emphasizes to trainees, is that working with Chinese officials requires a special mindset and attitude—a combination of polite respect and humility (giving face) and rock-hard perseverance (see, further, the case study "Displaying the Right Attitude"). Yu explains: "When you do consulting services, you meet all kinds of restrictions, all the time. I tell my staff that, when a [Chinese] government official says, 'This cannot be done,' you can't come back to tell me 'This cannot be done.' You've got to find a solution. There is always a way to do it. Nothing is impossible; it is just how hard you try. This is very important."

Yu says that an attitude of polite persistence works well, even when facing a difficult situation. For example, when she sought to launch her business in 2003, there was no precedent for it. "In China, there was no concept for our type of business—a serviced business center—and there is still none even now; it falls in a gray area," she says.

Yu's strategy was to see how other companies that similarly lacked a defined business category had managed to launch their operations. She says: "Since I studied law, I know the rules in China. If you can't find the regulations covering your business, you've got to find the key players in the market and follow them." So, Yu visited the local district

TIP Determine which local district or city most favors your type of business before you choose your location. If your goals match those of the local government, applying for a business license can be quick and painless.

> *I tell my staff that, when a [Chinese] government official says, 'This cannot be done,' . . . you've got to find a solution. There is always a way to do it. Nothing is impossible; it is just how hard you try. This is very important."*

Maggie Yu (Taiwan), Founder and Managing Director, Asian BizCenter & Consulting

TIP If you are in a new or emerging field, find out how other successful companies in your field have navigated the legal system in order to gain government approvals.

government offices where she planned to launch her business, and very politely asked to see how other companies in related businesses had legally set up their operations. "The officials were very kind, actually. They wanted more foreign investment."

Through the local government officials, Yu learned that other companies offering serviced offices had simply registered as a "consulting" firm. "Many foreign investors provide many kinds of services that are prohibited for them. To get around this, they just set up a 'consulting' company—which can be a very broad concept. Everything falls under the umbrella of 'consulting services.' We just followed those big companies and started

CASE STUDY

DISPLAYING THE RIGHT ATTITUDE

Does the "right attitude" solve government troubles in China? "Yes," says Taiwanese businesswoman Maggie Yu, founder of Asian-Biz Center & Consulting. Her business, offering serviced offices to business clients operating in Shanghai, depends upon quickly satisfying customers in setting up their offices. But one troublesome regulation plagues Yu: when a tenant leases one of her offices, that address is logged in by the Shanghai municipal government's Industrial and Commercial Administration (ICA). Later, if that tenant moves location, it must officially change its address with the ICA before a new client company can rent the office from Yu. The problem is that few client companies bother to complete this time-consuming task. As Yu cannot lease the empty office to a new client until the paperwork is completed, she must track down the original tenant and convince them to re-register.

In one particularly frustrating case, Yu spent four months trying to locate a former tenant. Searches via the internet, former employees, and customers all proved fruitless—and the ICA refused to allow Asian BizCenter to re-lease the former tenant's office. It was a stalemate. Says Yu: "I sent my staff to the government offices to find a solution, but they all came back with: 'It's impossible. We have to find this missing company.'"

our operation. We found a way to avoid any negative outcome, as everyone does."

Now that her company is up and running, Yu continues to track the industry's large-scale operators whenever Chinese laws and regulations change (which happens fairly often). "We know that if the policy changes, for sure that will affect the big players. They will do something to seek a solution," she says. Yu says this strategy has helped to ensure her company's survival, as the regulations governing her industry have undergone many (sometimes drastic) changes in recent years. "Obviously, [my business] is related to real estate, and the government has strengthened its control over the property market. They have

Comply with regulations as much as possible, but don't become paralyzed when the rules are unclear, contradictory, or inconsistently applied. In such instances, rely on good relations with government officials.

Then Yu herself went to the ICA offices. Her plan was simple: wear down the officials through displaying the right mindset—an attitude of humble respect and polite persistence. "Whenever a problem comes up, I always go to see the government officials myself. I always show greatest sincerity, and I am very humble. I say: 'I'm very sorry, but I need your help. Please tell me how to solve this problem.' I just don't leave."

In this case, when one ICA clerk told Yu he couldn't help her, she very politely tried another. "I just went upstairs to another office and kept on sitting there until someone would see me. I just kept sitting there and kept asking for help, very humbly." Finally, after several hours, someone took pity on her. After being told by dozens of officials over the previous four months that there was no solution, the official told Yu that she could re-lease the office space if her company issued a letter stating that Asian-Biz Center & Consulting would take responsibility in the event that the previous tenant disputed the new lease. In fact, having offered this solution to the stalemate, the bureaucrat then immediately changed her mind and issued the permit on the spot. Yu's four-month ordeal was over.

The lesson? Yu stresses the importance of being respectful toward government officials, and at the same time being doggedly persistent—that is, giving face, but not giving up. It is a lesson she stresses to her employees. "Some young staff don't know how to talk to officials; they might not be persistent enough."

Be respectful, but persistent with local authorities whenever you encounter difficulties. Give face, but don't give up.

put lots of restrictions on foreign invested companies, and this has caused us some problems."

British entrepreneur Mark Pummell also advises foreign businesspeople in China to be flexible and practical when grappling with government regulations. "I believe the new model within Chinese politics is mainly pragmatism," he explains, adding that Chinese officials expect businesspeople to operate in gray areas. In other words, entrepreneurs should do their best to follow the regulations, but not become paralyzed if (and when) the rules are unclear, contradictory, or inconsistently applied.

Small Isn't Beautiful

One theme repeated by many of our international startups in China is that they struggled harder with government entities because of their small size, newness in China, and general lack of clout as compared with larger, more prestigious foreign companies. Logistics entrepreneur Jeffrey Bernstein describes a subtle-to-pronounced bias within the Chinese government against smaller companies: "SMEs do face challenges in working with the government in China, and especially in Shanghai. There is always the suspicion that SMEs will cut corners and not do things the right way. The onus is on the small businesses to prove otherwise."

Many of our entrepreneur interviewees warned that more time will be spent dealing with government officials in China than is necessary in most home countries. Bernstein spent 80% of his time negotiating with various government entities in the early startup phase of launching his logistics company. Since beginning operations in 2000, he has spent 20% of his time working with government on "operational" issues, and a further 20% on "building bridges with the government on a strategic level." Overall, Bernstein advises international businesspeople in China to expect to invest time in government relations. "In China, business development really involves government relations more than in other markets."

Strategies for Successful Government Relations

Our interviewees offered the following tricks of the trade, developed by trial and error, for negotiating with Chinese officials.

Rule #1: Build Connections with Relevant Authorities

Successful startups always need connections to relevant government officials, and this is a difficult network for foreigners to build up. As Taiwanese businessman Michael Yang says: I'm ethnically Chinese, so I have a lot of direct or indirect friends in China. If I have any questions about registering a company, I will ask friends who work in the *Gongshangju* [the Industrial and Commercial Bureau]. If I want to look for products, I go through my friends in that industry. I have the connections to do the job easily. For real foreigners [that is, Westerners], that's very tough. You don't even know how to find the right channel. You don't know who is the right person to talk to."

Yang continues: "Connections are very important. If I face a problem I don't know how to solve, I call my friends, and they can introduce me to other friends who are experts in that field and can give me a lot of advice. That's how I look at it. Having connections is very useful."

> "
>
> *Connections are very important. If I face a problem I don't know how to solve, I call my friends and they can introduce me to other friends who are experts in that field and can give me a lot of advice. That's how I look at it. Having connections is very useful."*
>
> **Michael Yang** (Taiwan), Founder, East West Restaurant

Rule #2: Keep Perspective, Stay Positive

The right mindset is also critical. In the face of difficulties, try to stay positive. One of the key qualities of a successful entrepreneur is perseverance. Also be aware that, despite the multiple obstacles, China in general welcomes foreign investors, and the local authorities are usually helpful and positive. Consider the experience of American software business operator Eric Rongley, who describes his business start in this way: "It went pretty smoothly. Considering that I am a foreigner in a country that was closed just a few years ago, it was pretty easy. . . . I think the government here is very interested in helping people to come and get started. I would say it's much easier to start a company here than it was for the company I started in India, in terms of the government, and logistics such as hooking up electricity and other basics."

Although building connections and having the right mindset do not guarantee success, they do improve the odds of a smooth business start. The next challenge is seeking the appropriate business license and finding the right business partner. We will cover those two critical areas in the next chapter.

Investing in Post-WTO China

When China joined the World Trade Organization (WTO) in December 2001, adventurous businesspeople around the world celebrated the dawn of vast business opportunities in the world's most populous nation. In the first five years following WTO accession, the Chinese government passed scores of new laws opening up market sectors to limited or full foreign investment. The move clearly is one reason why China is ranked among the top destinations in the world for attracting foreign investment.[1]

Despite this positive change and the opening of many industries to foreign investment, the seasoned China hands we interviewed warned that foreign investors cannot assume they will have easy access.

Entrepreneur Shah Firoozi, who set up the China offices of his engineering firm in 1995, compares launching in China to his group's experiences of launching in Brazil and Egypt: "Compared with other countries, China was the most difficult operation for us to set up—perhaps even more difficult than in Brazil, which was also very complicated." In the past few years, he says, regulations have backtracked to become more complicated and restrictive in order to limit growth in certain sectors. "Recently, it's gone back to being a more complicated scenario for engineering consulting firms, because the government wants to limit the number of companies."

Today, entrepreneurs wishing to establish a presence in China will encounter widely varied regulations depending upon their industry. Investors in government-preferred industries can expect smooth approval processes and perks; those in "low value added" or overcrowded sectors will find more restrictions (and slower approvals).

[1]United Nations, *World Investment Report 2007.*

Rule #3: "Sell" the Project by Matching it with Government Goals

Many of our interviewees stressed that another critical component to success is making the right government officials aware that your project matches their goals. Eric Rongley advises the following when pitching your project to officials: "You want to talk big. Whether you are big or not, you should talk as big as you can. Officials in China have a lot more power than government guys in the [United] States, so you need to be very respectful. You need to smile a lot and show them respect,

Mexican businessman Juan Martinez also acknowledges the somewhat chilly reception that foreign firms now receive. He set up his import–export business in 2003, two years after China's WTO accession. "The government is still receptive [to foreign investment, but it's changing now. They don't want just to have *any* investment. They want to be more selective about the investment that comes into China."

American entrepreneur Jeffrey Bernstein, who founded Emerge Logistics in 2000, also stresses that China's entry into the WTO didn't immediately result in a more welcoming environment for foreign invested enterprises. In fact, in some cases, WTO accession brought about new challenges for FIEs. Bernstein explains that the government entities that actually implement business regulations may take a very conservative stance in interpreting new regulations, to the point that it leaves even *less* regulatory head room than before the reform. "Even after the WTO entry, some officials in the Ministry of Commerce—both at the central and local level—had interpreted the rules to mean that [officials] have the ability to limit the business scope of foreign distribution companies by a number of product areas. This is a requirement that local companies don't face." After the WTO accession, Bernstein had to persuade the Chinese officials to agree to let his company deal with the same breadth of products as it had handled before the WTO reforms; otherwise, he argued, he had no way to enjoy the new "import privileges" opened to all foreign investors following China's WTO accession. Fortunately, in the case of Bernstein's company, the Chinese Ministry of Commerce eventually provided clarification and direction. The problem is that this clarification came after a delay of nearly 12 months, a wait that can be costly for young, small businesses.

You need to smile a lot and show [government officials] respect, and you need to tell them how helping you is going to make them look good."

Eric Rongley (USA),
Founder and CEO,
Bleum

and you need to tell them how helping you is going to make them look good."

Similar advice was shared by American logistics entrepreneur Jeffrey Bernstein: "First of all: get to know them from Day 1. It's not like in the U.S., where working with the government is an optional thing. Here, the government is like the air you breathe." Once you have accepted the power of the government and the necessity of winning them over, your next task, Bernstein says, is to determine how to sell your venture to every entity involved in your approval or operating process. "Whatever business you are in, you have to know where the government stands in terms of supporting or discouraging your project. Whichever government department your company will come in contact with—whether it is customs clearance, or goods inspection—you need to figure out how your company fits in with their existing policies and goals." If your business is lucky enough to match with an ongoing government initiative, then tap into it, Bernstein advises.

Rule #4: Search for the Solution

Real estate startup Bruce Robertson shares his strategy of staying calm and positive, and persistently looking for a solution, when government procedures prove frustrating. "Your initial impression will probably be that the government issues the most stupid rules to give you a difficult time or to cost you a lot of money. You can get very paranoid when bureaucrats don't come up with any solution, and just tell you what the rules are." Often, the officials themselves are embarrassed about an unreasonable regulation, he says. "They actually feel very upset about the situation, and yet they have to be the one to tell you that you can't do your project because of some new regulation." Even worse, he says, are officials who seemed friendly and positive yesterday, but who suddenly turn surly today.

Getting angry, Robertson says, is the worst response in such situations. "If you get mad, they may never talk to you again." Instead, he advises working with the officials to find a solution, no matter how long it takes. "Once, I had a list of a hundred different problems I had to find solutions to in order to execute the project the way we wanted." The only way forward, he says, was to try to remain patient and positive, while inching along. "Find out why the government official has the problem. Go into it. Ask questions. You may not get an answer in the first meeting, but don't give up; there will be a way to solve the problem."

Rule #5: Join Forces

As individual SMEs may lack clout when negotiating with the government, Japanese consultant Hiroshi Shoda advises smaller clients to band together in approaching the Chinese government: "When you are a small company, of course, you cannot call the Ministry when you have a problem. You have to go through a business organization. If you are a member, you can ask them to help you." Shoda points out that Japanese companies have their own chamber of commerce in China, which most companies join. He also encourages foreign firms to join a Chinese *xiehui* (association or confederation) for their particular industry. "You can get information from them. They can give advice and probably find a good way to solve your problem."

Conclusion

The business environment in China has changed enormously since the beginning of the reform process 30 years ago—from a business landscape with no clear rules and enormous uncertainties, to a more regulated and transparent environment. Nevertheless, foreign entrepreneurs in China still consider working with the government to be one of their most serious challenges. Therefore, in taking the first steps into China, it is critical to develop the right mindset for handling the complexities and inconsistencies in the regulatory environment. Our 40 entrepreneurs agreed that, while launching a business in China entails certain challenges, they are not insurmountable. They offered their own experiences as lessons on how to overcome the difficulties that startups in China may face.

CASE STUDY

THE TROUBLE WITH FACING SOUTH

Real estate company founder Robertson tells how he found a solution to a seemingly impossible standoff with local government officials in China. "My master plan [for a new housing complex] had been turned down by the Minhang District Planning Committee [in Shanghai] for this reason: one-third of our planned apartments were facing north. There was a beautiful park located north of the buildings, but [the officials] demanded that we turn the planned buildings around to face a parking lot," says Robertson. "They said, 'We have a south-facing apartment rule in Shanghai. All apartments must face south.'"

Robertson continues:

I was heart-broken, but I kept asking questions. Finally, after many attempts to get an answer, I found out that the planning committee had been sued by a Chinese resident whose apartment faced north. [This had to do with *feng shui*, and the bad luck brought on by the wrong physical location and positioning of a building.] The Chinese resident had started proceedings for a settlement of US$100,000 to compensate for the pain and anguish he was suffering from facing north. After that lawsuit, the government decided they would never again approve a north-facing apartment.

The next morning, I went to the officials and said: "How about if I promise never to have a Chinese person living in those north-facing apartments?"

"Only foreigners?" they asked.

"Yes, only foreigners. And foreigners don't have the right to sue for this," I said.

In the end, the officials agreed; all Robertson had to do was draft a two-line letter. "That was the way we solved a monumental problem that would have cost us a fortune in property value."

GETTING STARTED

DEALING WITH THE CHINESE BUREAUCRACY

Take calculated risks. Sometimes, you may need to act in the gray zone.

Determine which local district or city most favors your type of business before you choose your location. If your goals match those of the local government, apply.

If you are in a new or emerging field, find out how other successful companies in your field have navigated the legal system in order to gain government approvals. Ask officials to help you follow their lead.

Try to comply with the regulations as much as possible, but don't become paralyzed when the rules are unclear, contradictory, or inconsistently applied.

Be respectful but persistent with local authorities whenever you encounter difficulties. Give face, but don't give up.

RULES FOR SUCCESSFUL GOVERNMENT RELATIONS

Rule #1: Build connections with relevant authorities.

Rule #2: Keep perspective, stay positive.

Rule #3: "Sell" your project by matching it with government goals.

Rule #4: Search for the solution—there is always a way.

Rule #5: Join forces through business associations or chambers of commerce.

Chapter 2
Setting Up Shop (I)
Obtaining a Business License and Choosing the Right Legal Form

"The difficult part is, when you are a small company, you can't always do things in an official way or with the right legal structure. Sometimes, you need to move in and out of gray areas. It's sometimes out of your control. If you are a big company, you've got backbone behind you; you've got finance, partners, and legal departments."

Susan Heffernan (Australia), Founder and Managing Director, Soozar

INSIDE CHAPTER 2

Getting Help with Licensing

Choosing the Right Legal Form

Conclusion

Introduction

This chapter covers the first set of "initial steps" for foreign businesspeople setting up shop in China: seeking the right business license, and choosing the best legal structure and form for the company. Chapter 3 will cover two other critical aspects of a new venture: finding the money to finance it, and choosing the right partner.

Foreign entrepreneurs have basically two legal options: (1) to establish a company outside of China, and subsequently open a representative office there; or (2) to form a foreign invested enterprise. Foreigners as individuals are not permitted to set up a Chinese firm (except in the form of a joint venture), although some of our interviewees found creative ways to bypass this rule, with widely varying degrees of success. The option of forming a joint venture with a Chinese partner is covered in Chapter 3.

The chapter covers two main topics:

1. Finding help with licensing—choosing a China-savvy consultant, or hiring a Chinese assistant to help with license application procedures in China
2. Choosing an appropriate legal category for your business license

As this chapter deals mostly with legal matters, a word of caution is appropriate. Laws and regulations change very rapidly in China, and vary widely depending upon the industry, location, and size of a proposed venture. Readers should therefore consider the material included in this chapter only as providing an overview. We strongly recommend getting legal advice before deciding on what is best for your company.

Getting Help with Licensing

China's regulations are often incomplete or vague, requiring that business operators work in the "gray zone" described in Chapter 1. The good news is that incoming foreign businesspeople need not try to find their way through that zone alone, as assistance across a broad spectrum is available in China. At one end are the highly professional international law offices, whose fees few of our startup interviewees could afford. Happily, many other options exist. Our entrepreneurs used creative alternatives such as hiring small-scale international or domestic consulting firms, or using street-smart domestic staffers (even before they had officially launched), or—cheapest of all—hitting the streets in search of free or low-cost advice available through chambers of commerce, embassies, and business associations.

Most of our entrepreneurs who set up their businesses in China in the last 10 years have simply hired a small-scale consulting firm to handle the application process. Now that China has been open to foreign investment since the mid-1980s, hundreds of such firms exist in all the major cities. American software businessman Eric Rongley describes his experience: "After we started to seek [a business license], it went pretty smoothly. You pay a couple thousand [U.S.] dollars to a consulting company and they do the work. . . . From the time we started the process until we got the business license, it wasn't more than two months."

When U.S. entrepreneur Mark Secchia and his partner hired a domestic consulting firm to set up Sherpa's in 1999, he admits that his method for finding an agent wasn't very scientific: "We looked in a Chinese newspaper for registration firms and hired the cheapest one." Secchia admits that he and his partner were fortunate in choosing an honest, professional firm. "We were really more lucky than smart."

The China offices of international chambers of commerce can also be a low-cost resource for startups. Korean businessman Chun In Kyu needed only one month to set up a representative office for Shanghai Asset after he contacted the China offices of the Korean Chamber of Commerce.

Australian retail display designer and manufacturer Susan Heffernan advises using a mix of international and domestic firms for legal advice and assistance with procedures, especially if you plan to open as a wholly foreign-owned enterprise, rather

Alternatives TIP to expensive international law firms are: small-scale international or domestic consulting firms, street-smart Chinese employees, or free or low-cost advice from international chambers of commerce, embassies, and business associations.

"

I spent a couple of months looking for my first employee because I knew that person was going to be extremely important for my company. . . . I really needed to be able to trust that person . . . "

Eric Rongley (USA),
Founder and CEO,
Bleum

than adopt the simpler form of either a representative office or a domestic company (explained further below). "My advice is: don't use all of your money on getting a foreign firm to do the whole [business licensing process], but you definitely do need a good legal advisor. Then you can use a local consulting company in conjunction with a foreign law firm." In her own case, she paid an international law firm for advice, which she then implemented using a local consulting firm.

Finally, our interviewees—both entrepreneurs and consultants—stressed the importance of hiring competent local personnel to help with the initial navigation of the government bureaucracy you will encounter in establishing your company. American entrepreneur Steven Ganster tells of his own experience in establishing Technomic Asia in China: "One of the most valuable resources for me from the beginning was a 24-year-old Chinese woman who I could trust, who was dedicated and could get stuff done, and who was street smart. She started our rep office really quickly. With someone like that, you can get an FIE set up without spending US$15,000 at an international accounting firm. You need to have the local wherewithal."

Software entrepreneur Eric Rongley agrees: "[In the beginning,] I spent a couple of months looking for my first employee because I knew that person was going to be extremely important for my company. They were going to get the business license, and it would be written in Chinese and I wouldn't be able to read it. All of the startup information was going to be written in a language that I didn't understand. I really needed to be able to trust that person, so I spent as much time as I needed to find someone who I really thought would stick it through."

One encouraging message voiced by the China-business pioneers is that, while the regulations may be vague or confusing, the procedures are often not as complex as in developed nations. After 25 years of working in China, Belgian businessman Jan Borgonjon, who has operated InterChina Consulting since 1994, describes business regulations for starting a business in China today as "quite straightforward" and "not that complicated" compared to the situation in some European countries, though he concedes: "There are always some surprises in China." The regulatory complexity of launching a China-based business does vary by business category, Borgonjon says, so that launching a consulting firm, for example, is "quite a clear-cut business," while seeking approvals to launch a distribution enterprise is "necessarily more complex."

Choosing the Right Legal Form

One of the most important decisions an entrepreneur in China faces is the choice of legal category under which to establish his or her business venture. A business can take the form of a foreign company with a representative office in China, a foreign invested enterprise, or a domestic-owned enterprise (formed via a Chinese partner). Each category has different requirements and offers different benefits and drawbacks.

In this section, our entrepreneurs and consultants share their real-life assessments of the pros and cons of each of these common legal categories. As China's business regulations change frequently, and will vary depending on industry type, size, and business scope, this section isn't intended to serve as a road map detailing the best route for setting up a company. However, it does serve as a travel advisory, with our seasoned travelers (our 40 China-based foreign entrepreneurs) providing warnings of rough conditions and potential hazards along each possible path.

We will start with the safest, but also most restrictive, legal option for entrepreneurs in China: setting up an offshore company, and then simply "parachuting" into China to do business.

Legal Option #1: Offshore Company

When considering the possible legal categories for launching a China venture, the safest, lowest-risk (but also most restrictive) option is to set up an "offshore company" elsewhere, and then simply travel into China to conduct business. Among our

The business TIP activity you are permitted to carry out depends on the type of license you have. Make sure your license gives you sufficient scope to develop your business.

In China, if you are registered as a coffee bar, if you want to sell tea in the coffee bar, you have to get special government approval. If you want to serve sandwiches, you have to apply for a special approval letter. . . . So, I discovered that I . . . can do nothing else but sell cappuccino, espresso, macchiato—and that's it."

Oto Petroski
(Macedonia) Founder, Trading company

DEFINING THE BUSINESS SCOPE

When Oto Petroski sought to open a trading company in China, his goal was to import and export construction materials and other products between China and his native Macedonia. Petroski says he was initially met with a warm welcome by Chinese investment authorities and was led to believe that he could open a broad-based trading company. "The first time you go to the registration office, they offer you Coca-Cola and answer every question you ask with '*Dou-ke-yi*' [literally, "All can do"]. In the beginning, everything is *dou-ke-yi*," he says. He later realized that "*dou-ke-yi*" was better translated as: "All is possible."

Only gradually did Petroski discover the many restrictions placed on his original business plan. "Everything is 'easy' in China, but in the end, you learn there are many, *many* restrictions that you don't know about when you announce, 'I want to register a company.' When you first arrive, the officials say: 'China has joined the WTO and the market is open! Welcome foreigners to register a company!' Only later do they show you how it really works."

Petroski describes the climate for foreign investors in China when, in 2001, he actually began trying to establish his business: "At that time, there were limited activities foreigners could do, even as a JV [joint venture]. Some businesses were totally reserved for the Chinese government, others were half-and-half, and others allowed foreigners to own more than half." Since Petroski had owned and operated his own business for most of his working life (previously in Macedonia, then in Singapore), he decided to launch a joint venture in Shanghai, and to choose a Chinese construction company as the partner firm. "My dream was to operate in many areas," he explains, but he decided to start small. "The easiest way to establish myself [in China] was to open a company, so I told the government: 'I want to open a coffee bar.'"

Petroski's goal was to get licensed, then expand the scope of his business. "But once we got the business license, the first problem appeared," he recalls. "I said, 'I want to export some equipment from China for coffee bars.' But my secretary said, 'Uh-oh—we cannot.'" Petroski found that although the company was licensed, it was licensed only to operate as a coffee bar. "In every other country in the world, once you register a company, you can start to do all kinds of business. Not in China."

In fact, Petroski soon discovered that his business license had a very narrow scope. "In China, if you are registered as a coffee bar, in the coffee bar, you have to get special government approval if you want to sell tea. If you want to serve sandwiches with coffee, you have to apply for a special approval letter. If you want to make coffee with mineral water, you have a problem. So, I discovered that I have a 'goofy' company. I realized that I can do nothing else but sell cappuccino, espresso, macchiato—and that's *it*. For the next three years, it was like that."

Perhaps even more alarming, Petroski also faced restrictions on the sales volume he expected to reach. "The next question from the government officials was, 'How much will you export next year?' I said, 'Maybe US$2 to $4 million.' They said, 'With this license, you can only export US$1.5 million, maximum.' In China, the officials didn't want me to do too much business. If I do too much, I am competition, I am trouble. They restrict you."

The solution? Petroski learned that if he wanted to expand the business scope of his company legally, he would need to apply for a new license and prove that he had more minimum capitalization. "If I want to receive the same business scope as a local company, I would have to register at least US$2 million. Otherwise, you have no rights," he says. (In general, startup fees for local companies are much lower than those that apply to foreign companies, mainly because the capital requirements for local companies are far lower.)

At the time of our interview, Petroski was working through the process of establishing an FIE—a process he found extremely frustrating. "Now I have become a little bit Chinese, so whenever I hear '*dou-ke-yi*,' I ask another 10 questions, so that I know what it *really* means." The application process, he says, is rife with hidden problems and unanswered questions. "What is interesting is that even those who work in the government offices don't know the answers." Petroski's difficulties were compounded by the fact that, since he began the application process, the rules had changed. "This is a problem whenever a country is growing quickly."

Asked whether he has found a way to survive in China, Petroski says: "Yes, the government cheats me, and I cheat the government." For example, in the official documentation, he will describe exported construction materials as "decorative material," instead of "construction material." Petroski says that such corner cutting is the only way to survive. "Everyone cheats everyone, and everybody suffers," he says. What if he is caught? He shrugs: "I will pay the official. That's all."

To legally expand the business scope of your company, you will need to apply for a new license every time and prove you have more minimum capitalization.

interviewees, 14 had set up a company outside of China—mostly in tax havens such as the British Virgin Islands, and especially Hong Kong—but regularly visited the mainland on business. (Despite reverting to Chinese control in 1997, in legal terms, Hong Kong is still considered, in many ways, a separately governed location.)

Scotsman Jonathan Di Rollo, who launched Career Development China, a publishing and consulting business, as a Hong Kong "shell" company, lists the benefits of launching this way: "It's cheap, fast, easy, and not in mainland China." He explains further: "First, you can have your own company in two or three weeks. Second, it costs less—there is no fixed capital to invest, and no extensive paperwork."

In fact, Di Rollo advises easing into setting up the offshore company. "My approach was to start a legal entity only if I had to. If you can earn money by working as a freelancer, or in a team with other people or companies first, do that. Watch your cash flow." During his first eight months in China, Di Rollo worked as a freelancer hired project-by-project by market research companies. It was only when clients began requiring him to issue officially recognized invoices that he launched his own company. By then, he had secured a customer base and could launch with less risk, he says. "A friend, who is an experienced entrepreneur, told me that when you start your own business, you must have three things: contacts, capital, and confidence. I had contacts and capital already in place. When I finally got the third thing, that pushed me to start the business."

Dutch businessman Nic Pannekeet also launched his company, CHC Business Development, in Hong Kong, mainly to reduce launch-time and minimize taxes. "It was easier for us to set up the company in Hong Kong than in mainland China," he says. If you follow the rules, he adds, registering in Hong Kong is "no more difficult than setting up a company back in Holland."

But while establishing a business in Hong Kong (or in another offshore jurisdiction, such as your home country or an investor-friendly place such as the Virgin Islands) is often straightforward, this method has several limitations for China-based businesses. For one thing, offshore companies, by definition, have no legal structure in China. In consequence, the company cannot undertake business functions such as hiring Chinese employees. By law, hiring Chinese employees requires that your company at least establish a representative office within China. Even after taking this step, the offshore company cannot recruit directly, but must use one of the handful of officially sanctioned human resources companies in China that are authorized to serve as middlemen in hiring domestic employees. To avoid these hiring restrictions, some offshore companies hire domestic Chinese as contracted freelancers, rather than as employees.

Another restriction: offshore companies cannot freely carry out sales transactions with Chinese clients. This means that customers in China must go through the entire import process—customs goods' examination and approval, payment of import tax, customs tax and import value added tax, and other formalities—for which the assistance of an import/export agent is normally necessary. Finally, payment must be made in a foreign currency, which causes additional administrative procedures.

China-based legal expert Lluis Sunyer explains that establishing an offshore company in order to invest in China is "not in line with how Chinese authorities want foreign companies to [operate in China], which is through a legal structure in the mainland." When investors use the offshore method, the Chinese government loses out on the company's enterprise income tax and employee income tax revenues. So, the government has taken regulatory steps to address this problem, Sunyer says, including passing the new Enterprise Income Tax Law in 2008. In order to encourage China-based companies to pay taxes, the law introduces to China the concept of "taxpayer's fiscal residence"—which covers companies that have been established in a foreign jurisdiction, such as Hong Kong, but whose actual management organization is in mainland China.

Another hurdle for offshore companies operating in China are the visa restrictions, which often impact foreigners wishing to work in China. Foreign nationals entering the mainland to

TIP China's business regulations change frequently and vary widely depending on industry type, size, and business scope. Rules are often enforced differently across China, depending upon the interpretation of the local government.

"

My approach was to start a legal entity only if I had to. If you can earn money by working as a freelancer, or in a team with other people or companies first, do that. Watch your cash flow."

Jonathan Di Rollo
(Scotland), Founder,
Career Development
China

work for an offshore company will not be given "resident" visas, but must repeatedly apply for a short-term F-class "visitor's" visa. Chinese law allows foreigners to visit and stay in China under an F-class visa if they are invited for the following reasons (according to the Chinese Embassy of the United States): "a visit, an investigation, a lecture, to do business, scientific-technological and culture exchanges, short-term advanced studies or internship for a period of no more than six months." F-class visas are normally renewed every six months, but applicants can also apply for a 12- to 24-month visa.

To avoid the above restrictions, another popular option for foreign investors is to register a company offshore and open a representative office in China. Fourteen of our interviewees have taken this route.

Legal Option #2: Representative Office

Many of our interviewees took the route of establishing an offshore company, and then opening a representative office in China. According to the American Chamber of Commerce in Shanghai's *Orientation China Guidebook* (2007), this is "the most common way to invest in China, as [representative offices] are fairly inexpensive to establish and do not require capitalization."

Navigating China's Legal Maze

Attorney Lluis Sunyer, nowadays legal consultant at Guangsheng & Partners, has been helping clients of his Shanghai-based practice find their way through China's hazy legal maze since 2004. Sunyer offers below his views on the challenges that foreign entrepreneurs can expect to face in adapting to China's evolving legal environment.

The Chinese legal system is far from perfect. It can be labeled as a legal system "under construction," with the following primary features:

- *It is new:* Very few regulations date before the 1980s.
- *It is constantly growing and changing:* Chinese law is catching up with the opening and fast growth of the economy.

Israeli national Aviel Zilber, who launched his business development and investment company, Sheng Enterprises, in Hong Kong in 2003 and then opened a representative office in the mainland, describes the process of setting up a "rep" office as follows: "The procedure requires much more bureaucracy than in the Western world, but it's not that complicated." For Zilber, establishing a rep office was a logical first step into the China market. After four years of operation, the company then began "moving to form a trading company" within China.

The rep office option allows foreign businesspeople to reside in China (rather than constantly having to renew a "visitor's" visa), and to hire domestic staff indirectly through one of a handful of government-designated third-party Chinese human resources agencies. However, rep offices in China (with some exceptions, such as law firms and accounting firms) are still restricted to conducting "non-profit activities"—meaning promotion work only, with all sales transactions still conducted offshore. Thus, this option brings international investors one step further into China, but still offers the safeguard of maintaining all financial transactions outside China.

> **TIP** Launching an offshore company is often faster and cheaper than launching a China-based FIE. However, this option restricts your business operations.

- *It is not yet codified:* There is a jungle of regulations for each different legal field, with the main regulations mixed with circulars and implementation rules, and not necessarily issued in a logical or systematic way.
- *It is sometimes defective in its conception:* Normally, regulations are very simplistic, and often not in line with previous existing ones.
- *It is defective in its implementation:* Laws are not implemented uniformly throughout China. Local authorities at all levels still exercise a great deal of autonomy with respect to whether, or the way in which, a regulation is put into practice. Central government efforts to fix the problem are not always successful.
- *It is in Chinese:* Language, and China's non-Western business mindset, create important barriers for foreign investors in China. Since China's laws must be translated and interpreted, misconceptions and misunderstandings occur and these may seriously influence the success or failure of an investment.

Legal Option #3: Foreign Invested Enterprise

The ultimate goal of many longer-established or larger-scale foreign business operators in China is to set up a wholly foreign-owned enterprise (FIE) or foreign commercial enterprise. The FIE status ensures sole ownership of the company, sole decision-making power, and more control over business operations.

More than half (22) of our entrepreneurs set up an FIE after surviving their initial years of operation in China. In the past, many import/export companies, in particular, were established

Location, Location, Location

Our interviewees advise that the business terms offered to entrepreneurs by local government entities can vary widely across China. This is because China's regulations are often vague, and are therefore interpreted differently by different local (provincial, city, or village-level) governments. In general, the larger and more commercial the city, the more transparent and consistent the treatment from government.

Swiss national and 20-year China veteran Nicolas Musy, who founded the CH-ina (Shanghai) Co. consultancy business in 1997, explains why he chose Shanghai over other potentially cheaper locations. "It isn't fair to say that China is the same everywhere. There are two main reasons: the authorities and the legal framework." Musy's company researched Swiss companies in China and published the results in the book *Kaleidoscope* (2006). The company found Shanghai to be a more transparent location than Guangdong province or Beijing. "In Shanghai, it's much clearer, straight-forward, and freer of corruption than in Guangdong [in the south]. Beijing is also much higher in corruption than Shanghai. Shanghai is the lowest [in corruption] of the three places," Musy says. When advising foreign companies setting up in China, Musy stresses the need for careful research on the best location for a business, including the availability of human resources and determining which local government entities are most likely to need your business and thus be most favorable. Making this decision requires time and research; sometimes, the place you initially thought was a perfect match may not actually be the best choice, because of local government interests, Musy says. "Choosing [the right] location is one of the things we advise on a lot. We not only help to choose the location, but also a particular place within the area."

as an FIE in one of China's Special Economic Zones (SEZs), where the legislation allowed tax breaks. However, the government is progressively phasing out these perks through the implementation of the new Corporate Income Tax Law (2008). Even so, foreign investors are encouraged to look into the many SEZs on offer—they include bonded zones, bonded logistic zones, export processing zones, special development zones, and special technologic development zones—as they still offer attractive terms.

Turkish businessman Onder Oztunali, who launched the building materials trading company Globe Stone Corp. in Xiamen's SEZ in 2005, says: "Outside the SEZs, you still have many restrictions; it can be a big headache." U.S. entrepreneur Jeffrey Bernstein agrees, describing the launch of Emerge Logistics as an FIE in Shanghai's Waigaoqiao SEZ as "very straightforward." He adds: "The only challenge for a non-seeded company is that you need a certain amount of capital—US$200,000 at that time [December 1999]."

Today, many foreign entrepreneurs are also establishing FIEs outside the special zones. In such cases, location decisions are best made based on good government relations as well as the standard business considerations.

In general, the choice to set up as an FIE in China gives a company autonomy, but also requires both more money and more hassle compared to the fourth option: operating as a domestic company. (See below for details on taking this option.) For instance, foreign-owned startups must have far greater capitalization—three to five times more, depending upon the sector and business scope—than domestic companies. Also, when they are up and running, foreign-owned businesses must pay higher taxes as well as other expenses.

Attorney Lluis Sunyer explains that, since the implementation of China's Company Law in 2006, domestic firms must have a minimum capital investment of RMB30,000 (approximately US$4,300) for a limited liability company (LLC) with more than one shareholder, or RMB100,000 (US$14,300) for a one-person LLC, or RMB5 million (US$71,400) for a company limited by shares.

> **Forming a representative office in China is one step forward in making a commitment to China. This option offers advantages over operating as an offshore firm.**

"

I have to pay for an office which I don't use. The government says, 'You must rent this office or I won't register your company.' If you are a Chinese company, you can choose where you have your office. This is discrimination . . . ."

Oto Petroski
(Macedonia), Founder,
Trading company

On paper, China's new Company Law is also applicable to FIEs, but Sunyer explains that two caveats apply. First, in actual practice, the local-level government will often request FIEs to have a higher minimum capital investment, far beyond the minimum amount set in the Company Law. Second, in several specific sectors, regulations set higher capital requirements both for Chinese-invested enterprises and FIEs.

Oto Petroski is a case in point. When he launched his FIE trading company, the Chinese government first required a minimum capitalization of US$100,000 for a narrow-based business scope and US$2 million for a broad-based business scope. While the startup fees for a company such as Petroski's might be lower today under the Company Law, he still expects to pay more than his domestic competitors.

In addition to setting-up costs, operating costs are often significantly higher for foreign-owned companies than for local companies. Petroski, who now owns both a domestic-owned and a foreign-owned company based in Shanghai, says his foreign-registered company is required to rent an address in an expensive "international class" office building—a site he doesn't use. "For the foreign company, I have to pay for an office which I don't use. The government says, 'You must rent this office, or I won't register your company.' If you are a Chinese company, you can choose where you have your office. This is discrimination against the business rights of foreigners versus Chinese."

Adding further to their costs of operation, in January 2008, many types of FIEs in China lost their preferential corporate tax rate when the new Enterprise Income Tax Law was implemented.

Problems With Foreign Partners

Although many of our interviewees were pleased with China's new openness to investing as wholly foreign-owned enterprises, several also warned that forming a partnership with a fellow "foreigner" in China doesn't guarantee success. Many of the same risks—and some new troubles as well—that are present among Chinese partners were also found among international ones.

One problem that is typical of foreign partners, and less problematic with Chinese partners, is that they often simply leave China. Danish entrepreneur Simon Lichtenberg tells of the havoc wreaked on his company when his first partner decided to marry a Chinese woman and move back to Denmark. "In our business, we were handling real estate, timber, and furniture. I was the timber guy and he [his Danish partner] was the real estate guy. But then, the real estate market went bad, and he left in 1999. He went back to Denmark to become a teacher."

Another problem is simply that some foreign-to-foreign partnerships end in divorce. Swiss businessman Nicolas Musy describes how the first business venture he established in China ended in disaster. "In my first China company, formed with a Swiss partner, I was quite young and was the minority shareholder. My partner sold his shares to a new partner, and that new partner with the majority of the shares just kicked me out."

One of our entrepreneurs tells of another such case. "I had a pretty horrible experience with my foreign partner. It's a very sensitive issue for me." The underlying problem, he says, was an imbalance of power between the partners; although his team originated the project and "did everything," the other side had made more of the initial capital investment and thus held more power. "When you are small and your partner is big, you are at a severe disadvantage." Because the partner had paid in more capital at the beginning, disputes arose when the company began turning a profit. "Despite the fact that we gave [the partner] a very high return, they were still upset that we were going to make 50% of the profit without a commensurate amount of capital investment."

Relations between the two sides soured after the firm was established and the foreign partner no longer considered him as necessary. "It's always a tough position to be in because, frankly, as an entrepreneur, once you've given your financial partner your technology, once you've built the business, once you've hired employees, once you've opened a shop, once you've got all the customers, you're no good [to them] anymore; you're useless. They [the partner] can do it themselves. You basically work yourself out of the job."

> **TIP** Forming an FIE will generally give you more control over your business than forming a rep office or JV. FIEs can also take advantage of the incentives offered by Special Economic Zones.

Be wary of involving strong partners in your venture. Once they acquire the knowledge, technology, or contacts they seek from you, you may "work yourself out of a job"; Protect your interests legally from the start.

Looking back, our entrepreneur says he should have drafted the initial agreement differently, clarifying the terms for his side of the partnership; but even that might not have helped, he concedes. "The only thing that can protect you is your initial business statement. If something happens, you can go to court; but if the partner has money and lawyers, the dispute could last for 10 years."

Our entrepreneur says the reason his firm was eventually forced out boils down to "the imperfection of the Chinese legal system." He says, "There is no law firm that can give me any form of comfort. Chinese courts won't favor the little guy against the financial institutions, who are playing many other games—banking games, insurance games—much more consequential than my little lawsuit. There is a technical term, the 'bear hug.' If a bear hugs you, eventually, you have to give up."

One pleasant problem facing some startup FIEs is the flood of interest from potential foreign partners eager to link up with the

CASE STUDY

FIE vs. Chinese-owned Company

Several of our entrepreneurs have established both a domestically owned and an FIE enterprise, after weighing their respective benefits. Irish businessman Ken Carroll explains that he and his partner set up their initial "brick-and-mortar company," a chain of English-language schools called Kai En, with a local partner. This worked well, since the customers—Chinese seeking language instruction—are Chinese nationals. But when setting up his newest venture, website-based Praxis (online instruction for learning Mandarin, called "ChinesePod," and other languages), it made more sense to establish as an FIE. Carroll explains his reasoning: "A startup is so intense, so fraught with daily ups and downs, so we thought this time [for Praxis], we wanted to not have a local partner. In Kai En, we had a local partner, but that was okay because it was a slow, steady business, a brick-and-mortar business. But for ChinesePod, we wanted to keep the team lean and mean. My advice is to always do it with fewer people than you think you'll need."

China market. American entrepreneur Phillip Branham, who launched B & L Group, a construction project management and procurement company, in China in 2005, was quickly approached by many international businessmen seeking a co-operative arrangement. "I have met several entrepreneurs in the Middle East who wanted me to start businesses with them. I was invited to the home of an Iraqi in Dubai who, over a water pipe, really nice red wine and fabulous cigars, suggested that we start a business together. He wanted me to work in a construction company and help him to bring in Western techniques. The hesitation was on my part, because I wasn't sure that I wanted to be involved. Where had his money come from?" Another invitation to cooperate, Branham says, would have meant entering an entirely new line of business: "Another gentleman wanted me to start a business with him selling parts from China in the Middle East—a supply distribution business."

After less than a year spent building the business, Branham found himself facing more offers to cooperate than he could handle, and with some big decisions to make in terms of where the focus and direction of his new business should be.

Carroll says he sometimes feels at risk as an FIE. However, having set up his first company in partnership with a local partner, he feels that having a local partner for the new company would have been more of a hindrance than a help. "At Kai En, the Chinese partners keep telling us how much we need them and how important they are; but when we got into a crisis, they weren't of much assistance."

Another example is British entrepreneur Mark Pummell, who opened ChinArt as a domestic company under his Chinese partner's name, which Pummell says cut the government registration fees to between one-third and one-fifth of the cost for a foreign firm. At the same time, he registered Double Bass—a web-based enterprise that exports high-end musical instruments—as an offshore company in the British Virgin Islands. The arrangement allows that company to save on taxes and operate efficiently by selling to local customers through the local company, but to overseas customers via the offshore company.

Legal Option #4: Domestic-owned Enterprise

Although foreign nationals are not permitted to establish a Chinese firm, seven of our 40 interviewees chose to launch a domestic company, mainly in order to receive the benefits of a local business. This option allows the startup to enjoy significant benefits: lower taxes, lower operating costs, and fewer restrictions on hiring, location, and business scope. These foreign entrepreneurs established at least one of their China-based ventures as a domestic firm by registering the company in the name of their Chinese spouse, or a trusted Chinese partner. This method offers benefits but also carries risks (as several of our interviewees discovered), because all the legal rights are held by the Chinese partner alone.

U.S. businessman Phillip Branham is among those relying on their spouse (or spouse's family) to serve as the Chinese partner or legal owner. Branham and his wife, Rebecca Li, had completed the process for B & L Group just before our interview. "I thought it would be terribly difficult to get a Chinese, business license, but actually each government district has an agency, and you pay them and they help you to get your license—done," says Branham. "It's a Chinese company; that's the difference." Branham says the main reasons for setting up as a Chinese company—through his wife's brother and sister—were to save on time and startup fees. "I could actually form an FIE right now, but it would take about US$140,000 in capital. For the Chinese company, the required invested capital is very small," he says. "We now have an FIE with a different work scope."

Mexican entrepreneur Juan Martinez used both family and classmate connections to form an import/export company specializing in China–Mexico trade. His first company, formed in 2003 while he was still studying for his MBA at the China Europe International Business School in Shanghai, was set up as a joint venture with a Chinese MBA classmate, Snoopy Wen. As the business grew, the partners split the original company into two, amicably ending the partnership. Martinez went on to form Solis Holdings Import & Export (SOLHIX) through his wife Zhou

Chunli, a Chinese national. Today, another Chinese MBA class-mate, Winny Wu, and Martinez's brother Fernando have also joined the company. After five years of operations, Martinez says working with family and friends is still the best option for his company: "I have started the businesses with family, friends and classmates—people I know. Sometimes, it can bring problems or difficulties, but so far, we've had good relationships with all the people."

Taiwanese businessman Michael Yang also chose to establish the Golden Atrium restaurant chain as a domestic company via a mainland Chinese friend, because that route was the most practical. "Ten years ago, when I started, China wasn't very open. Government regulations for restaurants were very tight, both for foreign and local people," Yang says. The local partner registered the business in return for a "management fee," while Yang supplied the startup money and acts as manager.

Is Yang concerned about his lack of ownership rights? "My friend and I have a contract that specifies who owns the com-pany and who has the rights to run the restaurants," he says. If he and his partner ever have a dispute about ownership, Yang believes the contract would hold up in court. "I wouldn't lose the case, so I don't worry about it." (Several other interviewees have experienced serious difficulties with local partners, as described in the next chapter.)

In founding Sherpa's, Mark Secchia also initially used Chi-nese friends as domestic partners. Sherpa's hired an agent to serve as its Chinese partner. This partner holds the legal owner-ship rights to the company but is generally not involved in the company's day-to-day operations.

Secchia says that working through his Chinese partners has proven helpful, especially initially, because they have helped to guide him in the China market. "For example, when we first named the company, I wanted to insist on a particular name, but Steven said, 'Stop and think about it for one day.' The next day, when I woke up, I realized that I had chosen a stupid name."

For the past eight years, Secchia has worked as CEO of Sherpa's (now a business with turnover of between RMB3.5 and 4 million [US$500,000–570,000] a month) and the Chinese

I have started the businesses with family and friends and classmates— people I know. Sometimes, it can bring problems or difficulties, but so far, we've had good relationships with all the people."

Juan Martinez
(Mexico), Founder and Director, SOLHIX

A frequently used option for forming a domestic company, and avoiding the higher fees often charged to an FIE, is via a Chinese partner: a trusted friend, classmate, or—most often— the spouse.

"

Maybe 15 years after the WTO accession, it will be easier for foreigners [to launch businesses in China] as FIEs. But right now, it's a great advantage to be a Chinese company—a **great** *advantage."*

Mark Secchia (USA),
Founder, Sherpa's

You can
TIP combine the
advantages of
each legal form.
Launch a
domestic firm to
do business with
Chinese clients,
and an offshore
firm to work with
international
ones.

partners have stayed on the sidelines, meeting only socially. "The more active partner and I meet a lot. I'm his son's godfather. He works in another company in Shanghai," says Secchia. "We play tennis together and we talk about our work, but we don't talk about the work details. He's not allowed to work in the company. No company has two CEOs; it doesn't work that way. Very few people in the company know him."

What about the risk, especially since the Chinese partners are not tied to Secchia by family? "It's not fun to do so, but you have to think about [the possibility of] splitting the relationship. We were friends, but we formed an agreement because we knew a split could happen," he says. One safeguard against a bitter breakup, Secchia explains, is that when the company was formed, he put all the debt into the company, not into assets. "If my Chinese partner wants to take the business, he would have to pay off a couple of million Renminbi. That's one way to prevent it from happening." Another incentive for the Chinese partner to continue cooperating is that, because Secchia serves as the hands-on CEO, he oversees the day-to-day banking operations and ensures that all of the company's suppliers are paid on time. "If I take all the money and leave, [my Chinese partner] is going to be legally responsible for millions of Renminbi to pay out to suppliers. . . . My Chinese partner runs more risk than I do."

The bottom line, for Secchia, is that the benefits of operating as a Chinese-owned company—including lower capital investment and less initial hassle, but also lower taxes and more freedom in terms of business scope—outweigh the risks. He believes that, while the situation may change in the future, establishing a business as a Chinese company is currently the best route for small companies and entrepreneurs. "Maybe 15 years after the WTO accession, it will be easier for foreigners [to launch businesses in China] as FIEs. But right now, it's a great advantage to be a Chinese company—a *great* advantage."

One message voiced by many of our interviewees is that, although China has liberalized its markets (especially since joining the WTO in 2001), foreign investors are not guaranteed easy entry into the China market, especially if they seek to launch an FIE. Consider the case of Parisian fashion executive Valerie Touya, who launched a fashion distribution company in Shanghai in 2004. She went on to open a chain of designer clothing boutiques in Suzhou and Shanghai in 2006, two years after China officially opened its markets to foreign retailers. (Under WTO regulations, China opened its retail market to international investors in December 2004.) But since China's opening to retailers, shop licenses have been given out sparingly.

CASE STUDY

ADAPT AS YOU GROW

American businesswoman Marjorie Woo is a good example of an entrepreneur in China who has adapted the legal form of her business as it has grown in size and complexity. Woo was operating her training services company from Hong Kong when, in 1996, she decided to follow many of her key clients to the mainland. "I found it necessary to move to Shanghai to be closer to my clients. Seventy percent of my clients are American multinationals, and 30% are European pharmaceuticals."

She started out in China as a rep office of her Hong Kong company; then, in 1998, she registered as a Chinese company. After five years in the mainland, in 2002, Woo decided to establish an FIE and phase out the domestic company. Each legal category offered different benefits at different times.

"A representative office does make sense [as an initial method of entering China]," she says. The requirement of making sales transactions outside of China was doable, Woo says, since most of her clients were multinationals. When the company began attracting more domestic Chinese clients, Woo maintained the representative office but also registered a Chinese company, with three trusted employees, in order to be able to enter transactions within China, and to issue her clients with invoices.

"Since our business evolved, and after we had gained more experience in China, the next step in our development was to finally set up an FIE." Woo cites two main advantages of an FIE: "One is sustainability; the other is credibility. In our line of business and leadership development, we need to be global and credible in order to work with our clients. So, my choice was to form an FIE. I have now created the structure and the systems, together with proper finance accounting and a succession plan."

TIP **Prepare in advance the necessary legal documents to protect you in case something goes wrong with your Chinese partner. Get advice from a China-savvy lawyer.**

Thus, by the time Touya was preparing to launch her business, she was aware that only a few of the giant international clothing retailers, including Zara and H&M, had been awarded licenses in China. Furthermore, the capital investment required to set up an FIE—RMB1.6 million (approximately US$230,000)—was beyond her means. "Even the chambers of commerce told me it would be better to set up under a Chinese name, rather than as an FIE," she says. (For a more detailed assessment of China following its accession to the WTO, see the box "Investing in Post-WTO China" in Chapter 1.)

Touya therefore chose to form her company through a Chinese partner. "By working through the Chinese friend, approval took only one month. Only through Chinese people is this possible." After the business began growing, Touya discovered several drawbacks. First, when the retail stores became successful in Shanghai and Suzhou, she was approached by a businessman who wanted to cooperate with her in expanding the chain to Beijing. Touya had to turn down the opportunity so as not to overburden the Chinese partner with additional risk. "I felt that, if there was a problem, [the Chinese partner] would be held responsible, so I couldn't grow too fast." Then, after four years of successful operation, Touya decided to sell her company and move back to France. Again, because she wasn't the legal owner, the sales process became complicated. Touya's advice to incoming entrepreneurs is that, while setting up an FIE requires greater time and expense, it also allows for greater freedom—and financial reward—if the venture takes off.

Some of our other entrepreneurs have had far worse experiences with their domestic partners (see Chapter 3).

Conclusion

Choosing the business license category—offshore, representative office, FIE, or Chinese firm—is one of the key steps in correctly starting a new venture in China. Choosing the wrong legal method, or choosing one with limited scope, can hinder your growth. Our 40 China-based international entrepreneurs recommend using a small consultancy firm, or hiring a street-smart staff member, to help with the initial process of determining the ideal legal category and applying for a license.

SUMMARY OF TIPS

SETTING UP SHOP (I)

FINDING HELP WITH THE LICENSE

As an alternative to hiring expensive international law firms, consider using the services of a small-scale international or domestic consulting firm to help you establish your business, or simply use a street-smart Chinese employee to research the best options for your business venture. The cheapest choice is to use the free or low-cost advice offered through international chambers of commerce, embassies, and business associations.

Hire a trustworthy and competent local employee to help you with the initial navigation of the government bureaucracy you will encounter in establishing your company.

The business activity your company is permitted to carry out depends on your license. Make sure your license gives you sufficient scope to develop your business.

To legally expand the business scope of your company, you will need to apply for a new license each time and prove you have more minimum capitalization.

CHOOSING AN APPROPRIATE LEGAL CATEGORY

Be aware that China's business regulations change frequently, and vary widely depending on industry type, size, and business scope. Making operations even more complex, rules are often enforced differently across China, depending upon the interpretation of the local government.

Launching an offshore company is often faster and cheaper than launching a China-based FIE. However, this option comes with restrictions on your business operations.

Forming an offshore firm with a representative office in China is a step forward in your commitment to China. This option offers advantages over the offshore option but still places some limitations on your operations.

Forming an FIE will generally give you more control over your business than forming a rep office or JV. FIEs can also take advantage of the incentives offered by Special Economic Zones.

Be wary of involving strong partners in your business venture. Once they acquire the knowledge, technology, or contacts they seek from you, you may "work yourself out of a job." Protect your interests legally from the start.

CHOOSING AN APPROPRIATE LEGAL CATEGORY (*cont'd*)

A frequently used option for forming a domestic company, and avoiding the higher fees often charged to an FIE, is via a Chinese partner: a trusted friend, classmate, or—most often—the spouse.

You can combine the advantages of each legal form. Launch a domestic firm to do business with Chinese clients, and an offshore firm to work with international ones.

Prepare in advance the necessary legal documents to protect you in case something goes wrong with your Chinese partner. Get advice from a China-savvy lawyer.

Chapter 3
Setting Up Shop (II)

Finding the Money and Choosing the Right Chinese Business Partner(s)

"Forming a business partnership [in China] can sometimes go really wrong. I think everybody entering a business partnership should be very cautious. This doesn't apply only to Chinese people; people everywhere are complicated. People are quite greedy. When money is involved, it can be very difficult."

Mark Pummell (UK), Founder and CEO, ChinArt, Sinapse, and Music Pavillion

"When it comes to business plans, you have to make sure you are profitable within a year. It is nonsense to make a five-year plan before you can make a profit. Things are changing so fast [in China] that if your business model isn't profitable in a year, you have to seriously reconsider. Maybe that's not true in other places, but it is true in China."

Olaf Litjens (Netherlands), Founder and CEO, Unisono Fieldmarketing (Shanghai)

Introduction

This chapter covers the second set of "initial steps" for foreign businesspeople setting up shop in China: funding the new business, and finding the right Chinese business partners. Both steps are difficult for entrepreneurs in any business environment worldwide, but starting up in China offers several unique additional challenges.

In terms of startup funding, entrepreneurs in China generally choose one of three main sources of funding: their own savings; those of family or friends; or funds provided by professional investors. Unlike in developed markets, it is virtually impossible to obtain financial assistance from China-based banks. The first part of this chapter examines how our 40 entrepreneurs successfully secured startup money without bank assistance.

The chapter then covers the crucial issue of choosing the right business partner if the foreign party opts not to go it alone.

We have divided the lessons shared in Chapter 3 into two main topics:

1. Finding the money
2. Choosing the right local business partner(s)

Finding the Money

Entrepreneurs worldwide struggle to secure the funding necessary to get started and build their business. But for foreign startups in China, the options available are fewer and the financial bumps along the road can be more treacherous.

First, it is nearly impossible to obtain bank financing in China, as the nation's immature banking industry doesn't include channels for foreign entrepreneurs seeking seed money. A 24-year China veteran and founder of several companies, including his current fieldmarketing venture, Olaf Litjens explains the dilemma most foreign entrepreneurs face: "You can't get a loan from a local bank, because Chinese banks won't fund a foreign entrepreneur—and a foreign bank won't do it because you are small and China is still a very complicated country. So, it's extremely hard to get financing." His own solution has been to collect funding from partners, clients, or suppliers: "We always get money from other people. We are very good at this!"

Fellow Dutch entrepreneur Nic Pannekeet echoes Litjens' sentiments: "I used my own money [to start CHC Business Development]. I don't know of any local bank that would be willing to offer me funds." In fact, he explains, even some of China's most successful business ventures have been refused bank funding. A case in point is Shanghai's Xintiandi neighborhood, where historic pre-communist buildings have been architect-restored to create a very trendy and commercially successful shopping–dining–entertainment district. Says Pannekeet: "I know the guy who developed Xintiandi and his real estate company. When he was planning the project, the bank said that the idea was good but it would be very hard to make money, so they couldn't lend to him. But now, you see how Xintiandi has developed." His point: if the developer of Xintiandi couldn't convince the banks to extend him a loan, most foreign investors should also expect to be denied financing. Pannekeet himself says that the only time he was granted a bank loan was in the southern Chinese city of Kunming. But in that case, he turned down the offer. "In Kunming, I had to pay a commission under the table to the bank official to get a loan. So, I gave it up."

Lacking bank loans, all of our business pioneers had to use alternative means to acquire startup funds. The most obvious strategy, they agree, for those with either the time or the financial means, is simply to wait until you have enough funds to launch on your own. South African consultant Kobus van der Wath, who launched The Beijing Axis, voices a typical mindset: "My firm is self-funded. I started with my own savings. [In the initial stage,] I was approached by a few people wanting to invest in the company and buy equity, and therefore, take some level of control. I immediately saw that none of the people or entities understood my business. I

TIP Chinese banks are generally reluctant to loan to private enterprises. Consider using clients and suppliers as your funding source.

TIP Save enough money to survive at least during the first months of operation. Self-finance is the safest option for funding your business.

didn't want to have a board that didn't instinctively understand the business." So, Van der Wath waited until he could fund the business himself, and then in 2002 began registering entities in Hong Kong, Mainland China, and South Africa.

Home decorating manufacturer Wendy Tai has used a conservative policy to fund her China-based business after moving operations from her native Taiwan to mainland China 20 years ago. "Our business has grown with our own money, without the help of investors. The usual model is 30% self-finance, 70% borrowed from the bank. We only have self-finance," she says. Even when friends suggested channels for obtaining bank loans, Tai refused. "Many of our friends have suggested that we borrow money from the bank to grow faster. However, we insist on our way to develop our business. Now, when we look back and compare with the company in the old days, we're amazed by its rapid development."

Austerity is also the rule of thumb for British counseling and arts entrepreneur Mark Pummell. "It's very important to me that I never borrow money from anybody. Every penny [of our startup fees] came from us. If somebody pays 50% of your business here, they own 50% of your business—you don't have full control." In order to stick to the principle of not borrowing money, he started his China-based businesses with £100,000 of personal savings. Although the aim was to open several businesses eventually, his strategy was to begin with a small-scale niche venture that had the potential to be profitable. Pummell, who is a licensed psychotherapist in the United Kingdom, explains: "Therapy was my first business. Very quickly [after arriving in China], I saw the opportunity that nobody was providing psychotherapy [for expatriates]— literally nobody. A few people approached me and suggested that I start my practice." So, he rented a small office above a candy factory in Shanghai. "Each month, I kept my overhead very low. I just required some furniture, a few chairs, couches, and business cards. I placed some ads in [a free English-language weekly magazine for expatriates]. Then my phone started to ring and never stopped ringing."

After his first business became stable and steady, Pummell launched an art gallery/tea shop, and then a recording studio, and musical instrument export business for professional musicians. As the businesses grow, he has stuck to a principle of controlling costs. "I think the number one thing is to keep your overhead low. It's a temptation to spend money, particularly in Shanghai."

Irish national Ken Carroll and his business partner followed a similar plan of using their own funds to launch Kai En English Training Center, a chain of English-language schools, in China. "My partner and I had just US$200,000 between us. We got on a plane and came to Shanghai. We didn't know anyone, but we were committed to it. It was actually quite silly." Carroll followed a strategy of keeping costs very low and initially launching a safe, stable business. (The partners had managed a similar chain of English-language schools in Taiwan.) "We went without a salary for 15 months, which wasn't very nice," Carroll remembers. Still, the strategy worked. Kai En eventually grew to a five-school chain in Shanghai, providing a steady and stable income source. "It's not like a billion-dollar corporation but it's profitable—nice and solid," Carroll says. Today, he uses income from Kai En for his own salary and to help fund the growth of his new venture, Praxis, which offers web-based language-teaching services, including ChinesePod, SpanishPod, and ItalianPod.

One of our China business pioneers sums up the potential risks incurred with a self-funded venture. After five years of operation, he faced a dispute with his Chinese business partner that threatened to wipe out much of the earnings he had accumulated so far. He explains: "When I first developed my company, I used some of my own money and used a lot of my time. I also didn't pay myself a salary, just a stipend to survive on each month, for the last five years." The risk for him is that, in 2008, he ended his partnership with the Chinese partner and reopened on his own. "The hardest thing for me is that, if the [new] business fails, I will have wasted all the effort and struggle of the past five years."

Finding Investors

We didn't want to seek venture capital because the earlier you get investors involved, the more you have to give to them."

Aviel Zilber (Israel), Chairman, Sheng Enterprises

Not every entrepreneur has US$200,000—or more—in personal savings available to use in launching their China-based business. Below are strategies from business pioneers who had to borrow funding, mainly what some entrepreneur literature calls the "three Fs": friends, family, and fools.

In launching Sheng Enterprises in Shanghai in 2003, brothers Aviel and Jordan Zilber used their own funding plus "angel investors" from their native Israel—mainly their uncle and a small group of friends and acquaintances. Aviel explains: "We didn't want to seek venture capital because the earlier you get the investors involved, the more you have to give to them." However, as Jordan explains, even the strategy of borrowing from family and friends has drawbacks: "When I was looking for money, I was anxious to realize my dream. But now, looking back, I realize I gave away shares too cheaply."

When launching Emerge Logistics Shanghai, China veteran Jeffrey Bernstein also chose to target offshore clients as potential investors; he believed international customers would be most likely to understand the value proposition for his services. While this strategy is safer in terms of a stable payment stream once sales are finalized, it does require facing the initial difficulty of attracting customers located around the globe while being based in China. "One big challenge has been starting from Day 1 as a global company—meaning the operations are exclusively in China, but the client base is exclusively from overseas," says Bernstein. The geographical distance between the service and the customer creates "a resource and logistical challenge" that goes beyond the usual startup difficulties, he continues. "In most entrepreneurial companies the founder wears many hats, but one person can only be in one place at a time. The challenge is how you handle a global startup when you really need people on both sides of the globe."

In terms of the specific challenges he faced in launching Emerge Logistics as an FIE, Bernstein explains that he first had to raise capital of US$200,000. He had planned to use his own savings, plus funding from outside investors. But attracting investors was difficult without proven operations: "One main challenge is in finding external capital. There is the chicken-and-egg phenomenon—before the business starts and you have serious operating costs, that's the time to go on a road show [to attract investment]," he says. "But at that time, the business is just a concept, and it's very difficult to get investors to sign up."

Bernstein found himself in the difficult position of talking to investors while readying to launch. In the end, this plan worked: "We delayed as much as possible until we had ramped up, and then a high-school friend gave me the remaining capital at the last second, and the rest was history," he says.

Attracting Venture Capital

Consultants and interviewees stressed that there is plenty of venture capital coming into China, but that small-scale startups are at a disadvantage in attracting it. Says American consulting company founder Steven Ganster: "There's a lot of [VC] money out there. There's a lot more money than there are projects [in China], and there are many funds that are China-specific. If you have a good value proposition, there is a growing pool of venture capitalists who have [both] money and a fascination with China." Ironically, the trouble for startups, Ganster says, is that it is often harder to get a limited amount of seed money for a small-scale venture than it is to attract larger amounts for a bigger project. "Funding of less than US$1 million—that's hard money to get." He adds that when your business is running successfully, "money is easy to find."

But some of our interviewees did attract outside investors, simply on the strength of their business plan. Turkish business-man Onder Oztunali received funding from a Hong Kong investor for whom he had worked on projects in Turkey and Thailand. "That first investment is very difficult to get because you need people who believe in you and believe in your capabilities," says Oztunali. "My investor is a really smart guy; he immediately saw the fundamentals of my business." After receiving financial support, Globe Stone Studio eventually opened entities in Turkey, Hong Kong, and mainland China.

One main challenge is in finding external capital. There is the chicken-and-egg phenomenon—before the business starts . . . that's the time to go on a road show [to attract investment]. But at that time, the business is just a concept, and it's very difficult to get investors to sign up."

Jeffrey Bernstein
(USA), Founder and Managing Director, Emerge Logistics Shanghai

"Show Me the Money"

For advice on early-stage finance resources for foreign startups in China, we interviewed David Chu, co-founder and managing director of Shanghai Venture Partners. "There is plenty of capital available to support good businesses in China, regardless of a founder's nationality," Chu says.

Foreign startups will generally find three main types of early-stage investors available in China (excluding friends and family): (1) angels (high-net-worth individuals); (2) venture capital firms; and (3) strategic investors. Each of these types of investor is different, and there are many differences within each category, so China-based investors should spend time researching each.

Early-stage financing generally refers to the beginning stages of a company's life cycle. In [Table 3.1] the first two stages are typically considered early-stage. As a company matures, its business risk is generally reduced, and the amount of capital it can raise and its valuation typically increases. Different types of investors can be approached, depending on the size and business plan for the venture [Table 3.2].

The best method for reaching early-stage investors in China is through word-of-mouth—networking with someone those investors know and trust. The investors' personal network is a natural filter for screening the numerous

TABLE 3.1
Characteristics of Companies by Stage

	Stage	Milestone	Amount of Capital Raised	Business Risk	Valuation
Early stage {	Seed/startup	Proof of concept	Low	High	Low
	Product development	Beta product or first customers			
Later stage {	Shipping product	Profitable			
	Expansion	New markets and/or IPO	High	Low	High

TABLE 3.2 *Types and Characteristics of Early-stage Investors* — Investor	Stage Preference	Typical Investment Size	Desired Return (%)	Exit Horizon
Angel	Seed/startup and product development	US$10,000–US$500,000	Higher than VCs, since they typically invest earlier than VCs	< 5 years
VC	Mostly product development and later	US$500,000–US$5,000,000	Greater than 10 times the initial investment	3–5 years
Strategic	Product development and later	US$500,000 – several million	Some looking for VC-type returns; information on new markets and technologies; complementary to business	Some 3–5 years; others have longer-term horizon due to strategic value

projects that come across their desks. There are informal angel networks beginning to form [in China], but they aren't that active yet. Since most angels don't actively promote themselves on a website, persistent networking at entrepreneur/VC-related events can usually be fruitful.

For VCs and strategic investors, you can Google "Top China Venture Capitalists" and turn up several VC ranking lists, then Google the VC's name to find their website. Again, sending an unsolicited business plan is less effective than being introduced through a trusted source, so remember to network.

Last, but not least, you can enlist the help of a placement agent or financial advisor to secure funding. Make sure you look at their track record and talk to past clients to help ensure your chances of success, and avoid wasting your time. Good luck!

If you have a good value proposition, there is a growing pool of venture capitalists who have [both] money and a fascination with China"

Steven Ganster (USA), Founder and Managing Director, Technomic Asia

Marc van der Chijs, founder of the online video download-ing website Tudou (similar to U.S.-based YouTube) and other i-businesses, started his first venture with his own funds, then attracted several VCs. "It's not difficult to find VCs, as they're all looking for opportunities. But it took almost a year for the evalua-tion." Today, Van der Chijs enjoys excellent relations with his investors. "[Our relationship with them] is very good, because we have met all our business targets so far. We're really close, and we go out for drinks. It might be very different from the VCs you work with in other companies. Most of them are Chinese VCs, and some are U.S. VCs. We have in total seven to eight VCs. Some of them are on the board of directors, depending on how much money they've invested." Van der Chijs finds the contribution of VCs very positive. "They really helped us to grow and are really successful. I think Tudou was very lucky with its VCs. We chose the right ones, and they have helped us tremendously over the past several years." Today, Van der Chijs is in the enviable position of being able to choose from among willing investors: "Now, we are very success-ful, so we can choose which company to work with—just like a beauty contest."

TIP Keep your initial costs low, and try to establish a positive cash flow as quickly as possible.

As a final word of advice on financing, many of our inter-viewees stressed the need—after receiving initial funding—to keep costs low and to quickly establish a positive cash flow. Dutch businessman Olaf Litjens gives this advice to incoming foreign entrepreneurs to China: "People always tell you to 'think long-term' in China. But I say: 'When it comes to business plans, you have to make sure you are profitable within a year.' It is nonsense to make a five-year plan before you can make a profit. Things are changing so fast here that if your business model isn't profitable in a year, you have to seriously reconsider. Maybe that's not true in other places, but it *is* true in China. If you are an entrepreneur with a relatively small business, you have to make sure you are profitable in a year, or you have to seriously consider whether you are in the right business." It seems that, in China, the following financial principle holds true even more strongly than elsewhere: profits are the food of the business, while cash flow is the oxygen. You can live without food for some days, but for only minutes without oxygen.

Choosing the Right Chinese Business Partner(s)

Few China entrepreneurs launch a business venture entirely on their own; for practical and professional reasons, many of the 40 business founders/owners we interviewed launched their China venture with at least one partner. Finding the right partner is another critical decision in the birth of any new company. In this chapter, we share lessons learned in choosing a Chinese business partner. (For advice on working with a fellow non-Chinese as your business partner, see "Problems With Foreign Partners" in Chapter 2.)

In practical terms, using a Chinese–non-Chinese partnership is a logical blend; the domestic partner handles domestic issues such as government relations, distribution, and insight into domestic clients or customers; while the foreign partner provides technology or expertise in home-country standards, as well as managing foreign regulators, suppliers, or buyers.

Unfortunately, many of our interviewees working with Chinese partners have had some negative experiences. One such case is described here by U.S. entrepreneur Bruce Robertson, founder of Asia Pacific Real Estate. Under their partnership agreement, the Chinese partner was to handle government issues, while the foreign side would handle on-site issues. Problems arose when the Western side became suspicious of the way the Chinese partner managed the use of utilities for the venture. "We got the impression that the cost we were paying for utilities used on-site was way above what it should have been," says Robertson. "We were never able to prove this, but we thought the Chinese developer was getting a discount on the outside cost and that we were paying a premium because the same utility company was doing both the off-site and on-site utility distributions. We intervened and negotiated the right to take over the cost and the administration of the off-site part. After that, our on-site distribution costs went way down. From our experience, I would say that it pays to conduct your own negotiations with the Chinese authorities, rather than leave such matters entirely in the hands of your Chinese partner."

"

The first time I came to China, I chose to establish a joint venture with a very powerful [Chinese] partner; [he was] so powerful, he lost us millions of dollars. That way didn't work."

Oto Petroski
(Macedonia), Founder, Trading company

China hand Olaf Litjens shares another battle tale: "When we operated an export business [in the mid-1980s], we had four shareholders—my current partner Martin, a Chinese guy, a guy in Holland and myself. The Chinese guy was in charge of purchasing and quality control. The business was very successful—from year one, it was profitable—and we each took 25%. The thinking of the Chinese partner was, 'Great, it is working and we are all making good money. If I had the business alone, I would have made four times more money. I am missing out on three-fourths of the profit.'" In year two, before the next buying season for the company, the Chinese partner secretly launched a parallel company. "He reproduced everything and tried to approach our clients with the message that he wasn't sure our company could deliver but that he himself *could* deliver. He really had a big plan to corner the business," says Litjens. But the plan backfired. "The first client he approached called me immediately and told me about it." This led to a bitter 18-month divide within the company, Litjens says. Eventually, Litjens and his partner closed down the business. Today, the two Dutch partners operate both an FIE and a rep office in China, but use no Chinese partners.

Macedonian businessman Oto Petroski also experienced such serious problems with his initial Chinese partner that he eventually dissolved the company—but only after suffering serious financial losses. "The first time I came to China, I chose to establish a joint venture with a very powerful [Chinese] partner; [he was] *so* powerful, he lost us millions of dollars. That way didn't work. Another friend of mine lost US$1 million through the cheating of his Chinese partner, just like that. He paid a lot of money to the partner to set up things, and then the Chinese partner disappeared." After those experiences, Petroski formed a second business through the Chinese wife of a new business partner, this time, a trading company operating as a domestically owned firm. In this case, the Chinese wife serves as a silent partner who is not directly involved in the business but enables the company to attain "domestic" status. Petroski says that using this route was "the only possible way" for his company to begin importing and exporting. (See the case study "East–West Partnership Gone Sour.")

EAST–WEST PARTNERSHIP GONE SOUR

One interviewee tells of his bad experience in starting a manufacturing company with a local Chinese person. The original idea was to operate the business partly via an offshore company and partly through a Chinese domestic company. The business was initially based on a friendly agreement, and lacked a concrete division of roles and of revenue. Trouble brewed as soon as the business's sales revenues grew. He says:

> Around the time I started to do business on my own, I made contact with a Chinese person who was in a related business and with whom I had contact previous business connections. I made many mistakes. Initially, we used this person's entity to facilitate our business. In hindsight, it wasn't a good thing to do. There weren't clear lines of ownership. Most clients were invoiced through my offshore company. We never had clear guidelines about who had what. I just needed someone to facilitate the operations in China. This is my problem; I had orders, but I had no way to run a local operation because I needed to hire local staff. I should have opened a rep office, but I thought starting a company was too complicated. I later realized I could have hired a company to do it for me.
>
> At first, my company ran pretty smoothly. The Chinese person didn't interfere very much, which was what I needed. I was in charge and the driver of the business. The local person was supposed to support me with technical things, but he never really did. What I often come across is that these people tell you that you can't do without them, which actually isn't true. You *can* do without them.
>
> In the first year, the Chinese person had less input and less involvement in the business. Then suddenly, when the company revenues grew and he saw the money in the bank at the end of the year, he thought it was half his.
>
> It was really messy to run a Chinese company and an offshore company together. They are very different companies. You have a working spreadsheet and an invisible company, and then you try to match them together. That works when you want to know how much cash flow you've got, but when it comes to separating out the real value, you can't.

It may be better to go it alone unless you have total trust in your Chinese partner and legal precautions are in place.

The foreign entrepreneur says he has learned some important lessons. "You can run a business by yourself in China. You don't need a local person to help you. One of the reasons I got a local person involved originally was that I didn't have the money to set up an FIE. The minimum requirement was US$140,000. Now, when I look back, I can see that it wasn't actually all that much money. Now, I would rather just write a business plan and get an investor who has nothing to do with running the business and pay back the loan over three years or something. I would say, 'Go solo.' I hear the stories over and over again. People ask me, 'Why don't you just get your cash out [of China] and stop?' But I think I'll give it one more chance."

Effective Partnerships

Despite some cautionary tales from interviewees, many of our profiled entrepreneurs had positive experiences in forming partnerships with Chinese counterparts. For them, teaming with the right Chinese partner was an effective way to enter and expand in the China market. Japanese businessman Fumito Suzuki, who founded AOI Business Consultants with a Shanghainese partner in 1999, believes that cross-cultural partnerships can work for foreign investors. He explains the division of work between the partners: "I am the CEO, responsible for HR, marketing, and getting information about China. My partner, Mr. Ye, is the CFO, responsible for accounting, marketing, and the development of our strategy. I am a Japanese who is not quite Japanese, and Mr. Ye is a Shanghainese who is quite Japanese." Suzuki says the secret to their successful partnership is mutual respect. "We quarrel a lot in business, actually, but quarrelling is not a bad thing. It constantly reminds us of the possible mistakes so that we can prepare in advance. We complement each other a lot." The other secret, Suzuki says, is trust and understanding. Suzuki met Ye at university in Japan, which is why Ye speaks "perfect

Japanese." The partners' history as classmates, and their shared language ability, help to build trust, creating the foundation for cooperation.

Swiss executive Nicolas Musy admits that he found the Chinese partner for his cashmere factory by chance, but says that the relationship has worked well for both sides for nearly two decades. "I met my Chinese partner in a hotel in 1991. I worked for a Swiss trading company and was setting up their operations. As was usual at the time, I was living in a hotel and he was working there as key account manager. We talked and got along very well, and he wondered whether there was a chance that we could work together. At the time, I had just filled a position. Eight months later, I came across him in the street. 'I have a position for you here now,' I said. We started working together in the office, and we are still partners today."

Why has the partnership worked well? Musy says the main reason is that he chose the right person to work with. "In my case, there are three important elements for success. One is that the Chinese partner should understand a Western mindset. My partner actually thinks the same as me. The second is ethics and trust. We won't go for short-term gains at the expense of the relationship. The third is ability. He is a very capable person."

> *There are three important elements for success [in choosing a Chinese partner]. One is that the Chinese partner should understand a Western mindset. . . . The second is ethics and trust . . . the third is ability."*
>
> **Nicolas Musy** (Switzerland), Founder, CH-ina (Shanghai) Co.

Ingredients of a Good Chinese–Foreign Partnership

The skill of forming successful Chinese–foreign partnerships is extremely valuable for a foreign businessperson in China, whether you are establishing a domestically owned company or setting up an agreement with a domestic supplier, buyer, or retailer. In this section, our China-based entrepreneurs and consultants offer advice on the following ingredients, which they consider essential for a successful partnership:

1. Due diligence in seeking the right partner
2. Shared goals and clear communication

Before TIP seeking a Chinese partner, determine exactly what qualities you need based on your business plan. Screen each candidate with a background check, customer assessments, and financial profile.

3. Careful, thorough initial negotiations

4. Mutual respect and trust

Ingredient #1: Due Diligence in Seeking the Right Partner

Several of the consultants we interviewed were surprised by the number of foreign entrepreneurs who choose their Chinese partners casually, without a thorough investigation of their background, clients, market reputation, and financial holdings. South African consultant Kobus van der Wath put it bluntly: "Don't choose your [Chinese] partner at the first trade fair you attend. Some people bump into Chinese businesspeople at a trade fair in Germany or Shanghai, and three months later, they have a partnership agreement. Then six months later, they call us and say, 'I have a problem with my Chinese partner.' That's silly. They should have done due diligence and checked the track record." Van der Wath also warns businesspeople outside China to conduct due diligence on foreign companies selling themselves as "China experts" abroad. "You find many 'China experts' in the market, but how long have they actually been in China?"

Doing your initial homework well, Van der Wath advises, begins by researching exactly what kind of partner you need, based on your business plan: "Come in with a clear idea of the direction in which you want to go. I call it the 'Day One' strategy." During the second step—screening qualified partner candidates—Van der Wath advises setting up clear "processes," such as keeping clear documentation of all negotiations, and sticking to a timeline. "For me, it's all about process—being intelligent and systematic. In the early stage, the crucial factors are the people, the initial research, and the initial concept."

Ingredient #2: Shared Goals and Clear Communication

Readers may have heard horror stories of foreign companies forming totally dysfunctional partnerships with Chinese companies. Such disastrous pairings are fewer in China than a decade ago, but are still a reality. Mismatched goals from the two sides can still be a common problem in forming a partnership (or even a long-term sales contract) with a Chinese entity.

Fourteen-year China veteran entrepreneur Shah Firoozi says that one common danger is that both sides misunderstand the value they offer to the other side; this leads to disputes, he says. For example, foreign partners often believe that they carry most of the clout in the partnership because they offer financial resources or technological skills. "Most foreigners feel that if they bring investment and technology, they have the most power. Well, frankly speaking, the investment isn't a key issue for many partnerships because there are many sources of money available in China. Nor is technology all that important, as it's also attainable elsewhere." Firoozi advises foreign entrepreneurs to "always ask yourself: what advantages am I bringing to my local partner? What do they really expect from our relationship?" The real answer may surprise the foreign side, he warns, adding that the Chinese side will only answer this question truthfully once trust and goodwill have been established on both sides.

> **Find out what advantages you bring to your local partner, in their eyes, and what they expect from you. The answers may surprise you.**

Finally, one of the most common instances of "misaligned goals," according to our interviewees, is when the Chinese partner sets up a parallel business and steals customers from the original business. Consultant Ruggero Jenna tells of one client who discovered recently that his Chinese partners were developing similar products and distributing them to their clients at a similar price. "It was really difficult to distinguish the [copied] products from the originals. The clients wouldn't know the difference." In such cases, the foreign side of a partnership may not know about the problem for months or even years. "It's tricky, because it's the company's own distributors that were doing it. We are talking about a market in which the distributors really own the clients." Jenna warns foreign investors who are forming partnerships with local Chinese that this problem is common. "Many Chinese partners do this. Eventually, they want to develop their own technology and brands. That is their long-term strategic goal."

Ingredient #3: Careful, Thorough Initial Negotiations

One way to avoid forming a "poisoned partnership," in which the two sides have differing goals, is to spend more time and effort upfront in forming the agreement and building the relationship. Consultant Ruggero Jenna says the main reason that many partnerships in China fail is simple: "Usually, the interests of the two partners are not aligned. The upfront negotiation hasn't been thorough, so there are a number of unspoken issues in the initial stage that the partners didn't realize existed. At the beginning, everything looked nice and both sides were excited. When problems appear later that weren't contemplated in the initial agreement, then the partnership usually breaks apart."

To protect the foreign side against such a fate, and taking into account China's often vague rules and the difficulty in enforcing regulations, Jenna advises clients to maintain a strong position in the partnership. "It is very difficult to enforce rules [in China]; and besides, rules are unclear in many cases. In this situation, it's really a matter of who has the strongest position—the one with the strongest position can impose his view on the other side. It is important to have a position in the partnership that is sustainable over time. Then, in order to protect yourself, you should write a contract. The terms [of the partnership] must be set up in a way that gives you a safe and strong position from the start, and control later on."

The phenomenon of Chinese partners eventually competing with their international partner is "happening more and more," warns consultant-entrepreneur Jan Borgonjon. The best safeguard, he says, is "very careful assessment at the beginning," coupled with close communication and monitoring after the partnership is operating. He says that, unless the foreign partner has created a rock-solid relationship or offers sufficient incentives for the Chinese partner not to go into business himself, the international entrepreneur should actually *expect* such a development. "You shouldn't be surprised that it's happening. As your Chinese partner gets stronger, he can easily enter the same business and use the knowledge he has gained through you. How are you going to stop that? It also happens in the West. Here, it's simply a risk of doing business in China—and you take it, or you don't take it. No one is forcing you to come to China."

In cases of clear breach of contract, attorney Lluis Sunyer says foreign investors in China can go to court. "Many foreign and Chinese companies are trying to solve their cases in Chinese courts of justice these days," he says. He adds, however, that this option still "normally is not the most time-effective and cost-effective way to solve disputes. In China, as in Spain, we have the popular saying, 'Win the lawsuit, lose your money' (赢了官司输了钱)." Instead, companies generally try to avoid this route by including in their contracts an arbitration clause spelling out how to solve potential differences. For example, Sunyer says it is "very common" to set the Shanghai Arbitration Commission or the China International Economic and Trade Arbitration Commission as the designated body for submission and solution of disputes between contractual parties.

Our consultants stressed that one of the best safety nets against such a dispute is to hammer out a workable agreement and contract, and to build a good foundation for the relationship in the initial stage. Shah Firoozi warns clients against the common mistake of delegating the crucial initial negotiations to an assistant or a consultant who has Chinese-language skills but perhaps lacks the right personality. "The Chinese are very personal people. In every relationship, there is a personality in it. What makes the substantial difference is whether both sides connect and relate well. In my opinion, what is not important is language. I've seen many companies use a delegate just because he speaks Chinese. This person may or may not present the right communication skills and right personal skills to deal with the Chinese counterpart. The perception of many companies is that if you speak the language or because you are of Chinese roots, of course you can make a deal. It's very difficult for Chinese returnees sometimes to adapt well to China. In my opinion, I would look at the character of the person. The Chinese have an incredible way of sensing a genuine person from a non-genuine person."

> *As your Chinese partner gets stronger, he can easily enter the same business and use the knowledge he has gained through you. How are you going to stop that?"*
>
> **Jan Borgonjon**
> (Belgium), President, InterChina Consulting

Take the time upfront to build a solid relationship with your Chinese partner, then hammer out a workable agreement and contract. Maintain a power advantage in your favor to guarantee a degree of control after operations are up and running.

Ingredient #4: Mutual Respect and Trust

Lack of respect between partners is another common "poison pill" for ventures, our interviewees explained. Spanish consultant Josep Giro tells of a typical situation created when respect hasn't been established: "In one of our client companies, the Chinese side contributed to the partnership machines which were very old but that they had valued very highly. The Spanish side accepted this because they were busy doing other things. Both of them disliked each other and they cheated each other. If you cheat each other, you can only have a bad result."

Another critical factor in establishing respect and trust is to send the right foreign managers to China. Foreigners with personalities that clash with Chinese business norms can easily harm, or even destroy, the partnership. Says Shah Firoozi: "I've personally seen how the strong personality and character of the partners' representatives can make all the difference in how the partnership is formed and sustained." He advises foreign negotiators to "stay very cool with the potential partners and get to know them as people; establish a good relationship with them." Firoozi believes that a negotiator with a patient, respectful personality is most useful in winning a solid partnership agreement. "In the Chinese partner's eyes, the critical qualification is not only how much you know about your business, but what kind of character you have. Because, in the Chinese partner's eyes, you are the window to your company. How *you* behave is perceived as the character of your company."

Other consultants stress that successful cooperation can only take place if both sides are culturally sensitive and respectful. Kobus van der Wath explains: "You have to be culturally astute. I can tell within five or ten minutes of talking to them if they are going to do well in a negotiation. In the first few minutes, you can see whether they are going to be brusque, rigid, or rude."

Another kiss-of-death for a partnership occurs when both sides undervalue their partner, says Josep Giro. "When I was negotiating a partnership for a client recently, I asked him, 'Do you think your company is more important than the Chinese one?' The client said 'yes,' although his company in Spain had only 100 workers while the Chinese company had 200 and the same turnover. I posed the same question to the Chinese side. They also said 'yes.' I realized that both were in conflict. They didn't respect each other." He adds that unless both sides change their thinking, the partnership "will be a disaster."

Giro also warns foreign partners against making other common mistakes, including changing the foreign management team too often or quickly firing the Chinese managers. "I know of foreign companies that change their top management [in China] every year or two years. If you hire somebody from the competitors, three months later, you fire that guy and you bring a team of expatriates. Before those guys can make an impact, you replace them again. In this kind of case, you cannot blame the partnership failure on the Chinese side."

Then, too, some foreign businesspeople behave unprofessionally in China, damaging the partnership's and their company's image. Says Giro: "Sometimes, people do things in China that they wouldn't do in Spain. During negotiations for the JV, the Spanish people say, 'Okay, tonight we go to the bars for drinks.' I say, 'Come on, we are negotiating.' They don't do that in Spain, but they do it in China. They know they are not acting professionally, but they do it in China."

Dutch internet entrepreneur Marc van der Chijs believes that respect stems from both sides meeting both "technical and emotional" criteria. "As to the emotional side, we should choose a partner at the same level, with a similar educational background. Thus, we can show mutual respect to each other. We can't look down upon our partners or control them," he says.

> **TIP** To create a successful Chinese–foreign partnership, both sides must be culturally sensitive and respectful. Personalities matter.

Conclusion

In terms of finding the money to launch your China-based business, entrepreneurs are advised to be thrifty during the initial period of their ventures, and to exercise careful control over their expenses. Many of our interviewees used their own funds to start their businesses, and only invited venture capitalists to join them after some period of operation. When using outside sources of funding, the entrepreneur should consider the pros and cons of having more funds to grow the business faster in return for giving up some control.

The second topic covered in this chapter is choosing the right Chinese partner—a decision that will have an enormous impact on the future of the business. Our entrepreneurs have had mixed experiences; for some, their partners are like family members, while for others, they proved to be their worst enemies. Before entering into a partnership, they advise foreign entrepreneurs to research and clarify the benefits and obligations offered by both partners to the other, and then to establish an initial agreement that ensures the foreign side maintains its value in the eyes of the Chinese partner. The more time and effort that is spent upfront, the more chance there will be of avoiding a divorce within a Chinese–foreign venture. The four "ingredients" in a successful cross-cultural partnership are: (1) due diligence in seeking the right partner; (2) shared goals and clear communication; (3) careful, thorough initial negotiations; and (4) mutual respect and trust.

SUMMARY OF TIPS
SETTING UP SHOP (II)

FINDING THE MONEY	WORKING WITH CHINESE PARTNERS
Don't count on banks to finance the start of your business in China. Chinese banks are generally reluctant to loan to private enterprises; and as a small, foreign enterprise, it will be nearly impossible to find a loan. If you need outside funding, consider using clients and suppliers as your source.	It may be better to do it alone unless you have total trust in your Chinese partner. Make sure legal precautions are in place.
Save enough money to survive at least during the first months of operation. Self-finance is the safest option for funding your business.	
Be ready to sacrifice your own time and finances until the business takes off.	
Keep your initial costs low, and try to establish a positive cash flow as quickly as possible.	

INGREDIENTS OF A GOOD CHINESE–FOREIGN PARTNERSHIP

1 *Due diligence in seeking the right partner*

Do your desk research and be clear about what you want from a partnership. Only then, begin screening qualified partner candidates.

2 *Shared goals and clear communication*

Develop good communication and trust in order to fully understand the goals of the Chinese partner. Ask yourself what advantages you are bringing to your local partner and what they really expect from you.

3 *Careful, thorough initial negotiation*

Take the time to build a solid relationship with your partner, and to hammer out a workable agreement and contract. Time spent this way will save you many headaches in the future.

4 *Mutual respect and trust*

To create a successful partnership, both sides must be culturally sensitive and respectful. Personalities matter.

Chapter 4
Targeting the Right Customers . . . and Getting Paid

"If you are a small company, it is not a good position to be in. I didn't understand how the game is played. We were a small, foreign, underfunded company, [so] some customers took the attitude: 'Why do we have to pay them? If they go out of business, it doesn't matter.'"

Eric Rongley (USA), Founder and CEO, Bleum

Introduction

Having battled to acquire the startup money and to win the necessary government approvals to launch your business, the next goal for most foreign entrepreneurs in China—as every-where—is to start bringing in revenue. But achieving this goal in China involves some unique challenges. Here, startups face difficulties not only in attracting and keeping customers, but also in actually getting paid. In fact, "getting paid" was one of the most difficult challenges for many of the startups we profiled. Many had faced customers who disputed, delayed, dodged, or simply disregarded making payments. Two findings to note: first, the smaller the startup, the more acute their collection difficulties; and second, the problem was particularly acute among startups selling to Chinese customers and clients.

As young, small-scale newcomers to the market, many of our profiled entrepreneurs quickly learned the disadvantages of lacking clout—to the point where some saw their initial business models fail (as the opening quote describes).

This chapter covers two main topics:

1. Finding the right customers
2. Getting your customers to pay you

Targeting the Right Customers

The first step in creating your business strategy in China is to identify your target market or markets. The 40 foreign entre-preneurs we interviewed had tried a wide range of strategies for finding the right clients or consumers. Here, we introduce the main target groups for foreign entrepreneurs in China, explain-ing the benefits and drawbacks of each.

Strategy #1: Export Your Products or Services Back Home

Among our interviewees, 13 had launched their business by targeting customers located outside China, and exporting back home or to other markets in which the entrepreneur had professional or personal connections. In other words, they set up business models based on sales to fellow foreigners. In many ways, this is a logical business model, since the entrepreneurs could take advantage of their insight into customers in their home country or other international markets to successfully find buyers. Many used their foreignness as an advantage over Chinese competitors.

One successful case in point is Solis Holdings Import & Export (SOLHIX). Co-founder Juan Martinez built the business by selling China-made products to buyers in his native Mexico. Today, 70% of the products traded by SOLHIX are China-sourced products—mainly fashion accessories such as bags, shoes, and jewelry, plus electronics, medical products, and promotional items—sold to buyers in Mexico, Latin America, the United States, and Europe. Over the past five years since the launch of the company in 2003, Martinez has built a strong enough customer base that his next goal is to focus on four to five main lines of business. "We have the customers now, so we need to improve the way we operate for those customers," he says. Meanwhile, Martinez uses his network in Mexico to supply goods for import into China—the other 30% of SOLHIX's business. The company sells specialty products of his hometown of Guanajuato, Mexico—leather, and Mexican food and beverages—and also promotes Chinese investment into Mexico.

Following a similar model of exporting out of China to his home country of Macedonia is Oto Petroski, who explains the business scope for his import/export company in this way: "I do general exporting of all kinds of commodities," he says. "My market is Macedonia, a market of two million people. The market is too small to focus on any one area, so I am doing a lot of things, from everyday commodities to construction tools, equipment, logistics, to market research." Petroski tells of one time when a Chinese supplier tried to cut his company out of a deal, in a bid to work directly with the Macedonian client. "Neither side could talk to each other, so after a while, both were crying," he jokes. The buyer told Petroski about the incident and continued to do business with Petroski's company.

> **TIP** Use your foreignness as an advantage over Chinese competitors. You can set up your business model to export back home or to other foreign markets where you have professional insight and connections.

💡 Consider
TIP targeting
China-based
foreigners.
Understand their
needs, and
develop products/
services aimed at
meeting them.

Strategy #2: Target Foreigners in China

For suppliers of high-end products or services, another model followed by some of our interviewees is to target China-based foreigners. American real estate entrepreneur Bruce Robertson found success for his Shanghai-based company, Asia Pacific Real Estate, by renting luxury apartments and country-club memberships to upper-income expatriate families moving into Shanghai. The business model hinges on finding an unmet need among expat families in urban China. Robertson explains: "Our main customers are foreign families—especially the mother in the family. She is the person who makes the decisions [on family housing]. We are very focused on that market segment."

Robertson realized in the late 1990s that the needs of many expat families were not being served. "It was a segment identified to me by the multinational companies 10 years ago, when Motorola faced a big problem—executives were turning over because their spouses didn't want to live in China." After investigating, Robertson found that the problem didn't lie in the quality of the homes provided to expatriates in China, but in the lack of community available for the families of expatriate managers. "It wasn't really a housing problem; it was more of a friendship problem," says Robertson. "These people got off the airplane and they didn't have a single friend in China. Their children could survive at school and could make friends, but the mother was really in trouble." Robertson says that spouses— typically, wives—faced two main difficulties: lack of meaningful activities during the day, when the husband and children were away, and lack of wholesome recreation for the children after school. "The families were living in Chinese apartment buildings. When the kids came home after school, what could they do? There was nothing [the mom] could do but endure the next 12 hours until the kids went back to school," says Robertson. "So, we solved that problem."

The solution? In 1998, Asia Pacific Real Estate began marketing a newly built, expat-oriented gated community called the Shanghai Racquet Club. The development featured spacious,

Western-style homes, plus a wide range of sports and leisure activities. Most importantly, the compound of 116 luxury apartments offers an environment in which families—especially the supporting spouses of expat managers—easily link up with an active social community. Robertson explains: "The Shanghai Racquet Club is building a community of mothers and children who can instantly establish friendships."

He offers proof that the concept works. "We work a lot with the Shanghai American School. Before we opened the Racquet Club, the school turnover rate for teachers [all expatriates] was 33% per year. After we opened and 75 teachers moved in, the turnover rate went down to 6%. Now, the superintendent doesn't even make a trip abroad to recruit teachers. He just reads applications coming to him. Shanghai American School has become the greatest place for foreign teachers to work in the world [in terms of benefits]. That's a true story."

Today, the Shanghai Racquet Club has mushroomed into one of the largest country clubs in the world. The compound has a waiting list of families for its rental apartments, and has also attracted more than 1,000 families to join the sports and leisure facilities—mostly the families of expat managers of multinational corporations (MNCs). Apartments rent for US$2,500 to US$7,000 monthly, and family memberships at the club are priced at US$4,000 annually.

Following a similar strategy of targeting the expat community in China is Sherpa's. Co-founder Mark Secchia says the company actively targeted foreign families in Shanghai by offering home delivery of upscale restaurant cooking—especially non-Chinese foods, such as Mexican, Italian, and Indian meals. "We basically have foreign customers," says Secchia. "If you sit in on our call center, you'll hear that two-thirds of the calls are in English. One-third are in Chinese, but those callers will typically be ordering a double cheeseburger for RMB140 [US$20]. Not many Chinese customers would be interested in that kind of food, at that price, unless they had spent a long time overseas. So, we think that 80% of our customers are either overseas Chinese people or foreigners living here."

Again, Sherpa's has built its success based upon identifying and meeting a need among foreign customers in China. Says Secchia: "Our customer segment has money, but no time. So, we try to fill that niche." Given that dynamic, Secchia knows his customers place a premium on convenience and efficiency. "We have seven people working in the call center even though three

CASE STUDY

WEB 2.0 BUSINESS MODEL IN CHINA

Can foreign entrepreneurs succeed with a Web 2.0-based venture in China? Yes, according to the founders of Praxis. The company, launched in 2005 by three expatriates, offers a Mandarin-language training website called ChinesePod (among other sites). The site delivers RSS feeds of free Chinese lessons (at different levels) daily to subscribers, including audio downloads that can be saved on an iPod. Or, users can visit the website directly to download any of more than 100 lessons. Those seeking more advanced instruction can pay for additional services, such as vocabulary drills and quizzes. Three years after its launch, ChinesePod was attracting 25,000 visits to the website daily and boasted 300,000 paid subscribers for the RSS feed.

Co-founder Ken Carroll, an Irish entrepreneur, says the business could not have grown so quickly had the Web 2.0 technology not allowed for instant, continuous feedback from site users, who can upload comments on any lesson, at any time. When the site launched, users began uploading comments directly to the site within hours. Carroll and his partners were overjoyed. "We thought we were strapped to a rocket!" Since then, the partners constantly monitor user comments, adapting the product as they go. "We have no marketing or sales department because *everybody* is in sales and marketing. The store-front, so to speak, is on our computer screens—it is so transparent! We can see who is in the store, what they are buying, and whether they are happy or not happy. None of us can hide from that—we all have the same screens on our computer."

Another factor in the quick popularity of ChinesePod, says Carroll, is the deep familiarity of the founders with their users—because all three founders also struggled to learn the Chinese language. "We are targeting the North American market. Hank, Steve and I personally can understand all the feedback. We read it and, culturally, we would be enough. We want to have more than enough people. We spend money to ensure that our service is quick."

Taiwanese businesswoman Maggie Yu also targets incoming foreign companies seeking serviced offices and consulting assistance. Nearly 95% of her client firms are non-Chinese, with 30% coming from Japan, and the rest from "all over the

---

know where the users are coming from," he says. The founders read and adapt to user comments constantly. "The feedback goes right into the nerve center where the decision-makers are."

In 2007, Praxis also launched a Spanish-language site now called SpanishPod, followed by ItalianPod and FrenchPod. The lessons are taped in the company's Shanghai studio using native Spanish, Italian, and French speakers as hosts, plus sound effects to make them appear to be on location in Europe. As of late 2008, Praxis had attracted subscribers to the four sites worldwide.

But not all of Praxis's ventures in China have succeeded. What about using Web 2.0 to target the vast Chinese market for language training? Not so easy, says Carroll. Back in 1996, he and his partners planned to start with EnglishPod, a site designed to teach English to Mandarin speakers. But the site failed.

Carroll says that the EnglishPod site was simply ahead of its time, especially since it was targeting Chinese users. First, the population of Chinese internet users wasn't yet comfortable with online interactivity, iPod downloads, uploading user comments, and paying online for language training. Chinese users simply didn't send feedback to the site, and didn't connect with it—or pay for it. "It's an interesting cultural phenomenon for us, but Chinese tend not to say anything. Americans will tell you that your product sucks, and you should never do that again, but Chinese audiences are less critical. They would say 'Very good, thanks. Very nice.' [even if not satisfied]. Critical feedback is vital for a startup."

Also problematic: the founders themselves lacked the Mandarin skills to interact fluidly with users. "I can read Chinese but it's too slow. We would need another layer of management who could interpret for us, but that adds a level of complexity," says Carroll. Still, Praxis's founders are keeping an eye on the market, and may launch EnglishPod when the market matures.

💡 **The easiest, TIP most logical target market for a foreign entrepreneur in China is buyers in your home country, or other overseas markets, or fellow expats in China.**

world"—from Europe to Latin America to Southeast Asia. Her competitive advantage for Asian-Biz Center & Consulting is her understanding of the needs of small-scale foreign companies in terms of business facilities, administrative personnel, and consulting services.

Strategy #3: Target Chinese Customers

Among our 40 interviewees, fully half had built a business plan around targeting Chinese consumers or client companies. The interest of our profiled entrepreneurs in this market isn't surprising; today, a growing percentage of foreign investors are in China for the China market, rather than to export out to other markets. For instance, among the nearly 300 American companies that participated in the 2007 *China Business Report* published by the American Chamber of Commerce in Shanghai, some 75% reported that their main business focus is "in China for the China market," as opposed to exporting from China to other markets.

One group of foreign SMEs that is now streaming into China, says Technomic Asia consultant Steven Ganster, is suppliers serving major Western retail chains. "We also work with many SMEs who are coming [to China] to follow their customers. We are helping the companies that sell to Best Buy or Home Depot. These suppliers are under duress to come to China because their key customers are here. They need to have a presence here and some direct control. That's kind of a new animal in the last few years." Technomic Asia helps such foreign SME suppliers to "make the transition" into China and to improve operations, such as streamlining supply chain systems.

💡 **Unless you TIP have a product or service aimed specifically at Chinese consumers, try using a progressive path. Begin by targeting more familiar foreign clients, then target Chinese customers as you gain more experience.**

Several profiled entrepreneurs began with mainly foreign clients, then expanded into targeting Chinese customers. Unisono Fieldmarketing, founded by a 24-year China veteran, Dutchman Olaf Litjens, initially targeted only foreign companies with its China-based field marketing services. Customers were mainly foreign companies seeking to succeed in placing their products on the shelves of Chinese stores. Today, the company is also attracting a growing base of domestic clients. Litjens explains: "Now we are starting to work with Chinese companies. The

Chinese companies traditionally do everything themselves, but more and more companies now are starting to outsource the marketing and inventory, and then they use our service." Litjens' customer split is now 80% foreign, 20% domestic Chinese companies, with the fastest growth occurring among the domestic firms.

Others among our interviewees are hoping to follow this strategy, gambling that launching with foreign clients will put them in an ideal position when the domestic market for their product develops. A case in point is accounting service provider Fumito Suzuki, who launched AOI Business Consultants in 2002 to target Japanese SMEs in China. This narrow-focus strategy worked well; within a year, the small firm of four employees was serving a pool of 15 client companies.

The company maintains an advantage over both Chinese competitors and Chinese intellectual property rights (IPR) thieves by emphasizing after-sale services. Says Suzuki: "We provide the accounting software with training and assistance, without which the software is useless. We train the employees of our clients in how to use our software. That way, we are not afraid of illegal copies because we are not selling just the software." Another key to the success of AOI, Suzuki says, is that Chinese accounting software makers haven't yet entered the field. "We don't have Chinese competitors yet, because few Chinese companies issue professional accounting reports," he says. Instead, domestic firms tend to "deliberately make their financial statements vague."

By the time Chinese companies develop a need for professional, world-class accounting software, Suzuki hopes AOI will be well positioned to provide it. "At the moment, Chinese companies are enjoying the quick development brought to them by the high GDP growth. They haven't realized the importance of financial statements for the internal management of the company. To them, the financial statements are prepared to meet the requirements of the government, which only asks for very rough reports. In the future, when China's GDP growth rate finally slows down, domestic companies will pay more attention to internal management. Only at that time will they realize the importance of financial statements." When that happens, AOI

You may need to educate Chinese consumers before they appreciate the value of your product/service, and are willing to pay the price you expect.

will be well positioned to break into an emerging domestic market, Suzuki hopes.

Challenges of the China Consumer

Those among our foreign entrepreneurs who are targeting Chinese consumers faced several specific problems. First, those targeting Chinese end-users with higher-quality, but also higher-priced, products or services tended to face a steep learning curve in educating potential shoppers. In short, many faced initial reluctance from Chinese buyers to pay more, no matter how good the quality.

High-end retail display designer and manufacturer Susan Heffernan explains: "If Chinese companies are buying finished products such as chairs, they would look at my chairs, which feature high quality and minimalist design, and say, 'Why does one chair cost RMB1,000 [US$140]? There's nothing to it.' That level of sophistication is still developing in China."

But Heffernan was surprised to find that, among some commercial clients, there is already an appreciation for guaranteed quality. Shortly after the launch of her business, Soozar, Heffernan began being approached by Chinese companies— especially retailers—interested in hiring her company to oversee quality control for the interior products for new retail outlets. "In China, I have worked with a lot of architects and designers outfitting new stores who come to [my company] and say, 'Can you spec all the carpets and sofas?'" In another case, Soozar was asked to produce all the stainless steel display products for a Chinese company constructing retail outlets for a U.S. retailer. "At first, it was kind of strange. Domestic firms have the capacity, so why are they coming to a foreign company? But then, I realized that they've seen our quality and they think we can guarantee them the same. So, I worked as a consultant between the two local companies for that project. Their client is a big American retailer that demands very good quality." In other words, the local construction and design company felt that working through Soozar would deliver high quality with no cutting of corners—a service they were willing to pay for to ensure the satisfaction of the U.S. buyer.

Belgian entrepreneur and consultant Jan Borgonjon agrees that home decoration and furnishings is a good industry in which to witness the dramatic changes that have been occurring in China's consumer patterns. In addition to his consulting firm, Borgonjon started a furniture and home decoration distribution business in China. "Ten years ago, Chinese consumers would spend a fortune on bad furniture. Now they know much more about what is available internationally—there are magazines, and more people go abroad. It's completely changed." Most noticeable of all, Borgonjon says, the market for upscale, foreign-designed furniture in China has changed in terms of scale. "Obviously, there are more consumers interested in upscale furniture. Now you really have quite a big market—mostly in Shanghai and Beijing, but it is extending to other cities." Changes in the furnishings sector reflect broader changes across Chinese consumers, he says. "Of course, Chinese consumers have become much more sophisticated. They know much better what is going on abroad. It's day [versus] night compared to 10 years ago."

Of course, Chinese consumers have become much more sophisticated. They know much better what is going on abroad. It's day [versus] night compared to 10 years ago."

Jan Borgonjon
(Belgium), President, InterChina Consulting

Changing Mindset, Growing Means

The central message that our consultant interviewees tell their clients planning to target Chinese consumers is that the consumer population is changing rapidly and dramatically in all categories. Says Italian consultant Ruggero Jenna: "The biggest change is that Chinese consumers are becoming richer. A fairly large number of people can afford mid- to high-end things now. Of course, this is creating business opportunities that didn't exist before."

Some of our interviewees have made a good business out of selling surprisingly "foreign" products and services to local clients. Brazilian-born Chinese entrepreneur Winston Ling found success by introducing Brazilian food and drink products to the popular Brazilian barbeques in China. "It's a natural channel for us, but it's a channel with a lot of competition from other brands. Any *Cachaça* [a Brazilian liquor made from distilled sugar cane juice] brand that wants to enter China

The biggest change is that Chinese consumers are becoming richer. A fairly large number of people can afford mid- to high-end things now. Of course, this is giving birth to a number of business opportunities that didn't exist before."

Ruggero Jenna (Italy), Managing Partner for Asia and Asia Pacific, Value Partners

would think about Brazilian barbeques. We want to sell to all the Brazilian barbeque restaurants, but this isn't our main target. Our main target is the local Chinese consumer."

Other foreign business founders were surprised by the interest from Chinese consumers in relatively high-priced, Western products or services. When British psychotherapist Mark Pummell opened a private practice in Shanghai for English-speaking clients, he found right from the start that 70% of his clients were Western-educated Chinese professionals. His practice grew quickly, mainly through word of mouth. One reason for this rapid growth is that Pummell had little competition locally, and filled a need among Western-educated clientele familiar with the benefits of psychotherapy. "Psychotherapy is extremely new here. There is still not much going on," he explains. The Chinese government has recently acknowledged the need for psychotherapy, Pummell says, thus giving his business legitimacy.

Pummell, who has also opened an art gallery and an entertainment business, advises foreign entrepreneurs coming into China not to underestimate the sophistication—and the potential buying power—of urban Chinese consumers. His music booking agency organizes events and provides music for luxury-brand clients, including Ferrari. Says Pummell: "There are people with a lot of money here. They buy Ferraris and other beautiful things. If you were to ask me the difference between the promotion parties thrown in Shanghai and those thrown in New York and London, I'm not sure there is a difference."

Parisian fashion retailer Valerie Touya successfully found a niche market for her upscale designer clothing when she opened her Curiosity Fashion Store boutiques in Shanghai and Suzhou. A full 80% of her clientele are Chinese nationals, a set she describes as "25- to 45-year-old women, working in creative jobs such as media. People who like fashion, like to get dressed up and go out, need a lot of clothes. Curious people who want to keep updated on new trends. Women who already have a European lifestyle." Touya found enough of such domestic Chinese shoppers to expand, within the first year in business, from selling imported French designer wear to Chinese retailers to opening three of her own retail boutiques.

Touya is sticking with a business plan in which she finds clients for eclectic, high-quality, mid-priced designer clothing, rather than adapting European fashions to suit Chinese tastes. "I'm not trying to adapt my concept to the Chinese. I am very French with the style, the atmosphere in the store. This is my strength. I don't want to adapt to the local market; I want to be very different, even the fashions—I won't change the size, the cut of the sleeves, for example. If I did, I would not be selling a French brand!" Touya says the only aspect of her stores that she "localized" was the use of a frequent shopper VIP card offering discounts for repeat customers—a highly popular sales method among Chinese shoppers.

One lesson that Touya has learned the hard way is that what works in Shanghai may not work outside the megacity. Touya opened a boutique in Suzhou, a major foreign investment destination just a two-hour drive from Shanghai. But while sales in Shanghai were hitting targets of RMB50,000 to RMB100,000 (US$7,140 to US$14,285) per month for her small boutiques, sales in Suzhou were one-tenth to one-twentieth that amount. "In Suzhou, on some days we might have no sales. I recently totaled RMB4,000 [US$570] for a whole month." Touya, who came to China with years of experience with French retailer Printemps, says the problem wasn't so much the location as the mindset of consumers. "In Suzhou, we are located in a good area for foot traffic, but the consumers in that part of town have a mindset that is too mass market," she says. "It is not the right place for my customer. My customer exists in Suzhou, but she doesn't go to that part of town. I need to make an effort to go and get the customer. The local and expat customer in Suzhou is more traditional, not trendy."

Since Touya had paid a full year's rent in advance on her boutique, moving to a different part of Suzhou wasn't an option. To boost the low sales volume, she had to undertake expensive promotional efforts that hadn't been necessary in Shanghai, such as hosting a fashion show in a hotel and nightclub, which attracted 400 people plus media coverage. Her underlying message for entrepreneurs: don't move into China's second- and third-tier cities too quickly.

> *There are people with a lot of money here. They buy Ferraris and other beautiful things. If you were to ask me the difference between the promotion parties thrown in Shanghai and those thrown in New York and London, I'm not sure there is a difference."*
>
> **Mark Pummell**
> (England), Founder and CEO, ChinArt, Sinapse, and Music Pavilion

Be aware of the diversity of demographics in China. If you are targeting sophisticated consumers, don't rush into the second- and third-tier cities. What works in Shanghai may flop elsewhere.

Our other interviewees agreed that consumer sophistication, tastes, and buying patterns vary widely across different regions of China. This means that what works in one part of the country may fail in other areas—a fact that some of our entrepreneurs learned the hard way. Turkish startup owner Onder Oztunali, founder of Globe Stone Corp., explains how he addresses the divergent markets for his stone business within China. "My clients are mostly Chinese, but I never talk about one China, but many different Chinas. Different parts of the country have different cultures, customs, ethics—many things are different." For example, Ozuntali says his first China experiences were in Beijing, where he quickly came to appreciate the culture and business pace. But when he traveled to the southeast province of Fujian, he found a very different culture among the local people. "When I came to Beijing, I said: 'This is much different than I expected. Beijing people are into culture, and hip and trendy things. They are big-picture people.' But the Fujianese are completely different. They are so focused on making money all the time. I think they are the toughest customers in China. They don't really care about the big picture; just *now*."

While designer clothing, Ferraris, and even psychotherapy finds a market in the urban centers, other high-priced imported products and services are not yet attracting Chinese consumers, our interviewees warn. "Able to spend" doesn't mean "ready to spend." Our consultants warned against entering the China market armed only with data on rising salaries. Entrepreneur Jordan Zilber explains a case in point. He recently helped an Israeli company eager to introduce to China a high-end product for the dental market that had been very successful in the United States, Japan, and Europe. Zilber says the China market wasn't ready for the product, but the Israeli company was impatient. "The market in China isn't yet prepared for such a product, but they aren't open to hearing this. They think their Chinese partner understands the Chinese market. The president came here for three days and he believed he knew China better than I do," says Zilber. "The Chinese aren't willing to pay so much for dental services even though they can afford a BMW. Things will change, but now is just the beginning. You have to lower prices, change the marketing—do everything differently."

One common message, loudly voiced by our interviewees, is: look before you leap. Those who jumped into the China market without fully understanding the customer base—especially the difficulties inherent not just in finding customers, but also in actually getting paid—got burned. Consider the following case of Bleum, which nearly went bankrupt after following a disastrous initial business plan (see In Search of Paying Customers, next page).

 **Don't jump into the China market without fully understanding the particular customer base you are targeting.**

Getting Your Customers to Pay You

Identifying the right customers for the products or services of your China-based operations is only half the battle. The other half—often the most difficult—is getting those customers to pay you. Many of our interviewees reported facing anywhere from a slight to a serious problem with not being paid on time, not being paid in full, or not being paid at all.

Retail display designer and manufacturer Susan Heffernan first experienced payment difficulties when she started selling to the China market. "Selling locally is very different from the export business, which is very clean. In the China market, you may have to revise the quotation 50 times, and getting payment is very difficult."

Another common payment problem, Eric Rongley says, is that Chinese companies tend to be very political, meaning that many different parties may be involved in (and possibly creating obstacles to) your payment request. "Everybody along the payment path [in a Chinese client company] has to be made happy. You need to invite them to dinner and give them gifts—do things for them. If any one of the people along that path doesn't feel they were treated right, they will exercise their right to hold up payment." Thus, companies selling to Chinese clients

CASE STUDY

IN SEARCH OF (PAYING) CUSTOMERS

Problems with cash flow—specifically, getting paid by customers and clients—can be fatal for startups anywhere in the world, but the toll is especially high for foreign ventures based in China. Consider the rocky start experienced by Shanghai-based Bleum. U.S. software executive Eric Rongley launched his specialized software company using his personal savings, which he then had to top up with another US$50,000 borrowed from friends.

The business was difficult to start because of a Catch-22: Bleum needed a big team of software engineers in order to attract customers—but it also needed customers in order to pay the employees. In the beginning, it was lopsided, Rongley recalls. "I had a payroll of 30 people, but no customers."

During the first year of operation, projects began pouring in and Bleum was busy—but still going broke. After the first 12 months of operation, the company had burned through most of the startup funding, and little money was coming in.

Rongley says his main mistake was in not following his business instincts. After having spent two years working in China for a U.S.-based company, he had launched Bleum knowing that the safest business plan for his high-end services was to focus on offshore clients. But just after launching, he switched tactics. "I didn't have enough money to attract offshore clients at first," he says. "So I thought: I'll do local projects first, and build up the company's strength and the team while I save more money."

But as an unknown startup in an emerging field for the China market, Rongley found that domestic customers were quite happy to try Bleum's services, but were very slow (or even unwilling) to pay for them. "In the first year, we focused on the local market, which promptly depleted all of my cash," he says.

The main problem, he says, was his own lack of understanding of Chinese business culture. First, Rongley and his Chinese clients had a very different concept of a business contract. "This is the difficult thing when doing business in China. In the West, we negotiate a deal and we struggle through the initial negotiation because we don't want to struggle after that. But in Asia, the first agreement is just one part of the ongoing process of working together—the perception is that both sides will keep negotiating as they do business." In other words, an agreement for payment is just a guideline, which the Chinese side expects to discuss and alter as actual business begins.

Second, Rongley didn't fully understand the Chinese business mindset and the bias against young and weak startups. He thought his experience in launching operations for a U.S. company in India would help him succeed in China. "I figured that I knew how to adapt the business model to China. But after I launched my own business, I found I didn't understand how business is done in China," he says. "[Chinese] businesspeople have a different set of goals when they engage a vendor. I was hitting my head on a bunch of walls. We weren't getting paid; we had customers making unreasonable requests of us; and, most importantly, the customers in China, especially five years ago, were very immature." Because Bleum was a young company with few resources, clients felt free to break deal terms and refuse to pay. "I found it a very vicious marketplace for us as a small, underfunded company."

Chinese clients were extremely short term in their thinking, he remembers. Stated bluntly: many clients didn't expect Bleum to survive long in business, so they didn't feel inclined to pay for its services. "It's kind of ironic that people in the West think Asians are very long-term thinkers. Actually, I see business here as extremely short term—'I'm going to burn up this vendor because there is another sucker right behind him; and after I burn *him* up, there will be another one right behind him.'"

At the end of the first year of operation, Rongley faced a do-or-die situation: "All our cash was gone," he remembers. Faced with a crisis, his first decision was to stop working for local client companies. Bleum even refused job requests from domestic clients that had paid their accounts.

His second move was to rely on his relationships in international markets to find paying customers and turn the company around. "Because of my reputation and my network in the software industry, I was able to pick up a few projects and got started from zero again," he says. At last, contracts—and payments—began rolling in. Says Rongley: "By the end of the second year, we weren't doing any local work. We had to tell some of our local customers 'We are done working for you.'"

Today, Rongley says he was correct in taking this "cold turkey" approach. The lesson learned: for high-end services and products that are new to China, foreign entrepreneurs face an easier time selling to international customers that are more familiar with the value of the service or product—and are more willing to pay for them.

> *Everybody along the payment path [in a Chinese client company] has to be made happy. You need to invite them to dinner and give them gifts—do things for them. Because if any one of the people along that path doesn't feel they were treated right, they will exercise their right to hold up payment."*

Eric Rongley (USA),
Founder and CEO,
Bleum

spend a lot of time and effort chasing payments. "Companies that do a lot of local business here have large sales teams and spend a lot of money on payment collection," says Rongley. "More importantly, they spend a lot of *energy* on this—energy that should go into productive things."

Putting the challenges into perspective, American entrepreneur and consultant Steven Ganster says the issue has improved over time. "Five to 10 years ago, getting paid was a horrendous issue. I would say that, today, it's not so much about not collecting payment, but about financing the 120 days it takes to get paid." In other words, the China market has grown more sophisticated and more in line with international practices. "In the mid-1990s, people lost a lot of money—they never collected at all." By contrast, today, while the issue varies in importance from industry to industry, Ganster's clients generally spend less time chasing payments. "It's an issue that our clients still suffer from, but it's not in the top list anymore."

Below, our interviewees offer their China-tested methods of coping with payment issues.

Payment Tactic #1: Cash Only, No Delays

The advice on payments provided most often by our China-based international entrepreneurs and consultants was simple: insist on cash only, and don't tolerate delays. Veterans of the China market said while such a policy may make getting started difficult, it is not impossible. The alternative, they stressed, is serious cash flow problems.

American entrepreneur Mark Secchia explains why Sherpa's operates on a cash-only basis for his meal delivery and other services: "We take cash on delivery. We don't do credit cards. We don't do accounts receivable. Nothing." This policy ensures money in the bank at the end of each month, which Sherpa's can use to pay suppliers and employees. "It's all a matter of cash flow. Profit really doesn't matter. You can be a very profitable company, but if your customers never pay you, you will go bankrupt."

Nic Pannekeet, a business development entrepreneur with 18 years in the China market, also insists on a prepaid, cash-only model for his company. "We always ask the customers to pay cash. This is our rule." He warns foreigners entering the market not to allow credit payments or delayed payment in their eagerness to break into China. "There are certain principles, and I stick to them. If you let it go, one month's credit becomes two and three, and you create a problem for yourself. Some people are so eager to get into a certain business that they forget the principle of the business: cash is the most important thing in a society like this one." Because the Chinese market allows for fast growth, companies with loose payment systems can quickly suffer from cash-flow troubles. "If you don't manage your cash, and the business grows fast, you face problems. Many businesses [in China] grow 30–40% a year, or even more. In that situation, you will have a problem if you aren't careful with your cash.

Based on "quite a few" bad experiences (see box, pages 94–95), software executive Eric Rongley also warns startups in China against offering special discounts and delays, even in the early stages. "As an entrepreneur starting [in China], especially if you are trying to break into an open market and your company is unknown, customers will keep saying: 'You need your first reference account, so make us a good deal—do it for free or for a little money, and we'll pay you a year later.' Don't fall for any of that because it very seldom works out," he says. "It's very much like in [the U.S. cartoon strip] *Peanuts*, when Lucy is holding the football and Charlie Brown is kicking it. Don't believe it."

Rongley advises startups to hold their ground, not offering first-time discounts or allowing payment delays. "If you are weak, [customers] will never be generous. One piece of advice is: if the [customer] isn't going to pay a reasonable amount—trading value for value—and pay upfront, don't deal with them. There will always be another sucker behind you who will fall for that trick."

Importer Juan Martinez, founder of SOLHIX, also warns against offering credit. "It's difficult to collect payment here.

TIP Insist on cash only, and don't tolerate delays. The alternative can be a serious—even disastrous—cash-flow problem for your business.

"

It's all a matter of cash flow. Profit really doesn't matter. You can be a very profitable company, but if your customers never pay you, you will go bankrupt."

Mark Secchia (USA), Founder, Sherpa's

TIP If a new customer isn't going to pay a reasonable amount and pay upfront, don't deal with them.

"

At the beginning, don't give credit. It's bad to think that people would cheat you, but some people would actually do it. It's better to take measures to avoid it."

Juan Martinez
(Mexico), Founder and Director, SOLHIX

We had some bad cases. The first time, I gave two pallets of leather to a company and they never paid us. We understood the lesson very well: don't work on credit." Until you have built trust with customers, he says, it is critical to insist on upfront payment. "My suggestion is to get payment in advance, cash on delivery, or a letter of credit. It might become a nightmare if they owe you a lot of money. At the beginning, don't give credit. It's bad to think that people would cheat you, but some people would actually do it. It's better to take measures to avoid it."

Retail display designer Susan Heffernan explains the challenges she faced in demanding a cash-before-delivery system. "In the very beginning, I was very strict with my payment terms—50% deposit, and 50% before delivery." She says the strategy was accepted by offshore customers, but not by local domestic buyers. "I lost jobs because of this," she says, but adds that sticking to her rule was worth it. "My advice is to stick to your rule, and stick to it more and more and more. People would say, 'If I pay you 50% of the payment before delivery, what if something happened and you cannot deliver?' Now I say the delivery isn't included. 'You can come to my warehouse, and inspect everything on the site. You can use my delivery company, but that fee is extra. My deal ends with the production of the product. If something happens on the delivery, you can make a claim.'" She says taking a tough line is necessary. "My strict payment terms are what have made me so successful."

Refusal to pay isn't a problem only experienced by foreigners. "At the beginning, I thought the Chinese were playing games with me because I am a foreigner," says importer/exporter Oto Petroski. "But when I discovered the problems they experience between themselves, I found it is 10 times worse."

Finally, China veteran Olaf Litjens stresses that, in many cases, when Chinese buyers fail to pay, they are suffering from their own cash-flow problems. "Oftentimes, it's not because the Chinese buyers don't want to pay, but they don't have money themselves. Financing for them is also a problem."

Payment Tactic #2: Choose Your Customers Carefully

In my experience, dealing with small companies is more risky. They can just shut down in one day and disappear with the money."

Juan Martinez
(Mexico), Founder and Director, SOLHIX

Several of our entrepreneur interviewees stress that taking the time to research major customers before selling to them is time well spent. When selling for his music and entertainment companies, British entrepreneur Mark Pummell says he and his business partner are "definitely very selective about who we do business with." He explains: "We put a lot of energy into whom we choose—we are very relationship focused." He says that, at a typical trade fair, he may end up making sales to one or two companies. "We go slowly and we choose people carefully. If we feel that someone isn't being fair with us, we take the view that we have more than one business and there are many options here in China, and we just politely walk away." When in doubt that a new customer or client will pay, says Pummell, "We say, 'Good luck in your business. Bye bye.'"

Import/export trader Juan Martinez agrees, adding that he and his business partners at SOLHIX are especially wary of selling to smaller businesses. Says Martinez: "In my experience, dealing with small companies is more risky. They can just shut down in one day and disappear with the money."

Japanese consultant Hiroshi Shoda comments that it is easier now to choose larger and more reliable Chinese partners—and to use more sophisticated payment systems—because many industries have matured. For instance, he witnessed a transformation in the retail home appliance industry in China during his previous job as president of Sony China. "The market [in China] has also changed. In 1993 or 1994, there were some aggressive small (home appliance retailers) like Guomei. Now, Guomei is a big retail chain and a big success. Back then, we collected cash-on-delivery from Guomei, but as their ordering volume grew, we granted them credit," he says. "In the past 10 years, the retail system has changed. Small shops are gone and only big chain stores like Guomei and Suning have survived. They have big business now, so we changed our policy accordingly."

Payment Tactic #3: Build up *Guanxi*

Business development founder Jordan Zilber offers this advice for small companies struggling to get paid: "You can control it in different ways. First, you must have strong *guanxi* with [your customers], so they have strong interest in paying you. Second, don't give them everything at the first stage; wait until they pay."

Trouble with Foreign Clients

Selling only to non-Chinese customers isn't a foolproof solution for getting paid. Several of our entrepreneurs stress that selling to multinational corporation clients requires delays in payment that aren't necessary when selling to domestic clients. Engineering company founder Shah Firoozi says: "The process of getting the invoices approved and payments made is very challenging. Many times, our foreign invoices have to go through bank approvals and payment of tax in advance before getting the money. [SMEs] can lose a lot of money by not understanding how much time you will have to wait." Firoozi says his firm has an easier time collecting from local companies than MNCs. "With local companies, once we have a contract or an agreement, the system runs very well. With a multinational company, however, we found that we run into a lot of unforeseen conditions because of the changes in the regulations on MNCs or because the financial situation of an MNC has changed, and so on. There is always something that delays payments. With local companies, once you get established, payment isn't really a big issue. Generally speaking, our experience with local companies for payment is much better than with MNCs."

Moroccan exporter Aziz Mrabet shares the same experience: "Up to now, I've never been cheated by a Chinese. However, I've been cheated by a Swedish client. He asked me to ship by air some goods he had purchased from us. If you ship by air, you don't have a bill of lading for payment. Usually the bill of lading goes with the goods. The goods arrived, but he didn't pay me. At first, he promised that if the buyer didn't have any claims, they would pay everything. In the end, he changed the whole story and found excuses never to pay me. The lesson is: You can't run a business without trust. Most of the time, you are a winner if you build good partnerships with people."

Zilber adds that while most Chinese companies are "serious" and "70% of all payments are okay," he still takes extra precautions because collecting missing payments is very difficult. "You do have to be aware that the legal system is not as good as in the West."

Dutch flower exporter Nic Pannekeet agrees that the best protection against not getting paid is to build a trusting relationship with clients. "It can be difficult to get the money from the customers sometimes—extremely difficult. Chinese customers are very demanding and suspicious; they have no trust in the supplier, especially when it is a new one." Before working with a new client, he says, his company does "rounds and rounds of negotiations—the procedure can be very complicated." The only solution, he says, is taking the time to build up a win–win relationship. Pannekeet says he also uses his long experience in China and his Mandarin language skills to win clients' trust. "Now, everybody in this flower industry knows me, a Dutch guy speaking Chinese. It is an advantage to be a foreigner, as you are conspicuous. Once people know you, they are willing to do business with you." Pannekeet says that, in recent years, the trust built with Chinese clients has served his company well. "We have had some [payment] problems, but are lucky enough to have them solved over time."

Once *guanxi* is built up, our interviewees said, relations with clients, suppliers, and buyers can sometimes be even stronger and more reliable than is standard elsewhere. Dutch businessman Olaf Litjens tells of a case in point. In 1997, he and his business partner had made a business of importing a brand of milk powder—called Dutch Dairy Cow—from Europe to sell in China. Litjens explains the incident: "From 1997 to 2000, we sold this milk powder brand. In 1999, there was some incident in Belgium regarding the contamination of the animals' feed, and the problem affected our brand. Belgium, Netherlands, Germany, and France were all affected. We appeared in every newspaper and on every Chinese TV station for about two months. The locals took advantage of the situation to claim that foreign brands were no good. We learned a bit about crisis

Don't rely on the Chinese legal system to help you claim payment; it is immature and still not very efficient. Better to spend time upfront forming a strong working relationship before you begin doing business.

Chinese customers are very demanding and suspicious; they have no trust in the supplier, especially when it is a new one."

Nic Pannekeet
(Netherlands), Founder, CHC Business Development

"

This is the incredible thing about the Chinese people: if the relationship is there, the trust is there, they do incredible things for you. People complain that they don't pay, but [Chinese business people] can also really help you when you need it."

Olaf Litjens
(Netherlands), Founder and CEO, Unisono Fieldmarketing (Shanghai)

management at that time. We lost all the money we had made up until then in just six months."

Litjens' products were blocked from store shelves for two months. "I had imported 80 containers-worth, and now I had to pay warehouse time—a huge amount of money," says Litjens. When he explained his predicament to his wholesaler, with whom he had done business for many years, an unexpected thing happened. "He just gave me the money—unbelievable!" says Litjens. "Because of the relationship we had built up for so many years, he understood us and helped me get through it. That would never happen in the West. Never." He stresses that such deep loyalty is more common in China than in Europe or the U.S. "This is the incredible thing about the Chinese people: if the relationship is there, the trust is there, they do incredible things for you. People complain that they don't pay, but they can also really help you when you need it."

One reason you can stick to insisting on cash payments is that Chinese companies often demand such a transaction themselves, especially when dealing with a new customer. Says Italian consultant Ruggero Jenna: "The first time you work with wholesalers in China, they demand cash payment. After a while, they will allow some financing. After the relationship is built, they will accept if you can have some delayed payments, or something like that. Again, you are building a track record. It's fundamental."

TIP Don't give up when a client defaults on payment. Be persistent until they pay.

Payment Tactic #4: If Necessary, Go Collecting

As a last resort, our entrepreneurs stress that they sometimes must go collecting in order to get paid. Some even hire employees specifically for this task. Mark Pummell demands a 50% deposit when arranging events and booking music, but he still has had to go collecting personally in some cases. "You have to be extremely firm. Payment is one of the areas where I must be very hands-on. I will go and knock on the door and make people very uncomfortable," says Pummell. "I make it very clear that if you are going to do business with us, you have to pay. We have a 50% deposit model, which I think is a good method."

Conclusion

Our foreign entrepreneurs found that they can sometimes turn their foreignness into an advantage. A usual path is to start their business model by selling products and services to fellow foreigners in China, or by exporting/importing to/from their home countries. An export/import business seems to be a natural option for many of our entrepreneurs. From that initial business, they can expand their range of products and services and eventually start selling to Chinese customers. This gradual approach seems to be a usual pattern among our entrepreneurs.

One key factor stressed by our interviewees is payment collection. Success, they say, isn't about generating profits but about managing your cash flow. Startups should be aware of unscrupulous buyers that may take advantage of the startup's strong desire to sell. An easy sale can become a death sentence. It is better to refuse a sale when the conditions are unfair. One repeated warning is to ask for cash payments until a level of trust with the buyer has been built.

SUMMARY OF TIPS
TARGETING THE RIGHT CUSTOMERS . . . AND GETTING PAID

FINDING THE RIGHT CUSTOMERS	GETTING PAID
Use your foreignness as an advantage over Chinese competitors. You can set up your business model to export back home, or to other foreign markets where you have professional insight and connections.	Insist on cash only, and don't tolerate delays. The alternative can be a serious—even disastrous—cash-flow problem for your business.
Consider targeting China-based foreigners. Understand their needs, and develop products/services aimed at meeting them.	If a new customer isn't going to pay a reasonable amount and pay upfront, don't deal with them.

FINDING THE RIGHT CUSTOMERS

The easiest, most logical target market for a foreign entrepreneur in China is buyers in your home country or other overseas markets, or fellow expats in China.

Unless you have a product or service aimed specifically at Chinese consumers, try cracking the China market step by step. Begin by targeting more familiar foreign clients, then target Chinese customers as you gain more experience.

You may need to educate Chinese consumers before they will appreciate the value of your product/service, and are willing to pay the price you expect.

Consider Chinese consumers in your business model. They are becoming wealthier, worldlier, and more sophisticated, which creates opportunities for foreign entrepreneurs.

Look for products and services that are still new to the China market. The number of such opportunities is decreasing quickly, as Chinese competitors rush into new sectors.

Be aware of the diversity of demographics in China. If you are targeting sophisticated consumers, don't move into the second- and third-tier cities. What works in Shanghai may flop elsewhere.

Don't jump into the China market without fully understanding the customer base you are targeting.

GETTING PAID (*cont'd*)

Build good *guanxi* with your Chinese clients. Don't give them everything at the first stage; wait until they pay.

Don't rely on the Chinese legal system to help you claim payment; it is immature and inefficient. Better to spend time forming a strong working relationship before you begin doing business.

Don't give up when a client defaults on payment. Be persistent until they pay.

Chapter 5
Human Resource Challenges

"As a small company, you are really at a disadvantage because many capable young Chinese want to go to a brand-name company that gives them face with family, friends, and professors."

Jeffrey Bernstein (USA), Founder and Managing Director, Emerge Logistics Shanghai

"If you can manage human resources in China, you can manage China. I think it's the key factor."

Prakash Menon (India), President, NIIT (China)

Introduction

After they had got their China-based enterprise up and running—having found the startup funding, secured government approvals, and identified the right market for their product or service—our China-based international entrepreneurs found their single-most difficult challenge was finding, training, and keeping qualified and capable employees. While this goal is likely a top-priority one for entrepreneurs operating worldwide, in China, it can be a truly make-or-break factor as the market presents several unique challenges.

The first of these challenges, according to our China entrepreneurs, is the cultural gap between a non-Chinese business owner and his or her Chinese employees. This gap affected nearly all our interviewees, who hailed from 25 different nations; however, those from the West, East Asia, and India identified different gaps. (See the boxes on comparative management skills, later in this chapter.) The bottom line: China's business and social norms differ from those of most other major trading nations significantly enough that culture clashes persist. The first task for a non-Chinese business owner, then, is to discover where the gaps exist. They must then learn to fill them effectively, in order to form and grow a successful team.

This chapter covers five main topics:

1. Strengths and weaknesses of Chinese employees
2. Bridging the skills gap: Training, training, training
3. Recruitment and retention challenges
4. HR strategies: Selling "small is beautiful"
5. Solving the salary question

Strengths and Weaknesses of Chinese Employees

Typical Strengths

Our 40 international business owners acknowledged several key areas in which Chinese employees excel, when compared with their counterparts elsewhere.

First and foremost among the special skills of Chinese employees is, of course, their insider's knowledge of China. All our interviewees stressed that a strong team of domestic Chinese staff is crucial for the success of their China-based enterprise, in all aspects of the business. Israeli business development/investment entrepreneur Aviel Zilber says that one of the secrets of his and his brother Jordan's success in launching Sheng Enterprises in 2003 was encouraging their Chinese staff to take the lead in explaining the Chinese way of operating before deciding on the method Sheng would adopt. Zilber explains: "I tend to give [my Chinese staff] credit that their way of thinking is probably the right one. We are in China. They are Chinese, and they know the business culture here and how to do things in China. If we have a discussion and they think we should do something in a certain Chinese way, at the beginning, I always consider their way first." In other words, Zilber tends first to ask his staff for their recommendations on how to handle a certain issue; he then weighs the benefits of using the "Chinese way" before deciding whether to adapt it or modify it to a more Western method.

Another commonly mentioned strength of Chinese personnel is their sheer diligence and ambition. Co-founder of Sheng Enterprises, Jordan Zilber explains: "China is an amazing place, for several reasons. One is the discipline of the Chinese students. At the end of a class, if a university professor says, 'I haven't completed this lesson yet—do you want me to complete it today or tomorrow?' The Chinese students will all reply: 'Today.' In Israel, the students would be gone before you could even finish that sentence." He says that Chinese people's hardworking, better-now-than-later attitude is shown at work as well. "People here are very motivated to do business," he says. Thus, working overtime, studying on the side to advance one's career, and constantly seeking career advancement are all common among the Chinese workforce, especially white-collar workers.

Taiwanese manufacturing business owner Wendy Tai also finds positive attributes in mainland China employees. She compares her staff in China with those in her native Taiwan: "Employees from mainland China are much better than those from Taiwan; they're more diligent. More importantly, people

> *I tend to give [my Chinese staff] credit that their way of thinking is probably the right one. We are in China. They are Chinese, and they know the business culture here and how to do things in China. If we have a discussion and they think we should do something in a certain Chinese way, at the beginning, I always consider their way first."*

Aviel Zilber
(Israel), Chairman, Sheng Enterprises

from the mainland have broader horizons, because they live in a big country; while Taiwanese live on a small island."

Spanish consultant Josep Giro advises his China-based Western clients that the work ethic commonly found among successful Chinese students carries into the workplace. "Chinese students study for long hours every day," he says. "For European students, if there is a party, they will join the party. For Chinese people, there are no parties—they study 24 hours every day." This all-work-no-play ethic often continues when today's graduates begin working, Giro adds, especially if the new employee believes that hard work will lead to career advancement.

Other interviewees also stressed that Chinese employees tend to face tremendous pressure from their families to succeed professionally. Unlike in other cultures, many professionals in China are expected and encouraged by their families to work long hours and to sacrifice social and family life. In other words, rather than viewing work–life imbalance as damaging to family, in China, it is often considered as a noble sacrifice that executives make in order to support their family. Especially in the case of parents of young children, it is widely accepted in China that both fathers and mothers will focus on their careers, leaving the primary childcare duties to nannies or grandparents.

Typical Weaknesses

While China's rigorous and often brutally competitive education system tends to produce professionals with a hard-driving work ethic, the system also leaves gaps in the job skills needed by international employers in terms of leadership, independent thinking, creativity and initiative, and accountability—all skills that are necessary in an international business environment.

One weakness of Chinese employees in general is pointed out by Chee-Chin Wu, a Canadian business owner who has operated a luxury floor tiles business in China since 2003. "In China, there is an old saying that 'Everyone sweeps his own snow in front of the door.' That is to say, they don't care much about others. Chinese people are hard working, but most of them don't have any idea of how to help others to work together." Such a mindset makes the concept of working in teams particularly difficult for Chinese employees to grasp.

Another weakness, Wu adds, concerns the Chinese concept of "face." Wu expresses the frustration typically experienced by Western employers in China: "Chinese people are reluctant to ask questions while they're attending meetings. They won't tell you that they are unable to do things beforehand." In North America, the situation is the opposite. Chinese people have to learn how to express themselves and how to communicate with others. I tell my employees, 'If you can't handle the work, please ask for help in advance.' Chinese people have to take more initiative. When they encounter a problem, they need to think of how to solve the problem, instead of just complaining." Wu comments that the tendency for Chinese employees to want to avoid appearing incapable before their colleagues or peers, and to generally lack initiative in solving problems, is "the consequence of the educational system in China," which emphasizes passive listening and discourages challenges to authority. One oft-used contrast is that Westerners follow the adage "the squeaky wheel gets the oil," while a popular Asian (Japanese-origin) saying is: "The nail that sticks up gets pounded down."

Irish entrepreneur Ken Carroll, founder of the Praxis internet-based language learning systems, agrees with those observations. He identifies the key gaps he has seen among Chinese employees as: reluctance to voice an opinion, to take business risks, and to be accountable. "The education system in China makes [students] great learners, but what they don't learn is to put their hands up and say: 'I'm going to risk it. I'm going to do it.'"

Carroll also says that this aversion to risk-taking is a learned response to the Chinese education system. He points out that his daughter, who is attending a Chinese-language primary school, is learning in the traditional Chinese way. "There is a lot of chanting at her school. All the kids are just repeating after the teacher." Speaking up as an individual is rare. Says Carroll: "I can see that the discipline [of Chinese schools] is good, but I really doubt whether this strict approach is the way to go into the future."

> *Chinese people are reluctant to ask questions while they're attending meetings. They won't tell you that they are unable to do things beforehand."*
>
> **Chee-Chin Wu**
> (Taiwan), Founder, Novalis Int'l.

"

It's not difficult to find intelligent people [in China]—there are plenty of very intelligent people. But it is difficult to find people who are able and willing to take on the challenge, to be accountable, and willing to make decisions and really manage."

Olaf Litjens
(Netherlands), Founder and CEO, Unisono Fieldmarketing (Shanghai)

Carroll adds that the Chinese government is under pressure to modernize the education system, and says he expects reforms over the next decade to promote more independent thinking and speaking out. "The schools and universities are not encouraging creativity. The thinking is: 'If I pass my exams and I study really hard, I will be fine.' In the world of entrepreneurship, passing exams has nothing to do with it," he says. "But, in 10 years, Chinese employees will be more creative. I think the thinking will change, because they are bright and very ambitious."

Others among our interviewees were less optimistic in terms of the time frame needed to overcome the weaknesses created by China's current education system. Prakash Menon, president of NIIT (China), explained: "Another weakness [among Chinese employees] is the ability to provide solutions for new problems. This is related to the education system. Forming a human mind takes less than one year, but conditioning a mind takes a lot more time—a generation. That's the educational problem that China faces."

In the meantime, until the education system is reformed, international SME owners face a situation in which their Chinese employees, even highly skilled professionals, tend to lack ability in key management skills. This lack is created in the traditional education system and reinforced in traditional Chinese companies, which operate based on a highly hierarchical structure. Most are managed in a strictly top-down style, where younger, less experienced employees are rarely encouraged to voice opinions or given complex responsibilities. As veteran China fieldmarketing entrepreneur Olaf Litjens explains: "It's not difficult to find intelligent people [in China]—there are plenty of very intelligent people. But it *is* difficult to find people who are able and willing to take on the challenge, to be accountable, and willing to make decisions and really manage." Scottish publishing entrepreneur Jonathan Di Rollo agrees: "Domestic Chinese professionals do have weaknesses. They don't see the big picture; don't understand how to manage foreign nationals in terms of personal relationships— soft skills."

Lack of Management Skills

China's acute shortage of qualified management-level employees can also be attributed to historical and associated economic causes. In China, those aged over 45, whose education was interrupted by the Cultural Revolution, began their working careers under the state-run economic system. Thus, employees of this generation tend to lack management skills. "I see a lot of difference between the 40+ generation and the 40– generation. The difference is huge — as if they were from different countries," says Prakash Menon. "It is a lot more difficult to work with the older generation. Young people in their thirties are a lot more international."

As a result of these factors, "young and inexperienced" is a common descriptor for the workforce available to many international employers in China. One case in point is the IT sector, explains software outsourcing company founder Eric Rongley. Looking at the computer engineering sector in particular, he stresses that China's universities are swelling in student numbers, producing a flood of inexperienced graduates. "In 2002, China produced around 40,000 computer science graduates per year. By 2005, that number had grown to more than 200,000 — a 500% increase in just a few years. Only China can do that," he says. But these fresh graduates aren't meeting the demand for experienced middle managers, Rongley says. "The problem is that there is a flood of people who have only a few years' experience. People who are today's middle managers are part of the 40,000 people who graduated in 2002."

Consultant Ruggero Jenna says the problem is one that extends across industries and around the country, affecting nearly all foreign-invested companies. "Good people, especially at the senior level, are very difficult to find in China," he says. "It's very easy to recruit junior people — junior employees are cheap in China. But at the manager, senior manager, or partner's level, they are very difficult to find and are very expensive. Their salary level is even above that of managers in Europe, because there are very few available."

> *I see a lot of difference between the 40+ generation and the 40– generation. The difference is huge — as if they were from different countries.*
>
> **Prakash Menon** (India), President, NIIT (China)

> *It's very easy to recruit junior people. . . in China. But at the manager, senior manager, or partner's level, they are very difficult to find and are very expensive.*
>
> **Ruggero Jenna** (Italy), Managing Partner for Asia and Asia Pacific, Value Partners

The upshot: lack of qualified personnel has become a serious inhibitor to growth among international companies in China in recent years.

Bridging the Skills Gap: Training, Training, Training

Given the lack of experienced managers, the availability of young and naive graduates, and the lack of focus within the Chinese education system on leadership skills and innovation,

The China HR Paradox: People Shortages in the Land of Billions

While unemployment is a growing concern among China's population of unskilled workers, the demand for qualified personnel among foreign enterprises outweighs supply. Many China-based international chambers of commerce have found that their member companies face white-collar turnover rates of 12–20% in key fields, while salaries are increasing by 6–10% in many positions. As a result, many chambers in China focus much of their effort on helping their member organizations to cope with the current "war for talent" among employers battling for white-collar workers.

The 2008 *Business Climate Survey* published by AmCham China (in Beijing) and AmCham Shanghai, and representing responses from 800 U.S. companies, found that "management-level human resources constraints" was the Number 1 "business challenge" among respondents. Thirty-seven percent of companies polled listed this as a "top 5" concern, and 80% reported problems in recruiting, training, and retaining managers and skilled workers (up 10% on the 2007 report).

In another example, the *2007 Swiss–China Human Resources Management Survey* found an average annual employee turnover of 11.9% among China-based Swiss companies. Yet, success stories from Swiss pioneers operating profitably, and with employee turnover rates of 3–4% per year, allowed the study to identify the following tips for attracting, managing, and retaining good employees:

most of our interviewees described facing a similar challenge in managing their China-based startup: what to do with a team of young and ambitious, but inexperienced, employees?

Nearly all our entrepreneurs agreed that the solution lies in providing more thorough and frequent training to Chinese personnel than would be needed elsewhere. Because most startups cannot afford to pay for expensive training courses, many business founders end up developing—even implementing—staff training themselves.

In the next sections, we present the advice of our profiled entrepreneurs on strategies for training entry-level employees and mid-level to senior staff.

TIP **Chinese employees generally don't cope well with unclear tasks and are uncomfortable adapting to new circumstances. They typically expect step-by-step instructions.**

- Qualified and capable Chinese have high expectations regarding their career and work-life. They generally don't change jobs solely for an incremental package increase offered by another company, but because they don't see a sufficient chance for their next career step with their current employer. As a result, providing opportunities for personal development, training, and career opportunities—along with salary advancement in keeping with the market—is one of the two keys to retaining valuable staff.
- Since life in China is so focused on work, and because work takes up so much time, Chinese employees tend to value a pleasant and enjoyable company culture. Thus, the second key to retaining staff is generating a friendly work atmosphere and creating the sense of social belonging to the company through an emphasis on social activities for employees.
- To stay competitive, HR management champions need to devise incentive and performance management systems directly linking income to employees' evaluation of their activity, behavior, and results in the company.

Note: The Swiss–China Human Resources Management Survey is a joint project of the Swiss Center Shanghai, SwissCham, the Swiss–Chinese Chamber of Commerce, and OSEC Business Network Switzerland. Many similar surveys and studies designed to help foreigners wishing to do business in China are conducted regularly by other international chambers of commerce based in China, especially the American, European, German, British, Japanese, and Korean chambers.

Because Chinese managers and skilled professionals tend to come from the younger generations, companies must invest more time in training.

Training Strategies for Entry-level Employees

In preparing entry-level Chinese employees to work in his company, restaurateur Michael Yang says he must provide broader and deeper employee training than is necessary in Hong Kong or his native Taiwan. Today, his company employs 150 Chinese nationals, many of whom, according to Yang, have large gaps in their educational or work experience training. "Most Chinese citizens who work in restaurants don't have a very good educational background. Some of them only get a couple of years of schooling; some don't even know how to write."

Yang teaches his staff many of the basics missing from the Chinese education system. "I have to let them know the fundamentals of business—such as: if we don't work hard, and if the

Management Skills: China vs. India

One telling illustration of the strengths and weaknesses typical among Chinese professionals comes through comparing the world's two most dynamic employment markets: China and India. Eleven-year China veteran Prakash Menon offers his insights into the differences between Chinese employees and those of his native India:

> There is a very big difference at different levels. In general, Indian employees would say that what matters most in their job satisfaction is the organization and the person they are working for—more than the salary. I think in China, it's completely reversed. The first factor people think of in judging job satisfaction is, "Am I happy in terms of my monetary requirements?" Then they will look at the organization and the other things.
>
> In terms of Maslow's hierarchy of needs, at the bottom is food, clothing, and shelter, and at the highest level is self-actualization. Chinese are indeed going through the different need levels, from the bottom to the top of the pyramid.
>
> But in India the order of the needs is reversed, because the need for self-actualization is much more pronounced than the need to make a good living. India is a very religious society. For example, my mother used to live in the south of India, close to a temple. At four o'clock in the morning, I would see a lot of

company doesn't make money, you won't have a job. You have to teach them Western business thinking. That's a very challenging job." As a result, Yang spends more of his own time on staff training than would be required in Taiwan, where employees tend to be more exposed to international business standards. "I spend a lot of time talking to the employees. Even with small things, I have to teach them several times," he says.

Macedonian entrepreneur Oto Petroski had a similar experience when operating his first China-based business, a European-style coffee bar in downtown Shanghai. He tells of starting with very basic service training for his wait staff because they were unfamiliar with international standards of service. In general, the concept of consistent standards and polite customer

people standing in a queue, waiting for the opening of the temple. Most of the people in the queue didn't have clothes to wear. I asked my mom why these people were standing in the queue at four in the morning [rather than trying to earn a living]. My mom told me that is what India is all about: the spiritual needs of people are so intense that, even if they don't have clothes to wear and don't know where their next meal will come from, they are still engaged in religion. This mindset doesn't exist in China.

The second difference has to do with the fact that Chinese work better as individuals, while Indians are better in teams. If you put three Chinese together on a team, it's so complicated to handle—it's not fun. I've tried [to do it] and failed.

The third difference is that Indians are outstanding at dealing with new tasks and processes. They have the initiative that if something unexpected happens, they can get it done. I think Chinese get stuck when the process is new and different, and when unexpected things happen. They aren't good at adapting in this way.

Fourth, Indians tend to be able to handle 15 different things at the same time. Multi-tasking is natural to them. Chinese prefer to do things sequentially, one after another. If Indians and Chinese are working on the same single task at the same time, the Chinese would likely be faster. But when they have to deal with a lot of things at the same time, it's just impossible.

service is lacking throughout China. "You have to teach them to provide service to people; I was very tough when I ran the coffee bar," Petroski says. He would draw detailed diagrams showing how to serve cappuccino—placing the cup on a saucer, with a chocolate, and served with a glass of water with lemon. He says training the staff in quality control and attention to detail was a challenge, given their total unfamiliarity with both European coffee culture and international service standards.

Taiwanese business founder Maggie Yu describes the challenges of training entry-level staff as follows: "Many companies face high staff turnover, especially of entry-level employees. The main reason, we have found, is difficulty for new hires in adapting to their new working environment or lack of understanding of their job responsibilities. For this reason, adopting effective training strategies is crucial." Yu

Management Skills: China vs. Japan

Consultant and entrepreneur Fumito Suzuki provides *China Entrepreneur* with a Japanese perspective on the typical business strengths and weaknesses of Chinese professionals. Like Prakash Menon, who compared the characteristics of Chinese and Indian employees (above), Suzuki found many areas of difference.

Generally speaking, both Chinese and Japanese employees are weak at timely communication and reporting. One difference is that the Chinese employees are more Western-like [in terms of work scope]; they expect a job description when joining a company and will work hard to complete the specified tasks, but will not do more than that. Japanese have the motivation to do things out of their responsibilities and will show more initiative.

Chinese are good at individual work, while the Japanese are more team players. . . . In Japan, when we have a problem [at work], we gather the people involved and talk about how to solve it. Once those people come up with a solution, everybody will follow it. In China, everybody in the group has a different opinion. It's a bit harder in China to come up with a solution. Each person thinks, urges managers to create a "well organized orientation." She adds, "Be sure that your managers spend enough time and energy on new staff members, especially in the first eight weeks, in order to orientate them." Other China-based foreign managers stress that the first two months are critical for screening any employees who are not working out well and should not be hired once past the mandatory probationary period. After the probation period has passed, Chinese labor laws place relatively tough restrictions against firing employees, as compared internationlly.

Several of our interviewees stressed that, despite the low starting point for training entry-level Chinese staff, the potential for learning quickly is very high. Brazilian trading company founder Winston Ling gives an example: "I hired my sales manager as an intern and taught him like a son. Now, he is

"My idea is better than yours." In Japan, if we come to a decision, then everybody will follow, even if they have different opinions. But in China, people say: "That's his idea, not my idea." Cooperating with each other—teamwork— is an area in which China has to improve. In the past, Chinese people had to obey orders. But the situation has changed. Now, they are more individualistic and have more freedom of thought.

The educational systems of the two countries are similar: Like the Japanese, the Chinese rely too much on teachers and memorization; consequently, are not good at understanding complex issues when they start working.

To be frank, I have to say that Chinese young people are much more diligent than Japanese young people. The youth in my country are spoiled by our developed society. Japanese lack ambition and are less motivated to learn. Young Chinese people have a much stronger sense of urgency [to succeed in their career]—not only young Chinese men, but also young Chinese women. In Shanghai, females are becoming a more dominant social group; they are more outgoing, more active at work, and earn more money than men. In Japan, women still cannot enter business society, which is wholly dominated by men. Therefore, the smart young Japanese women all leave the country, either for work or for study.

Be ready to provide training in basic international business practices and standards to your Chinese personnel, unless they already have international experience.

the manager and I'm still teaching him. I want him to grow. He has a lot of potential." Susan Heffernan, of Soozar, shares a similar experience: "I consider my key staff as my babies. I have closely trained three of my key staff who have been with me since the beginning. The one I spent the most time with now laughs at the behavior of the newcomers. I think the older and more experienced staff can pass down my methods."

Training Strategies for Mid-level Managers and Senior Staff

For white-collar professionals and middle managers, our international entrepreneurs stressed the need to provide training in basic international business practices and standards. Chinese university graduates, our interviewees said, tend to be far less business-savvy and less streetwise than their counterparts in other countries. The reason: most Chinese students finish their schooling without having acquired any work experience whatsoever. In China, it is relatively rare for students to work, even as part-time hires or interns during the summer holidays.

Thus, our interviewees explained, professional staff will need to be brought up-to-speed on basic business communication, quality control, and business etiquette. For many of our startup managers, providing this training means doing the educating themselves.

Another often-mentioned weakness of younger or more junior white-collar employees in China is a reluctance to speak out in front of colleagues, clients, or superiors. Web 2.0 entrepreneur Ken Carroll works directly with his engineering team to prepare them to negotiate with international business executives by first shaking off their fear of voicing an opinion or making a recommendation. "They are bright people, very smart, but they don't want to stand out because it's perceived as arrogant or rude. They prefer to keep in a background role." That means, in negotiations or meetings with Western clients, Carroll must push his Chinese team members to speak out. "They know their stuff, but how do you get them to say it and share it? I tell them. 'Americans like to "*blah blah blah*," but you're quiet. Americans will think either that you don't know anything, or that you are unwilling to share what you know. They won't think you are humble—a nice Chinese gentleman. So, speak up, guys!' I tell them." Carroll says he works to change this tendency with every new Chinese hire. "They have improved a bit, but it's still hard."

Another broad area in which entrepreneurs must work to train their white-collar personnel is in creativity, initiative, and innovation. Shah Firoozi, founder of The PAC Group, based in Shanghai, identifies "lack of innovation" as a key weakness he has observed in Chinese professionals. He uses the engineering sector as a case in point: "The quality of engineering education in China is very good from the academic point of view. Unfortunately, in the engineering consulting business, the academic part is only a small portion of what we need," he says. "We also need to know how to understand clients' needs and deliver results, how to lead project execution." He adds that the key skill needed is "not about inventing things, but rather about executing strategies and achieving results." Chinese graduates tend to struggle with the implementation of business plans, and with creative problem solving—due mainly to lack of real-world experience, Firoozi says. He adds that even Chinese professors admit that "Chinese universities still haven't reached a basic level of creating innovations. That is a very important characteristic for people working in knowledge-based companies."

How do foreign entrepreneurs offer training to Chinese personnel? Most of our interviewees lacked the funds for expensive or extensive outside training programs, so they mostly focused first on offering training themselves, and then offering outside training to the most promising rising stars in the company. Trader Winston Ling says he personally spends far more time training his personnel in China than was necessary in his native Brazil, but that his efforts help to retain talented staff. "It is difficult to retain them, because they just want to have a higher salary," he says. Thus, training in international practices and standards is one of the perks he can offer to keep talented staff longer. "I try to teach them all the time. I dedicate a lot of my time to building the team."

> ❝
> *[My Chinese staff]*
> *like the fact that*
> *they are handling a*
> *lot of responsi-*
> *bilities. If they*
> *worked for a big*
> *company, they*
> *wouldn't have this*
> *level of freedom and*
> *responsibility. . . .*
> *I involve them in a*
> *lot of decisions.*
> *They are doing*
> *different things all*
> *the time and don't*
> *get bored."*
>
> **Susan Heffernan**
> (Australia), Founder and
> Managing Director,
> Soozar

 Transform
TIP **the small size
of your company
into an advantage
by giving key
personnel a faster
career track than
they would find in
a big corporation.**

TIP Avoid correcting your staff in front of others. Loss of face can be devastating for Chinese employees, even causing talented middle managers to quit.

At Soozar, Susan Heffernan provides promising personnel with fast-expanding responsibilities designed to ready them quickly for working with international clients. "They like the fact that they are handling a lot of responsibilities. If they worked for a big company, they wouldn't have this level of freedom and responsibility. . . . I involve them in a lot of decisions. They are doing different things all the time and don't get bored." Heffernan also sends outstanding personnel overseas for on-the-job training—a very popular perk. "I make sure they go overseas. They would never have this opportunity so soon in other companies, especially when they are so young." Lastly, she offers "project bonuses" to quickly reward work well done.

Language Skills

One of the most common types of training provided to staff by our foreign entrepreneurs is language training—either in the mother tongue of the target market, or in English. Again, this type of training quickly expands the value of the employee at the company, leading to new responsibilities, and is a perk that competing companies cannot easily offer.

For example, when Mexican import/export entrepreneur Juan Martinez found that some employees were trying to learn Spanish on their own, he hired a teacher for them. "We cannot give [our employees] as good training as the big companies, but whatever we can do, we do."

Software startup Eric Rongley explains why and how he offers English training to all of his staff: "Our customers are in the U.S. and U.K. and our competitors are in India—and their English skills are better than those of Chinese." He says that some of his project work—mainly software development for Western clients—requires daily interaction with English-speaking customers. "At my company, junior personnel need to defend their design to the client company's architect every day. Everybody needs to speak good English. That's a challenge here in China." Rongley adds that the problem will improve over time, because English is now taught to Chinese school children beginning in eighth grade. "So, if you hire the best students from the best schools, they have the reading and writing skills," says Rongley. However, even book-smart English majors tend to lack confidence in actual speaking, he says. "We mitigate this challenge by creating an English-only work environment. The employees have to speak English all the time." Rongley says he facilitates interest in practicing English by this insistence on using only English during working hours, as well as by offering classes, lunchtime English-language movies, and regular English-language leisure games, such as the company's regular Scrabble tournament.

I talk to employees [in China] differently than I do in Israel. I do it much more delicately and in a much more positive way."

Aviel Zilber (Israel), Chairman, Sheng Enterprises

Warning: Be Aware of "Face" Issues

Several of our foreign business owners mentioned that when Chinese employees needed training, or simply needed to change a particular behavior or mindset, employers must discuss the issue with the individual (or individuals) in private. Loss of face can be devastating for Chinese employees, even causing talented middle managers to quit.

Israeli entrepreneur Aviel Zilber explains how he has changed his management style in terms of how he tells his Chinese employees when they need to change certain behaviors. "I talk to employees [in China] differently than I do in Israel. I do it much more delicately and in a much more positive way," he says. "It also depends on what stage of the relationship I have with the other person. If I have worked with him for a few years, and if we have built trust, then I can come to him and tell him that he made a mistake, but add that I know it happened because he was under pressure, or something. I try to do it in a more gentle way."

"If you want to correct someone [in China], you always do it one-to-one," says Prakash Menon. When determining career development and training for his personnel, Menon says he conducts all discussions in private, in order to save face. The performance management process used at NIIT (China) involves reviewing past performance, asking where the person would

> *The key to building any business is to find the core people who will stay with you and grow with the company. The real challenge for small companies is to provide business experience [that is appealing for employees]; what you can offer as an SME won't be interesting to everybody.*

Jeffrey Bernstein
(USA), Founder and Managing Director, Emerge Logistics Shanghai

like to be in two or three years, then advising them to ensure better performance in the next year. "We want to know what they expect from the organization and how we can provide them with training and development opportunities," says Menon. "We believe that if the person grows, the organization also grows. So, we need to look at their performance of previous years—their attitude, capabilities, ability to work with other people, and so on—and sometimes we need to give some negative strokes. It's very well accepted. Actually, there isn't a problem, provided the person sees [the feedback] as sincere. If the trust is built, they won't feel it's negative."

"Keep it private" is also the management motto of Danish furniture supplier Simon Lichtenberg. However, he adds that if a Chinese employee has worked for a Western company for some time, he or she will tend to be "thicker skinned" and more familiar with direct, European-style communication. "I am trying to promote as open and direct a culture as I can in my company. It's never going to be like in Denmark, but we have still started a lot of good practices."

Recruitment and Retention Challenges

One of the most frustrating aspects of operating an SME in China is that, once you have found, hired, and trained the right professionals, they quite often quit or jump ship. Eight years after founding his logistics company based on the outskirts of Shanghai, veteran China entrepreneur Jeffrey Bernstein names human resources as his main challenge. "In order to scale-up, you need very systematic procedures and the people who can design processes. But the workforce [in China] isn't very stable now; they are very edgy to find the next opportunity." Bernstein sums up the challenge facing his and other SMEs in China: "The key to building any business is to find the core people who will stay with you and grow with the company. The real challenge for small companies is to provide business experience [that is appealing for employees]; but what you can offer as an SME won't be interesting to everybody." A perk that many Chinese employees seek, he adds, is the chance to be sent overseas for training or a working stint. "This also can be very difficult for an SME to provide."

Serviced office supplier Maggie Yu describes the challenges of staff recruitment and retention. "The booming Chinese economy means there are abundant job opportunities. In fact, many companies that are expanding are recruiting more staff than they really need. This puts a lot of pressure on their human resources management. The revised labor codes add to the difficulty by shortening the required probation period. My advice is to approach recruitment in a more cost-effective way by building a lean organization and maximizing the productivity of each employee."

Shanghai-based businessman Aviel Zilber, who manages 20 employees at Sheng Enterprises, says: "It's difficult to find the right people, and difficult to retain them. HR is almost the most challenging thing for us. The economy is booming and opportunities are always behind the door. It's not easy to find good people, and not easy to make them stay."

China's talent shortage is worsening as foreign direct investment floods into the country and as domestic firms expand, leading to even tougher competition for qualified talent. Turning to the software industry as an example, U.S. entrepreneur Eric Rongley says he was able to attract a team of "superstars" when he first began hiring software engineers and other IT specialists in 2001, mainly because, at the time, his company was one of the few U.S. employers in China for specialists in the software field. "We were able to cherry pick the talent pool. We hired superbright people," he recalls. Today, however, the software industry has matured and his current company must work harder to find and keep top talent.

Below, our interviewees describe some specific challenges in terms of finding and keeping qualified personnel in China.

> *It's difficult to find the right people, and difficult to retain them. HR is almost the most challenging thing for us. The economy is booming and opportunities are always behind the door. It's not easy to find good people, and not easy to make them stay."*
>
> **Aviel Zilber** (Israel), Chairman, Sheng Enterprises

HR Challenge #1: Size Matters

" *It's hard to ensure loyalty from the staff. Sometimes, an employee can copy everything, leave the company, and start his own business.*"

Nic Pannekeet
(Netherlands), Founder,
CHC Business
Development

Dutch fieldmarketing entrepreneur Olaf Litjens explains the challenges he faces, as an SME employer, in this way: "When hiring people, the problem is that face is important for Chinese people. They like to say they work for a big company, and smaller companies don't have that. Really talented people have a tendency to go to work for the big companies."

One entrepreneur comments that the bias toward large, established firms is worse in southern China, especially in Shanghai and Guangzhou, where status and a large salary tend to be valued very highly.

Construction industry entrepreneur Phillip Branham also has met with a cool reception from potential hires. He says that many in the Chinese management talent pool are "reserved at the beginning, even skeptical" about working for a young startup. Some interviewees were openly negative about working for a still-young company, he says. "Some people came from very large foreign companies, and asked, 'Why would I move to a small company? I work for a big company now.'" Several applicants, when they realized that B & L Group had only a handful of employees at the time, were "very arrogant." Branham's advice: look elsewhere. "The people who were arrogant weren't ones I would want to hire anyway."

HR Challenge #2: Lack of Loyalty

Business development consultant and entrepreneur Nic Pannekeet faces two problems that can trigger talented Chinese employees to leave. First, many follow their ambitions to work or study abroad. "The Chinese staff like to study a lot. They come to the company, work for one or two years, and then go abroad, which is quite annoying." Second, the most talented and ambitious employees may learn the business, then leave to start their own similar enterprise. (In fact, this problem was so prevalent among our China-based entrepreneurs that it is covered extensively in Chapter 6 on ethics.) Says Pannekeet:

Boss–Employee Relations

One of the peculiarities of Chinese employees is that they have a different relationship with their bosses than what is typically found in Western countries. Internet video downloading entrepreneur Marc van der Chijs compares employer–employee relations in China with those in Germany, where he worked before moving to China. "In China, you're clear about who is the subordinate and who is the boss; whereas in Germany, you can be the boss but you can't order people to do certain things for you. Take making coffee as an example. In Germany, if I ask my secretary to prepare coffee for me, she would laugh at me and say, 'Do it yourself.' In China, it is the opposite. If I make the coffee myself, my secretary would probably ask, 'Didn't I make it the right way last time?'" Van der Chijs concludes: "So, the way of working is quite different. In China, you have to be hard in front of others sometimes, in order to gain respect. In Germany, if you're too hard, people don't want to work for you anymore."

Another difference identified by Van der Chijs is that bosses in China must rely on good *guanxi*—or social/professional relationships—with their employees. "Here, you don't hear things directly, so I have my 'spies' in the company. They come to me and tell me things. That's how I gather information. In Germany, you get information directly."

"It's hard to ensure loyalty from the staff. Sometimes, an employee can copy everything, leave the company, and start his own business. They learn a lot here."

Educational expert Prakash Menon says another reason for lack of loyalty is cultural; Chinese employees tend to form a bond with their direct supervisor, rather than with the company. This is a marked difference from the business norms in India, he says, where employees tend to create an emotional bond with the company, rather than with an individual manager. The upshot: if a favorite manager leaves the company, or even is promoted or relocated, Chinese employees in that person's team may quit the company rather than work with a new supervisor.

TIP Build good personal relationships with your key employees. Chinese employees tend to form a bond with their direct supervisor. They become loyal to a person, rather than to an organization.

HR Challenge #3: Salary Hopping

I train [my employees] to meet international standards, which makes them more valuable to the rest of the world. If somebody from a multinational company comes along and offers them twice the salary, that would completely break my salary structure."

Phillip Branham (USA), Founder and President, B & L Group

Many of the employers interviewed mentioned the difficulty they have in keeping key personnel if they are offered higher pay elsewhere. While this challenge is well known to SMEs worldwide, it is exacerbated in China where even a small raise can convince key staff to jump ship. With the nation's employment market tightening in key professional sectors, salaries are rising fast, both across professions and across the country. In many highly skilled positions, the salary gap between international expat wages and those of domestic Chinese hires is narrowing quickly.

Business owner Ken Carroll tells of a typical scenario that impacted his original business in China, language training schools: "We had lots of people working for us for a couple of years who went to work for Wall Street English [a competing school teaching English as a second language] after we trained them. That's the way it is. Wall Street paid higher and took them away from us." So, Carroll used a direct method to attack back. "We brought them back from Wall Street after offering another pay raise." Overall, Carroll says, poaching is a fact of life for many foreign entrepreneurs in China, across all business sectors.

Internet entrepreneur Marc van der Chijs agrees that pay is a more critical factor for many Chinese employees than for Europeans: "Money is more important here. In Germany, the company is considered as important. There, what really matters is whether you are happy in the company or have an interest in your job. Here, it's more money-based. If I don't give someone 10% yearly salary increases, they might leave. They may leave because of a small difference in salary."

However, Van der Chijs advises not raising salaries in order to keep people who come with offers from other employers. "Some of them come to me and say: 'I can get so much money from the other company. Do you want to match this?' I refuse. If I said 'yes' to one person, 40 people would come asking for more money." Instead, Van der Chijs offers attractive salary increases for talented employees who stick with the company over time. At Tudou, the video-downloading internet service that he co-founded, he offers stock options as well, but adds that employees must stay at least four years before cashing them in. "I gave stock options to everybody, but if somebody performs badly, he gets fired."

Think twice before getting into a salary "price war" as a way to retain your employees. Sometimes, it's better simply to let them go.

HR Challenge #4: Jumping Ship

A fairly common problem for our interviewees is when a superstar employee learns the business so well that he or she eventually jumps to a competitor or leaves to launch a competing business. Many of our entrepreneurs worried about—or had experienced—this risk. Construction startup founder Phillip Branham admits to worrying that a key employee may one day jump.

Says Branham: "I train [my employees] to meet international standards, which makes them more valuable to the rest of the world. If somebody then comes along from a multinational company and offers them twice the salary, it would completely break my salary structure. They'd be gone. That would bring me a lot of trouble."

Engineering firm owner Shah Firoozi also expects to lose a certain percentage of his China staff, especially after training. "The normal evolution is that if you work in a foreign company like ours, you can jump to companies like Fiat, GM, Chrysler. Our employees acquire experience that is very rare in this country. Therefore, they are in high demand and are recruited rapidly by other companies. Frankly, I can't blame them; people with the right know-how are in high demand. They are recruited very aggressively. The temptation finally prevails. Our company doesn't want to go into a price war, so we have to accept that they leave." Firoozi adds that the high turnover situation isn't limited to SMEs. "The big guys like Fiat or GM have high turnover as well. It really hinges on the supply of people with the required experience."

HR Strategies: Selling "Small is Beautiful"

> 💡 **TIP** Promoting your brand name among Chinese universities and business organizations will help to boost recruiting and retention.

Despite the wide spectrum of different industries represented by our interviewees, many of them use a similar strategy for improving the recruitment and retention of key staff by trying to turn the company's small size from a hardship to an advantage. Here are the key strategies shared by our 43 China-based small business owners and experts.

> 💡 **TIP** If a new hire isn't meeting your expectations, move him or her out during the probation period.

HR Strategy #1: Build Your Reputation

One China HR strategy employed successfully by Bleum is to work directly with the Chinese universities to build a reputation as a sought-after recruiter for fresh graduates. Eric Rongley explains: "This is my eighth year of doing college recruiting [in China]. We hire the best students out of the best schools. I think we have a pretty good reputation in the colleges." Today, after nearly a decade of building its reputation on campuses, the company receives applications from around 2,000 university graduates per year for approximately 35 positions. These applicants are screened through a detailed and difficult recruitment process (See below).

The firm also works to promote its name in the business arena through joining business organizations and networking.

HR Strategy #2: Recruit Rigorously

One way to avoid the problem of quick turnover caused by an imperfect fit with your company, our interviewees said, is to spend more time and energy upfront in the recruiting process. This can reduce turnover later, improving efficiency and enhancing success.

Swiss consultant Nicolas Musy, founder of CH-ina (Shanghai) Co., says his company uses a three-stage hiring method in China. "First we look at personality—whether the person fits into our culture. Then we look at their basic education, intelligence, and ability to learn quickly. The last thing we look at is their skills and experience. We would rather have someone who is a good person and a good fit in terms of the first two criteria, and then train him or her."

At his software outsourcing company, Eric Rongley uses a rigorous screening process for candidates, including an IQ test (the company requires a score of 130 for those with long work experience; 140 for fresh university graduates), an English proficiency test, then a technical test depending upon the job position. Finally, those candidates who achieve passing scores in all the preliminary tests are given a "behavioral interview" designed to determine their skill level in nine competencies important to the firm, such as "clear communication," "ability to take responsibility," and "integrity." During the interview, candidates receive a number score for each of the competencies.

Those who pass the first round of interviews go on for a second one, and a final decision is made after that. Rongley says this detailed and tough recruitment process culls applicants who are unlikely to fit in well. Of the 2,000 graduates applying to his company annually, only 300 pass the IQ test, 150 pass the skills test, and roughly 75 pass the behavioral interviews. "We end up hiring 35 out of the original 2,000 applicants," says Rongley.

HR Strategy #3: Cut Your Losses

If a new hire isn't working out, our entrepreneurs stressed the need to move that person out quickly. Mark Secchia, founder of Sherpa's, describes his company's tough recruitment procedures. "When we do interviewing and training, we treat our staff very hard. I want to find out as soon as possible at the end of the three months of training if any of the new recruits are likely to complain a lot. I don't treat them very well at the beginning on purpose, because I prefer they quit early during the probation period if they aren't going to be really committed to the job."

Under China's new labor laws, effective in 2008, employers face far tougher restrictions on firing employees after the end of the probation period. This makes testing out new hires during the initial trial period extremely important.

"

We usually try different people [during the probationary period] in order to get one that we like. Among two or three candidates, usually only one of them will stay in the company."

Juan Martinez
(Mexico), Founder and Director, SOLHIX

Trading startup Juan Martinez uses the probation period to measure whether a new hire has not only the skills, but also the proper work attitude, for his company. "For us, the attitude is very important. Our company culture is hardworking. We need to stay late sometimes. If people aren't very committed to what we are doing, they would have to leave." Since attitude is difficult to gauge in standard interviews, Martinez tests the work attitude of new hires during their probationary period. "We usually try different people in order to get one that we like. Among two or three candidates, usually only one of them will stay in the company."

"Sooner is better" is also the motto of logistics entrepreneur Jeffrey Bernstein when making a decision on new hires. "Either people leave quickly because there isn't a good fit, or they stay a long time—it's two extremes. The worst situation is that someone stays one year and then goes. It's better if they just stay through the [three-month] probation period." Irish entrepreneur Ken Carroll agrees: "Here [at Praxis], it is so chaotic and busy that if someone's not working out, we let them go. It's like 'Sorry. You did okay, but it's not working. Bye!'"

"

Some people like to be in a company that is just starting and growing, because in the future, they will be able to have positions in the small company that they might not get in a big multinational company."

Phillip Branham (USA), Founder and President, B & L Group

HR Strategy #4: Offer Job Security

One hiring difficulty for startups is that new hires may worry about the stability of the company. When Phillip Branham launched B & L in December 2005, he addressed such fears among would-be employees by guaranteeing them job security. "I guarantee that everyone who comes to work on a one-year contract will get paid for a year. If I don't have any work for them for six months, I will still pay them and pay the same benefits."

HR Strategy #5: Fast Tracking

Given the highly competitive and ambitious nature of many Chinese employees, one of the most important perks foreign entrepreneurs can offer is a fast track for career development. Phillip Branham stresses the opportunities for employees to grow as his company grows. "I think people see the opportunity for growth. Some people like to be in a company that is just starting and growing, because in the future, they will be able to have positions in the small company that they might not get in a big multinational company." One selling point: Branham can promise top positions to Chinese nationals—spots that might be reserved for foreign nationals in a large Fortune 500 company.

Trading company founder Juan Martinez uses a similar philosophy at SOLHIX: "In this company, I call the employees 'partners' and treat them like partners." This level of respect and responsibility can be very valuable for Chinese employees, he says. "If you are working in GM, you might be paid a lot but you are not the partners of GM and nobody will believe you are a partner of GM. In our company, yes."

Being a small-scale startup also allows SOLHIX to give critical projects to employees who have proven their capability. "We also try to give employees projects that make them feel motivated. It also shows them that, in the future, they can grow with the company. By growing, they can grow as a person, and of course grow their income." In general, career advancement prospects can be even more valued among Chinese employees than among their counterparts in other parts of the world.

Fast growth potential at his small-scale consultancy has been an effective way to retain high-flying employees, says entrepreneur Ruggero Jenna. "One advantage is in the growth opportunities we can provide employees. Here, you can write your own growth history. If you're a good manager, your path to partnership is much quicker. You can make more difference than in any of the more established organizations. It's our number one differentiating factor."

> **TIP** Offer employees projects that make them feel motivated so they know they will grow with the company, professionally and economically.

HR Strategy #6: Positive Work Environment (Software)

Providing a close-knit, supportive, and flexible work environment is one perk many of our entrepreneurs were able to offer—benefits harder to find at a large company. At SOLHIX trading

"

Show respect to the people you work with, and try to give them face. Second, don't work with a short-term mentality . . . Tell them how much reward they may gain after [staying with you] for three years."

Marc van der Chijs
(Netherlands), Co-founder, Tudou

TIP **Know your employees, and create bonds among them. This can be an advantage for small firms over big corporations.**

company, owner Juan Martinez says, flexibility can be as important as salary in convincing good employees to stay. "In my company, it's very important that we adjust to what employees need. For example, we trust people that they can manage their time. If they are key personnel, they would just need to inform me, not ask me for permission. We can be flexible."

Sixteen-year China veteran Aziz Mrabet stresses the importance of maintaining good relations in order to retain key employees. "I speak Chinese, and somehow have even become a little bit Chinese myself," says the Moroccan national. "To some extent, I find it quite easy to manage Chinese. Most of our staff have been working with me for eight years, and turnover is quite small. We have a very good relationship and there is trust between us. Even when the business goes badly, they still get their bonus. Furthermore, I never shout at them; I always show respect to them—this is most important for Chinese people."

Another suggestion for successfully managing Chinese employees comes from Marc van der Chijs. "The most important thing is to show respect to the people you work with, and try to give them face in and out of the office. Second, don't work with a short-term mentality; show the staff the long-term results. Don't tell them how many dollars they can earn in one year; instead, tell them how much reward they may gain after three years. Then, they may stay with you. That's the way I motivate people."

Others among our interviewees agreed that they sell hires on the close-knit, friendly environment that is possible in a small company. Consultant Ruggero Jenna comments: "We enjoy a more caring environment here. Compared with the big consulting firms, we have this advantage." Phillip Branham describes the environment at B & L Group in this way: "In small companies, people are more closely knit than in big companies. You can do things at different levels that the large companies can't. Large companies with several hundred employees cannot get together and go out for dinner every three months. We can do that."

Eric Rongley's company sponsors a company-wide soccer team, badminton team, and basketball team, in addition to holding happy hours on Fridays. Says Rongley: "We try to create lots of chances for employees to bond with each other and to have positive experiences here."

HR Strategy #7: Positive Work Environment (Hardware)

If you can't be big, be beautiful. This is the strategy retail display designer and manufacturer Susan Heffernan uses when wooing potential employees. When a promising possible new hire visits her company's Shanghai showroom, she says, he or she appreciates the value that the company places on quality, design, and high standards. Says Heffernan: "If I was in a tiny office, that would be really tough. Employees like the environment when they come to work here."

Eric Rongley also found that investing in attractive office facilities was money well spent in terms of staff recruitment, retention, and satisfaction. Rongley discovered through an annual employee survey that "work environment" was one of his employees' main complaints. As a result, he moved the company to an upscale highrise in downtown Shanghai, and created nicer service rooms for staff, including a "very beautiful gym." "Rather than throwing money at employees [in terms of salary hikes], we should make a more welcoming, fun environment. Then they will stay with us," he says.

HR Strategy #8: Keep Good Relations with Those Who Go

China veteran Olaf Litjens advises entrepreneurs in China to expect to lose a certain percentage of staff, no matter how much effort is spent on creating an ideal work environment. "I just accept the turnover; otherwise, I would get high blood pressure or have a heart attack," he says, with a smile. "What we try to do is to make the company attractive, equip people with good mobile phones, computers, and uniforms; we have a lot of

> **TIP** Investing in attractive office facilities can help motivate and retain Chinese employees.

> **TIP** When possible, maintain good relations with employees who leave you. They may be a future source of business and your best ambassadors.

company bonding events such as Family Day, and plenty of training. But in the end, in certain positions, you know there is going to be some turnover."

When you lose staff, entrepreneur Aviel Zilber stresses the importance of allowing the employee to leave on good terms, if possible. "We still have good relations with the employees who have left us. We keep in touch and try to find ways to do business together."

Solving the Salary Question

Setting the right salaries for China-based employees is a tricky business for any manager in China in the current climate, but particularly so for the owners of small businesses. The shortage of experienced white-collar professionals in many industries has triggered salary hikes for many positions, especially in China's larger cities. Nearly all of our featured entrepreneurs struggled with this issue, especially in terms of losing personnel to larger companies able to pay higher salaries.

"It is very hard to keep employees, not because they are not happy with our company, but because the offers they get from outside are incredible. It's very hard for people to say 'no' if the salary outside is 100% or 200% more," says fieldmarketing entrepreneur Olaf Litjens. The problem of salary hikes and poaching has worsened in recent years, he says, especially in his retail-oriented field of market research. As soon as he trains employees in any aspect of the work, they become valuable to competitors who are eager to offer a salary increase in order to lure over pre-trained personnel. Litjens believes the current cutthroat competitive environment will continue through to 2015 or 2020.

Spanish consultant Josep Giro adds that the job-hopping fever tends to run especially hot among personnel from Shanghai or other Chinese mega-cities, where the business culture is ultra-competitive. In Shanghai, for example, friends and family members frequently compare salaries, and react accordingly. For instance, employees who learn that they are receiving less than their peers may well quit.

Many SME owners, such as restaurateur Michael Yang, end up paying above market rates in order to attract employees to a small, little-known enterprise. "My salary philosophy is that I pay a little higher than other restaurants. If the other restaurants pay their waitresses RMB1,000 [US$140] per month, I pay RMB1,200 [US$170]," he says. "I pay more to keep them here. I don't have time to train new employees." Yang says the time invested in constantly training new hires requires far more expense than paying above market rates to keep staff longer. He adds that, for exceptional staff, he pays far above market rates. "I want them to feel that they cannot get better pay in other places." The stability this creates is well worth the extra expense, he believes.

In some industries, salaries for domestic professionals are rising to international levels. Entrepreneur Shah Firoozi explains that, at his engineering and consulting company, wages for domestic engineers tripled between 2000 and 2008, while costs for expats have been reduced by 20–30% through the cutting of benefits, including housing, transportation, and other costs. Also, interest in working in China is far greater today among expatriates than was the case a decade ago. Says Firoozi: "There was fear 10 years ago [among foreign hires relocating to China] and there is eagerness today. So, recruiting foreigners to China isn't difficult. Therefore, the costs of foreigners are coming down and the costs of the locals are going up."

In the current volatile market, which has seen salaries for some sectors of Chinese nationals increase rapidly, even figuring out what salaries to offer can be challenging. Construction startup Phillip Branham explains: "The pay scales are a very difficult issue. On the one hand, people working at the international companies are simply paid beyond what they should be. On the other hand, people from state-owned companies, and even private Chinese companies, are making much less." For a small business owner hiring employees from different work backgrounds (that is, from international companies, as well as from private domestic firms or SOEs), the result can be widely divergent salary expectations within a small employee group. A

The pay scales are a very difficult issue. On the one hand, people working at the international companies are simply paid beyond what they should be. On the other hand, people from state-owned companies, and even private Chinese companies, are making much less.

Phillip Branham (USA)
Founder and President, B & L Group.

One way to avoid paying perpetually rising salaries is to offer commissions and bonuses, or to use performance-based pay scales.

young engineer with a year or two of experience at an international firm may be expecting a salary twice as high as the manager you've hired as chief operating officer, an older manager with 20 years of experience in state-run companies.

The wage gap can be especially large—and politically problematic—when a young, foreign-trained employee is offered a higher salary than an older employee from an SOE background. "This causes headaches, because I cannot have the young engineers who don't know that much making more money than their manager," says Branham. "It is very difficult. If you don't match the market rates, you aren't going to get anywhere. If you want to attract someone away from the MNCs, you have to give more than what they are making there."

Another problem Branham discovered after hiring for B & L Group in 2007 is that young Chinese often have unrealistic career advancement goals, and may even lie about their previous salary in order to win a pay hike. He has experienced applicants blatantly exaggerating their previous salaries, he says.

Given the volatility, how can entrepreneurs determine reasonable salaries? Entrepreneur Eric Rongley says he researches the market rates by participating in annual salary surveys conducted by two China-based international firms. "We have a good sense of where our employees are within the talent pool," he says. Using that data, Rongley then offers salaries that are "between 65% and 75% of the market [rate]." Initially, his company had to pay 80% of the going rate or above, "but now, we are a more respected brand here, so we can lower that a bit."

Rongley stresses that it is the good reputation of Bleum, not high salaries, that attracts talented applicants. Currently, the company's turnover rate is about 10%—compared to 20% for Shanghai overall and far greater levels in India (for the software industry). "Three years ago, we had turnover of 50–55%. Now, we are doing better than the market, but we are not paying as high salaries compared to the market as we used to."

One way around perpetually rising salaries is to offer commissions and bonuses, or to use performance-based pay scales. Fashion apparel retailer Valerie Touya uses commissions with

EMPLOYEE MOTIVATION

One particularly clever way of handling salaries is demonstrated by IT education expert Prakash Menon, president of NIIT (China). Menon tells of how, when he began in his position in 1998, everyone in his office left work at 5.30 p.m. sharp, even if critical projects were still incomplete. "Normally, nobody in this industry leaves at 5.30 p.m. The IT field is about curiosity, learning new things," he says. "Worldwide, you see IT people staying late in their offices." Menon sought to address the issue by spending more time with his Chinese employees, eating with them and talking with them, in order to be closer to them.

The result? "People still left at 5.30," says Menon, exasperated.

Next, he tried offering more incentives, such as a family entertainment fund. This fund covered the cost of inviting all employees and their family members out once a year to thank them for their support. "My idea was to make employees feel that the organization was a part of their life."

Did it work? Menon sighs: "They *still* left at 5.30."

Frustrated, he asked other directors for their opinion, but no one could give him an answer. Finally, he asked a colleague directly: "Why do you leave at 5.30 p.m.?" The colleague answered: "It's very simple: if the organization pays me this low-level salary, then I will offer this level of effort."

That answer "hit me like a bolt," says Menon.

Menon revamped the payment system dramatically so that only 50% of salary for all employees was fixed; the rest was variable. "If you achieve 80% of the variable salary, then your salary is similar to the market rate. So, every employee also had the possibility of getting 20% more than the market rate."

The scheme met with an electric reception, Menon says. "No one went home at 5.30 from then on, and everybody's figured out how to get the 20% extra. Now the company is developing at a completely different pace." Menon explains that he didn't actually change the compensation amount under the new scheme. "I paid the people the same, but they felt differently. Before, they thought, 'This is a fixed salary, so why should I work harder?' It is different to India. If people in India are paid a decent salary, they immediately think they should work very hard and are loyal. They develop strong emotional ties to the company."

her sales clerks. "In retail, it is very hard to keep employees motivated. Commission is the only way to keep them."

At ChinArt, founder Mark Pummell offers profit-sharing to promising employees. He gives an example of how the company wooed a talented web developer. "We didn't have very much money, so we gave him 20% profit from the web business he developed. He remained very interested and very motivated. He drove the website to a higher ranking," he says. "This is our model to be really fair with people."

Trading company founder Juan Martinez adds that key employees "make money like a partner," meaning that top positions include profit-sharing schemes. "With most of our positions, we make them profit-sharing or we give bonuses or commissions. That way, employees really feel motivated."

Conclusion

If you are able to manage human resources in China, you can manage China, said one of our opening quotes. Anyone with business experience in China will agree that human resources can be one of the major headaches you will suffer in this country. HR can become your bottleneck for future growth, and even for survival. As soon as you start attracting the right candidates, you will find you are competing with the big corporations for the best people. Even if you manage to attract them, and train them to meet international standards, you run a high risk of losing them within a year or so, if they are offered a better salary or faster career advancement elsewhere. Or even worse, your most talented employees may leave to start a business in direct competition with yours.

While there is no magic wand that can erase these challenges, this chapter offers advice and strategies used by our China-based entrepreneurs in taking on these sorts of HR difficulties. Armed with this accumulated knowledge and experience of our China pioneers, readers will have a better chance of mitigating China's HR challenge.

SUMMARY OF TIPS
HUMAN RESOURCE CHALLENGES

MANAGING CHINESE EMPLOYEES

Forming a strong team of Chinese staff is crucial for the success of your China venture. Be sure to collect their input on important decisions.

Because Chinese managers and skilled professionals tend to come from the younger generations, be prepared to invest more time in training your Chinese personnel than would be needed elsewhere.

Transform the small size of your company into an advantage by giving key personnel a faster career track than they would find in a big corporation.

Build good personal relationships with your key employees. Chinese employees tend to form a bond with their direct supervisor. They become loyal to a person, rather than to an organization.

Chinese employees generally don't cope well with unclear tasks and are uncomfortable adapting a task to new circumstances. They typically expect to be given, and to follow, step-by-step instructions.

Be ready to provide training in basic international business practices and standards to your Chinese personnel unless they already have international experience.

Avoid correcting your staff in front of others. Loss of face can be devastating for Chinese employees, even causing talented middle managers to quit.

Think twice before getting into a salary "price war" as a way to retain your employees. Sometimes it's better simply to let them go.

HR STRATEGIES

Build your reputation—Promote your brand name among Chinese universities and business organizations to boost recruiting and retention.

Cut your losses—If a new hire isn't meeting your expectations, move him or her out during the probation period.

Recruit rigorously—Determine first whether the potential hire matches your business culture, then look at their basic education and intelligence. Finally consider whether they have the necessary skills and experience. A thoughtful selection saves costs later.

Fast tracking—A powerful retention tool for key employees is to offer a fast track for career development. SMEs can move their star players up the career ladder faster than can many larger companies.

Offer job security—This can be critical with startups.

Keep positive relations with those who quit—Your "alumni" may be a future source of business and your best ambassadors.

The salary question—One way to avoid paying perpetually rising salaries is to offer commissions and bonuses, or to use performance-based pay scales.

Positive work environment—Offer them projects that make them feel motivated so that they can see they will grow with the company, professionally and economically.

Invest in attractive office facilities can have a positive effect on motivation and employee retention.

Know your employees, create bonds among them. This can be an advantage of small firms over big corporations.

Chapter 6
Ethics and Corruption

"In China, there is an absence of religion. The moral concept is much weaker. In my mind, when a Chinese comes to a crossroad, the decision-making is about 'What is the benefit for me?' On average, the Chinese tend to think about their benefits first."

Prakash Menon (India), President of NIIT (China)

"I have seen so many foreign companies in which the foreigners had no idea what was going on in their own company, underneath the Chinese surface. Many of these expats get cheated on several levels and have no idea what's happened to them."

Simon Lichtenberg (Denmark), Founder and CEO, Trayton Group

Introduction

For foreign entrepreneurs in China, the "c" word—corruption—is often one of their most serious concerns when preparing to invest in a business. On one hand, rumors abound about China's *guanxi* (or relationships) system, in which backdoor connections to both government and private sources are necessary in order to operate a successful business. There is the widespread feeling that if you don't use backdoor shortcuts to getting business done, your competitors will. On the other hand, foreign-invested businesses are subject to the tough anticorruption laws of their home countries, such as the Sarbanes-Oxley Act regulating accounting for U.S. companies worldwide. This situation can make for an uncomfortable double-edged squeeze for foreign-invested startups in China.

While the importance of China's well-known *guanxi* system is often exaggerated in the foreign media, our interviewees did confirm that working in hazy legal "gray zones" is a fact of life in this country (see Chapter 2). In addition, as foreign-invested startup companies, they describe a clear disadvantage in comparison with large multinationals; at least to some degree, Fortune 500 firms in China are protected against the threat of corruption by their big name, high profile, and global standards and corporate processes.

This chapter covers seven main topics:

1. Putting corruption into context
2. Government *guanxi*
3. B2B corruption
4. Unethical employees
5. Strategies for avoiding government corruption
6. Strategies for avoiding B2B corruption
7. Strategies for fighting internal corruption

Putting Corruption into Context

One aspect of running a business in China that all our interviewees agreed upon was that managing ethics—and guarding against corrupt business practices—is a continuous struggle. The organization Transparency International, in its 2007 annual Corruption Perceptions Index, placed China in the 73rd position among the 180 countries included in the index. (In 2006, China ranked 71st among 163 countries.)

Although some of the 40 entrepreneurs we interviewed had experienced difficulties regarding corruption, none of them had given up on their dream of operating in China. In the end, each was able to launch a successful, legally operating business in China—an achievement that several said would have been more complicated in other countries in which they had previous experience. Construction entrepreneur Phillip Branham compares China to other areas in which he operates: "In Kazakhstan, corruption is even worse. In China, most of the things are under the table at least. In Kazakhstan, they are upfront, on the table." He adds that he has had to turn down business opportunities in Kazakhstan in order to avoid engaging in corruption—a situation he, and his company, encounters far less commonly in China.

Others among our entrepreneurs commented that China is significantly less corrupt than other emerging economies' markets. Says furniture entrepreneur Simon Lichtenberg, "Other countries are much worse than China. In the timber industry in Thailand and Malaysia, for example, they have a list of under-the-table rates for different services. The rates are official," he says. Lichtenberg adds that, while corruption is sometimes highly sophisticated in China—including operations via offshore accounts—and even occasionally lead to violence, "the overall system in China is improving." Italian consultant Ruggero Jenna agrees that China isn't at the "high" end of the corruption spectrum in the Asian region. "I don't think China is very different from other countries. There are some countries in Southeast Asia and Africa that are much worse in this respect."

American consultant Gene Slusiewicz agrees that corruption elsewhere in Southeast Asia is worse than in China. "A friend of mine in Indonesia got pulled over [by bribe-seeking traffic police] for 'traffic violations' many times, usually just before lunch or dinner and certain holidays. Ten thousand Indonesian rupiahs [US$1] was a common amount paid for 'traffic violations,' real or contrived," he says.

> *In Kazakhstan, corruption is even worse. In China, most of the things are under the table at least. In Kazakhstan, they are upfront, on the table."*
>
> **Phillip Branham** (USA), Founder and President, B & L Group

Spanish consultant Josep Giro believes that China compares favorably with, say, India in terms of corruption. "In China, corruption is useful—you use corruption to get what you want to get. Here, you pay the customs officer and you clear the goods—I like this kind of corruption. In India, you pay bribes and do favors, but you never get your tasks done. That's the problem."

Cultural, Historical, and Economic "Triggers"

The first step in managing corruption in China is to understand it. Our interviewees commented that the country's tendencies toward corruption are rooted in cultural, historical, and economic factors.

The first trigger for corruption in China is the nation's social norms built upon *guanxi*. Our interviewees explained that Chinese businesspeople today continue to follow the tradition of using social contacts, or *guanxi*, in both private and business contexts. Also, they report a general blurring of business life and professional life in China. At best, these social norms create a warmer, more "human" business environment than is the norm in developed nations; while at worst, the system leads to corruption. Another point is that corrupt *guanxi* is generally being phased out of the larger, more international-ized cities that now have a tradition of attracting foreign direct investment. As exporter Oto Petroski says, operating in Shanghai or Beijing is becoming more straightforward. "[However,] once you go into the other areas [of China], you still find in power the traditional *guanxi* system. That means: if you know people in the village, you can do every-thing. If you don't know people in the village, you cannot do anything."

Our interviewees also commented that the lack of religious beliefs among most of the Chinese population (especially among the younger generations who have grown up since the Cultural Revolution) creates another key social—and business—difference. Indian education consultant Prakash

Menon explains how this contrasts with his home country: "The average Indian is very religious. So, when he makes a decision, the moral aspect will influence that decision. If it's not the right thing to do morally, he will not do it." Menon believes that religion thus contains and curbs corruption in India, while China lacks such moral guardrails.

Consultant Josep Giro identifies a similar religious-based contrast between Chinese and Spanish social and business norms. "In Spain, because we have a Christian civilization, we believe in punishment for wrongdoing. If you do unlawful acts, you are going against God and will face the consequences. But in China, if you want to do it, you do it—so what?" In Chinese culture, Giro says, there is no tradition of spiritual punishment for moral transgressions. "The concept of committing a sin isn't integrated into their mindset," he says.

Dutch entrepreneur Olaf Litjens says that while businesspeople around the globe need to be aggressive in order to be successful, Chinese society tends to emphasize results over methods to a higher degree than elsewhere. "People everywhere want success, but in China, the thinking is: 'It doesn't matter how you get there—just make sure you don't get caught,'" he says. "Western society looks at *how* you reached success, and not just at *what* you have achieved."

Third, the socialist history of the country has also promoted the growth of corruption, says Giro: "To get things done under the communist regime, you had to use relationships and pay for favors." Today, Giro says, China is "at the third stage" in its development, in which corruption is "linked to business activities, like in the West." He says that most corruption today takes place "when somebody takes advantage of his position."

Finally, a new trigger for corruption in China has emerged in recent years: the explosion of wealth among some sectors of the population (especially urban residents) has created a serious income gap between rich and poor. This has resulted in new frustration and temptation among the "have nots," fostering crime and corruption. "When I first came to China in 1986, there were few thieves, but they are now growing in number," says

> **"**
>
> *People everywhere want success, but in China, the thinking is: 'It doesn't matter how you get there—just make sure you don't get caught.'"*
>
> **Olaf Litjens**
> (Netherlands), Founder and CEO, Unisono Fieldmarketing (Shanghai)

> *Part of the corruption problem can be attributed to unclear rules and regulations. [China] is a country where decisions are made based on interpretations, as opposed to clarity of the law. . . . There is a lot of room here for corruption."*
>
> **Shah Firoozi** (USA),
> Founder and President,
> The PAC Group

Josep Giro. "When the wealth of the country grows, corruption also grows—that's human."

Evolving Legal System

Another reason for corruption—or at least a lack of transparency—is China's still evolving legal system. Because many of China's business-related laws are new and vaguely worded (see Chapter 1), they are being tested and finalized, creating legal chaos.

"Part of the corruption problem can be attributed to unclear rules and regulations," says business development entrepreneur Shah Firoozi. "It is a country where decisions are made based on interpretations, as opposed to clarity of the law. Sometimes, the way a law is interpreted by government officials is in the interest of the public, and sometimes it's for self-serving reasons. There is a lot of room here for corruption." For example, Firoozi finds China to be more corrupt than Brazil, where he also operates.

The Good Side of *Guanxi*

Despite the hassles—and even dangers—caused by corruption in China, our interviewees also stressed areas in which Chinese business partners, clients, or employees tend to be more loyal than their counterparts elsewhere. Once a working relationship has been established, they said, Chinese tend to show more loyalty and commitment than is standard in developed nations. In other words, if a Chinese partner, client, or customer has formed a trusting long-term relationship with a foreign invested company, the Chinese side will support the relationship through thick and thin—showing more loyalty than is standard in the West. Spanish consultant Josep Giro explains: "I have experience with both Spanish and Chinese clients. The Spanish clients will get information from us and then hire [a cheaper consulting firm]. Chinese people never do this. I have had relationships with Chinese people for over 20 years and they are still honest. Even if we don't do business together, we still have a good relationship. In Europe, if you have ongoing business transactions, you have a relationship. If no business, no relationship."

China veteran Olaf Litjens also emphasized the positive aspects of *guanxi*, both in business and social life. First, he stressed that in China, the boundaries between business and personal life are much more blurred than in the West. A certain degree of blurring—as long as it doesn't go too far—can be practical and useful, he says. "What is corruption? If you go to the tax office and you become friends with the officials and they advise you how to do things, is that corruption? If you pay them money, that is corruption. What if you have dinner with them? Is it corruption?" In many cases, foreign companies in China end up blurring the distinctions between business and personal life, often operating just within the limits of their home country laws in terms of gift-giving, favor-swapping, or other "gray" business practices. This creates challenges for specific companies, as home country regulations vary widely from country to country. For example, U.S. law (especially under the Sarbanes-Oxley Act) is restrictive against giving or receiving gifts, which puts American-invested businesses at a competitive disadvantage in China.

Litjens adds that, after spending 24 years working and living in China, he finds the relationship-based culture—in both personal and professional life—to be more human. "I think one of the nice aspects of life in China is that relationships are important and you should take care of each other. I think it is actually quite a nice thing to take care of each other." As an example, he points to the differences in how Western and Chinese families tend to care for their aging parents: "In the West, we have insurance and can put our parents in a nursing home when they are retired. [In comparison,] the way Chinese take care of their parents by living with them is good." He sums up the East–West cultural difference in this way: "The corruption in China is not nice, but the strong relationships are nice."

> " *The corruption in China is not nice, but the strong relationships are nice."*
>
> **Olaf Litjens**
> (Netherlands), Founder and CEO, Unisono Fieldmarketing (Shanghai)

Government *Guanxi*

Learning to work effectively with the Chinese government is a significant challenge for any foreign startup—and that generally means building up positive relations (*guanxi*) with a host of officials at various agencies relevant to your business. The frequency and seriousness of government-related corruption experienced by our entrepreneurs varied widely, based on their industry, location, and connections in China.

At the "mild" end of the spectrum were cases such as those described by logistics entrepreneur Jeffrey Bernstein, who told of a bribe request from a government official who inspected a shipment of designer sunglasses being transported by Emerge

Clean Government

While our interviewees had encountered instances of fuzzy dealings with the Chinese government, many clarified that corruption tends to be most rampant in the lowest levels of government and in the least-developed regions of China. Thirty-year China veteran Robert Theleen, who has served in a Chinese central government lawmaking body (because of his background in finance) and now operates his own investment bank in Shanghai, stresses the upstanding nature of the Chinese government: "There is such a cliché surrounding the idea of corruption in China. I believe China's national leadership is less corrupt than that of any modern society on the face of the earth— and that includes Europe and the U.S." (Theleen says that corruption is most common at local levels of government, where central government oversight is weakest.)

One of the driving forces among China's top leaders is legacy, Theleen says. "They're concerned with what their forefathers, what their ancestors, are going to think of them. I truly believe that national leaders in China are clean." He says that while corruption exists within the central government, it is dealt with very harshly among top-level leaders. "Can you picture a European or American leader being sentenced to life in prison?" However, Theleen concedes that "down the ladder"—in the city, provincial, and local governments—corruption can be quite pronounced.

Logistics: "There was one inspector who wanted to try on a pair of expensive sunglasses and let his friend do the same. He was bragging to us that they both have pairs of Fendi glasses at home, too. These are people who earn only about RMB800 (US$114) per month in salary, local rural inspectors. They were hinting that they should be allowed to walk out wearing our glasses," he says. "These things happen, but less often in Shanghai than in other areas. I guess the answer is to know when to stay firm." Did Emerge let the officials keep the sunglasses? "No," says Bernstein.

Bernstein says that location is one reason Emerge has avoided serious issues with corruption: "The sunglasses incident is about as bad as it has gotten. Part of the reason is that I've been [based] in Shanghai, which is in general a cleaner place."

Other entrepreneurs also agreed that the problem of corruption tends to be far worse in China's second- and third-tier cities, where the legal system is less mature and businesses tend to be less familiar with international standards. "Shanghai is a little better. In other cities, corruption is still a barrier to doing business," says Korean financial advisor Chun In Kyu.

Simon Lichtenberg agrees that corruption varies between the urban centers and rural areas. "Shanghai isn't bad, but certainly not clean, sometimes at higher levels," he says. He points to the 2007 arrest and 2008 sentencing of Chen Liangyu, former general secretary of the Communist Party in Shanghai, as an example of the scale of corruption in Shanghai. Lichtenberg says that corruption is more widespread in China's small towns and rural areas, but tends to operate on a low level. "Once you get outside of Shanghai, the court system is sometimes really rotten. Some of the party figureheads at the village level or the district level are very bad. It is something that even the farmers are complaining about. I have seen terrible things." He adds that, at the national level, China is making a serious effort to crack down on corruption as a matter of necessity and national pride, and as a way to integrate with the global community.

Consultant Gene Slusiewicz describes the urban-versus-rural variation in transparency in this way: "Shanghai is more

> *Once you get outside of Shanghai, the court system is sometimes really rotten. Some of the party figureheads at the village level and the district level are very bad. It is something that even the farmers are complaining about. I have seen terrible things."*
>
> **Simon Lichtenberg**
> (Denmark), Founder and CEO, Trayton Group

advanced now, and business practices and lifestyle there are more like in Western countries. When you move inland, the cities are the way Shanghai was 10 or 15 years ago. Shanghai is more efficient now, while the central provinces are still a little bit slow. Today, cities like Wuhan and Chongqing are moving faster, while the smaller cities are still not following international practices—there, the mayor or the mayor's son cuts the deal." Slusiewicz adds that there is a "thin line" in China between being practical and expedient, and being corrupt. He gives a typically "gray" example: "What if you hire a consultant who has good connections with the government officials, who can push your case forward? You pay a little bit of money, but it's not under the table. Probably, it is not fair, but it is not cheating—and it is not illegal."

Sector by Sector

Corruption also varies by business sector, our interviewees said. In the stone business, for example, corruption is quite rare, says Turkish startup Onder Oztunali, founder of Globe Stone Studio. "We deal strictly with the bosses of companies," he says. When he launched the business, he says, "We didn't have to pay anything under the table; everything was very clear." Compared to business norms back home in Turkey and in Thailand, Oztunali says he faces minimal corruption in China. "For some licenses, we gave some money to a third party who helped speed up the application process, but it was a very small amount. I wouldn't actually call it corruption or bribery—just something to make them happy. For Turks, it is not a problem at all. In Turkey, it used to be pretty bad. After all, '*bakhshish*' is another international Turkish word, like 'Turkish coffee.'" By comparison, Oztunali describes the level of corruption in Thailand, where he also worked for several years, as "unbelievable."

Korean financial services entrepreneur Chun In Kyu agrees that corruption levels vary by industry, and according to the potential pay-offs to be had. "The real estate business has a lot of room for profit, so there is some corruption. As for other industries like manufacturing, corruption is much less serious."

Corruption Levels: From Annoyance to Danger

Our interviewees experienced vastly different levels of government-linked corruption. At the low end of the spectrum, they described facing complicated regulations, delays, and extra expenses in China. A case in point: Oto Petroski describes a typical scenario: "There are no corruption issues for me, but I have to pay lots of 'penalties' in this country," he jokes. "For example, I paid a penalty for not requesting a tax refund. I have paid maybe RMB200,000 [US$28,600] in penalties." When he operated his initial business—a coffee bar—inspectors visited twice to measure the air quality. Both times, he was fined for

Communication Clash

One problem for foreign entrepreneurs is that they may not understand when a bribe is being sought by Chinese counterparts. Brazilian trading entrepreneur Winston Ling explains: "Sometimes, when we bring in containers, the official's requests [for procedures and paperwork] don't make sense. At first, I got very confused, wondering why they are asking for so many things, and why their requests changed from container to container. I finally realized that they wanted a bribe." Ling sent one of his managers to visit the officials and find out what they wanted. Afterward, Ling began using agents as middlemen to negotiate terms with officials. "I always work through agents, because they can do this and I don't know how to do it." By using a third party, messages are sent clearly between the sides. Another benefit: if the foreign entrepreneur seeks to keep operations free of corruption, a message can be sent indirectly, without causing the officials to lose face.

Israeli Aviel Zilber faced a similar situation where, initially, he didn't realize he was being asked for a bribe. "At the beginning, we didn't think about it so much until we realized what was going on. But we always work through a Chinese associate. Both parties want to operate this way."

poor air quality—a measure that he claims was untrue. Each time, Petroski paid an RMB1,000 (US$145) fine. A traditional Chinese-style wok-frying restaurant located directly next-door, from which clouds of greasy smoke poured throughout the cooking process, was never tested for its air quality, he says. "The inspectors never visited my neighbor; they only went to foreign restaurants. This is another kind of discrimination. The only solution is just to pay the fine."

Others among our interviewees have experienced far more severe instances of corruption in China. In fact, Eric Rongley says he met with such serious corruption from both Chinese police and his domestic competitors that he changed his business model to sell only to offshore clients. "We stopped selling to local Chinese clients partly because domestic customers don't pay well, but also because, in competing with local companies for local business, local companies have better government networks than we do. We found ourselves getting into difficult situations a couple of times." (See the case study entitled "The Price of Weak *Guanxi*.")

Generally, our interviewees found different types of corruption depend on the size and scope of the company. At the young, startup stage, companies can be vulnerable based on their lack of resources, clout, or *guanxi*. Business founder Juan Martinez explains the dilemma he faces in operating a young import/export company in China: "Corruption is an issue. For example, we are now trying to get a new kind of import license, and the officials are hinting that they need *hongbao* (Chinese expression to indicate money inside a red envelope). The official keeps saying he will need to have a 'big talk' with his boss, and that our case is 'complicated.' We feel it is about the red envelopes. We are facing it right now; it exists. Maybe it is worse for us because they see us as being not very powerful."

As the owner of a small company, Martinez describes feeling "damned if you do, damned if you don't." "You need to move forward and get the license to do business, and it seems that red envelopes are the only way possible," he says. But, he warns, once a company begins paying off officials, it can slide down a slippery slope of having to pay extra "fees" constantly. "It's very tricky. You don't want to fall into a trap."

Such dilemmas don't end when companies grow in size and reputation. Software entrepreneur Eric Rongley says that when his company became more successful, new corruption issues arose. For example, when the company moved into upscale new offices in downtown Shanghai, Rongley faced extortion from the fire department in order to issue permits. "It happened because they saw us as a rich company. They thought, 'If we cheat them out of a little money, who cares, right?'" In the end, Rongley says, "We paid a few thousand dollars here and there and the problems went away. It kind of infuriated me at the time, but when I put it into perspective, it wasn't a big deal."

At another time, however, Rongley's company, Bleum, faced a very serious issue with local government, caused mainly (he says) by competing with a local company that had excellent government *guanxi* (see the preceding case study).

[Fighting a corruption case is] like when you have a room full of cockroaches and you turn the light on and they run away. That became my strategy: turning on the light."

Eric Rongley (USA), Founder and CEO, Bleum

B2B Corruption

Another notoriously corrupt sector in China is the food-and-beverage business. "The alcohol and F&B business is a very dirty business. There is a lot of money under the table," says trading company founder Winston Ling. He explains that many bars and most night-clubs charge "entrance fees" and "menu fees" — fees that suppliers must pay in cash without getting receipts, before selling or promoting their products in their facilities. Says Ling: "Outside Shanghai, you cannot do business if you don't pay the entrance fee." These fees, he says, may also be charged to suppliers of products for supermarkets or other types of retail business.

Olaf Litjens stresses that corruption in China not only harms the companies that are forced to pay kickbacks and bribes, but also destroys the normal benefits of an open market economy, where the best products and best services win the highest market share. When relations are built upon corruption, rather than market-based reasons, the result is poorer products and

CASE STUDY

THE PRICE OF WEAK *GUANXI*

In launching Bleum in Shanghai, American-born entrepreneur Eric Rongley had, in his own words, "a couple of crazy experiences that tested my commitment to starting a company in China." He relates one of those experiences, which occurred when his company was still in the process of getting a business license.

Our first customer was also a potential competitor, a well-connected local company. They were using us to make products, which they later sold to China Mobile (one of China's largest mobile phone service providers). They had a large deal with us. Later, China Mobile found out that the software was being made by us, and not by the local company. So, I guess they felt threatened that we would steal their customer away. That wasn't my intention, but they still felt threatened. They knew we hadn't got our business license yet, and that we were very poorly funded, so they decided to attack us. Their intention was to try to scare me out of China and force my staff to join them.

What they did was, they told the police in Hangzhou that we had placed an espionage code into the telecom system. That is a very serious offense in China. It wasn't true, but who knows whether truth is the deciding factor in these cases in China? So, one Friday afternoon, at 5.30, the police showed up at our office. It was a very dangerous situation because I didn't have a business license, so I didn't have any ground to stand on. I didn't have a lawyer either, as I'd never really needed a lawyer before. The police locked our door and put a seal across it. I thought I was going to be arrested for espionage! It was a scary time.

The local company just wanted to tie me up [keep me from doing business] long enough so either I would be scared and leave or burn all my money up. My friends suggested that I simply break into my office and get my equipment out. All my computers were in there. Without our computers, I couldn't do my business. So we did that; we broke in and took some stuff out. The police were chasing us down the street, but we had the receipts and proof that the stuff was ours, so they let us go. We went back to our office and got more stuff. For about three or four days, we were playing cat and mouse with the local police. Breaking into our office was the scariest moment in my life.

One of my Chinese friends told me that the other company was "playing poker." They were bluffing because they couldn't really take this case to court. How can they say to China Mobile: "You thought *we* were making your software. But actually, we hired this illegal company and they put an espionage code into it." Right? How could they ever do business with China Mobile again? They couldn't really push the situation forward. Secondly, luckily for us, they chose espionage code as their excuse [to attack us]. That turned it into an international incident. In America, I have good *guanxi*. My father knows some senators and they could communicate with the American ambassador in China. A lot of heat could come from the situation.

It's like when you have a room full of cockroaches and you turn the light on and they run away. That became my strategy: turning on the light. After several days of running down the street with the police chasing us for getting our own equipment and being hauled to the police station, we met with the police chief and a PLA general who was the *guanxi* guy of the company attacking us. I was also becoming a little braver because we'd been released several times. I was telling the policeman in English, with a translator: "You've got a couple of choices. One is you can arrest me now, and I want to go to the highest court in China RIGHT NOW!" I yelled at him. He was a bit shocked, because this wasn't the behavior of a spy or a thief. I challenged him to take me to court or let me go. I told him: "Another choice is: I'm going to release this code that the customer never paid for on the internet, RIGHT NOW, and the whole world will see that there is no espionage code there."

Then the PLA general started yelling at the cop, and the cop started yelling back at him. That shocked the hell out of me! People who know China much better than I do, and who have been here longer, pointed to this as an example of how China is progressing: 10 years ago, the cop would never have yelled at the PLA general, they said. The PLA general said to the police officer: "Look, if you've got an espionage case, this is the time to bring it forward. Otherwise, you'd better stop this, because the heat is getting to be too much."

The company that had wrongly accused us of espionage ended up paying some of the money they owed us, but it was much less than we were owed.

The funniest moment was when I was running down the street with one of our computer servers in my hand, which I had broken into my office to get. A Chinese policeman had his arm locked around my arm. Of course, there were a lot of people watching. I screamed out as I was running, "*Zhe ge shi wo de! Zhe ge shi wo de!* (This is mine!)" People were thinking, "What the hell is going on with that foreigner?" My pants started falling down, almost down to my knees. I was running with this server, dragging the Chinese security guard, yelling: "*Zhe ge shi wo de!*" Finally, he was laughing so much, he fell off my arm, and I got away. I got the computer back to my house. If you want to be an entrepreneur in China, you'd better be that committed.

" "

Sales staff in China know thousands of ways to cheat. They are very, very innovative in finding ways of cheating," he says. "There is a Chinese idiom that says, 'Whatever the emperor says, the guys on the ground have 10 ways to get around it.'"

Simon Lichtenberg
(Denmark), Founder and CEO, Trayton Group

services from suppliers. "The problem with corruption is that it stagnates innovation" Litjens says. "If I give kickbacks— which I know some of my competitors are doing—in the short term, it is good because it protects you from that client. But it creates no drive to excel or improve in order to beat competitors. For that reason, we simply stay away from it. I want my clients to stay with me because I offer them much better quality than anyone else. It still sometimes happens, although I'm finding that, very rapidly, China is becoming much more professional."

Unfortunately, corruption between business partners, such as buyers and suppliers, is widespread, with many of our interviewees having had first-hand experience of it. "I could write a dictionary of cheating methods," says 15-year China veteran Simon Lichtenberg. One example occurs when a buyer purchases, say, RMB10,000 worth of furniture and the seller issues a *fapiao* (invoice). "The seller has the authority to give the buyer a 3% discount, but he doesn't tell that to the customer. The customer pays RMB10,000 [US$1,430], and the seller writes out two invoices: one for RMB10,000 for the customer and one for RMB9,700 [US$1,385] for the store records. Then he pockets the difference." Lichtenberg says this is just one of many common forms of cheating. "Sales staff in China know thousands of ways to cheat. They are very, very innovative in finding ways of cheating," he says. "There is a Chinese idiom that says, 'Whatever the emperor says, the guys on the ground have 10 ways to get around it.'"

An example of borderline B2B practices is the year-end tradition in China of giving out *hongbao* (red envelopes containing cash) to family, friends, and business contacts during the Chinese New Year festival. "You do business with the company all year, and at the end of the year, you give red envelopes to the buyers or extra money to the supplier," explains American consultant Gene Slusiewicz. He adds that this "gray practice" is declining in larger, more Westernized cities such as Shanghai. Another entrepreneur comments that such practices are still business as usual. "It's a given that the supplier gives the buyer a gift [money] at the end of the year. Even if the buyer is totally honest, he or she expects a package from the supplier during the New Year holiday."

China's gift-giving culture presents another example of social customs seeping into the business culture to create "gray" practices. The giving of gifts may or may not be corrupt, depending upon the scope and scale of the gift. Business development startup Shah Firoozi explains: "I don't think relationship building is necessarily corrupt, and part of relationship building is the old tradition of exchanging gifts and showing hospitality. We do no more than is normal [in China]. We get the same treatment from our customers. My customers give us gifts and invite us to social events, so it's true relationship building and reciprocity."

However, some of our other entrepreneurs had clearly been exposed to corruption. Taiwan-born restaurant owner Michael Yang says the hospitality and retail industries are rife with the practice of kickbacks or payment shaving: "In my business, we have vendors [in China] who send us meat and vegetables every day. Sometimes, they give us less than we ordered or products of a poorer quality, but they still ask for the same money. They give my chef some money and ask him not to tell me. So, I have to check it out myself. I have to hire buyers who I trust and who wouldn't take kickbacks from vendors. Even with big supermarket chains, buyers always ask for something from vendors. Otherwise, they won't put the vendors' products on the shelves."

Procurement Problems

One type of business that is rife with corruption is product procurement and purchasing. Our interviewees recounted many examples of their buyers being tricked, sometimes expertly, into purchasing low-quality goods.

After seven years of trading between China and Macedonia, Oto Petroski says the practice of passing off low-quality goods as high-quality products is "everyday life in China—I don't find it happens just occasionally." He describes having bought ceramics, such as "Italian" ceramic tubs, that initially appeared to be of a high quality, only to find that "the color disappears after three months" or they break after a few days. "They are made with a very teeny layer of [genuine] material as a cover," he explains.

Petroski describes attending a trade fair and finding a Chinese supplier of toilets. "They had a 150-page catalog and a great website. My client saw beautiful products and wanted to order some." As soon as Petroski placed an order, he knew that something was wrong. "The order should have been completed in 45 days, but they said they needed three months. So I knew immediately that they had never manufactured toilets before," he says. "You learn these things only by experience, by knowing the business."

When he visited the company, he learned even more. "When I found the supplier's actual company, I found a house with pigs walking around the yard. In the end, a worker told us that the catalog and website showed samples that her boss had purchased in Italy. They were just waiting for an idiot to come and place an order—then they would try to make an imitation."

On another occasion, he ordered a set of porcelain tubs. While the sample shown weighed 2.5 kilograms, the model produced by the company weighed only 0.5 kilograms. Petroski rejected it. "In the end, after we had paid a deposit, after six months, they simply said 'Dui bu-qi' [Sorry], we cannot produce this'," he recalls. How can buyers avoid such situations? Petroski says the only way is, first, to know the business so well that you cannot be fooled by low-quality imitations; and second, "[to] spend time and build relationships with qualified suppliers."

On the other side of the corrupt procurement equation are buyers seeking perks, benefits, and kickbacks. This is also extremely common, according to our interviewees. Construction businessman Phillip Branham tells of procurement officers for companies openly seeking "gifts" in return for orders placed. "For example, when we were negotiating one purchasing contract, one [procurement officer] said: 'Why don't you take me on a shopping trip to Hong Kong or Macau?' That was her condition for getting the contract signed."

One consultant interviewee agrees that China-based buyers often demand perks and benefits when negotiating with suppliers. He says his clients, especially manufacturers, are often approached for kickbacks. In a recent and typical case, a China-based company ordered product from a manufacturer on behalf of a foreign client. The company rep told the factory to add 20% to the price charged the client—an extra fee that the company planned to skim off before paying the foreign client. "It is very common, and the worst offenders are Western companies in China," says the consultant. He adds that larger foreign manufacturers are refusing to pay these kickbacks. "They are big enough to say 'no,' but it's quite tough for small companies. SME owners feel very unhappy paying these fees, but if they don't do it, they don't get the order."

Stealing Intellectual Property

China is well-known for intellectual property rights (IPR) infringement, for good reason. Another common form of corruption faced by our entrepreneurs is the stealing of IPR—or, less severe, copying of business practices and methods—often by employees within the company.

Few of our interviewees voiced confidence in protecting their business practices or IPR. Language instruction entrepreneur Ken Carroll is a typical example. He says several competitors copied various aspects of his first China-based business, a series of English-as-a-second-language schools called Kai En English Training Center. "Some schools took our website, copying literally every part of our website, and just changed the logo," he says. Looking back, he says companies should simply expect to be copied, at least to some extent. "I think we need to have a sanguine attitude toward this. It's going to happen," he says. Rather than spending time trying to fight small-time competitors, especially with hard-to-prove cases such as copied websites, he and his business partners believe it is better to focus on making the product and services outshine those of their competitors.

> **"**
> *When we were negotiating one purchasing contract, one [procurement officer] said: 'Why don't you take me on a shopping trip to Hong Kong or Macau?' That was her condition for getting the contract signed."*
>
> **Phillip Branham** (USA), Founder and President, B & L Group

"

There's little you can do [about being copied]. You don't come to China and get upset because competitors copy you—that's how it is. It is you who were stupid enough to come here not knowing that you might get copied."

Jan Borgonjon
(Belgium), President,
InterChina Consulting

His second China business, web-based language instruction sites, now has "tons of competitors," but he says they lack "the technological element" offered by Praxis. Overall, Carroll considers copying from competitors an unavoidable hindrance when doing business in China, but in most cases not a serious obstacle.

Consultant and entrepreneur Jan Borgonjon agrees that IP infringements are a fact of life in China for nearly any successful company. "There's little you can do. Let's put it like this: companies that come here have to accept this as part of the game, as 'one of those things.' You don't come to China and get upset because competitors copy you—that's how it is. It is you who were stupid enough to come here not knowing that you might get copied." Borgonjon tells clients to expect to be copied, then to take measures to limit or fight against it. (See the sections on anti-corruption strategies, at the end of this chapter.)

Trayton Group founder Simon Lichtenberg has faced many instances of copying in his 15 years of operating furniture-manufacturing operations in China. "You can't say Chinese people are not very innovative. They are, but in very specific areas," he says. "Typically, they don't *invent* new sofas, but they are very good at *copying* new sofas. They can improve the sofas technically, but not aesthetically. Their ability in cost engineering is top notch—they figure out how we can make the same sofa more cheaply by taking out everything inside that can possibly be removed. They are very good at that." Lichtenberg argues that these strengths have roots in traditional Chinese culture. He points to the difference in Western versus Chinese appreciation of art. "Traditional European paintings are all different, but traditional Chinese paintings are mostly the same motifs. In China, the artistic master of any time period is the one who could create the best copy of a painting by an earlier master." Thus, the Chinese concept of artistic excellence focuses on expertly copying the works of previous masters, making copying a revered skill.

Unethical Employees

Corruption against a company from its own employees was one of the most harmful challenges faced by the foreign business founders we interviewed.

Wendy Tai recalls the problems she faced in 1989 when she relocated her silk flower manufacturing business from her native Taiwan to Xiamen, in China's Fujian province. "I handled the business alone in Xiamen, while my husband was still in Taiwan. One day, something weird happened: I only had enough materials to make 20% of the products as normal because some of the materials had disappeared. It was a big problem for me. I hired new women guards instead of the male ones to check female workers at the end of work. Surprisingly, that day, the missing materials showed up on the ground near the gate. The workers were scared of the guards, so they just threw away all the materials they had stolen."

Two decades later, Tai says her company rarely faces such employee theft these days. "Nowadays, we don't encounter such serious stealing problems. Maybe it is because people are getting richer and they don't care about stealing small things anymore."

But many of our other interviewees weren't as positive about today's environment for employee theft. At the low end of the internal corruption spectrum were instances of well-meaning Chinese employees who had cut corners for the company in order to save costs. For example, consultant Steve Ganster says many of his client companies—mainly foreign invested SMEs in China—tell of being urged by employees to avoid paying taxes. "For entrepreneurial companies, you are looked upon as stupid if you don't take advantage of the loopholes," he says. In fact, foreign managers who insist on following local regulations may find that their domestic employees have never followed the regulations fully before. Another common example of employee pressure concerns software. Says Ganster: "I insist that we use legitimate copies of software. But my employees come up

> *I insist that we use legitimate copies of software. But my employees come up to me and say, 'Are you an idiot? Nobody does that.''*
>
> **Steven Ganster** (USA), Founder and Managing Director, Technomic Asia

to me and say, 'Are you an idiot? Nobody does that.' "In their minds, buying illegally copied software is just how everyone does things." While domestic employees easily know where to buy pirated software, they may not know where to buy legal versions.

Another typical ethical challenge mentioned by foreign business owners in China entails suppliers and business partners offering perks and kickbacks to your employees. Entrepreneur Aviel Zilber explains: "It's very common for a travel agency to tell your office manager, 'If you buy plane tickets from me, I'll give you a kickback.' It's unbelievably normal in China." Zilber gives a real-life example: "When we moved from one office to another, my wife was responsible for all the relocation, design, and renovation. She got offers from each and every supplier telling her that, if she did business with them, she would get kickbacks."

With such tempting offers available, what can an employer do? Indian education executive Prakash Menon says the main weapon for combating unethical behaviour among staff is clear, zero tolerance communication with employees. Menon gives an example: when his purchasing director recently bought 96 computers for the training center he operates, the supplier offered to deliver one extra computer to the director's home, as a show of appreciation. "The purchasing director argued to me that the computer company got a good order, so they didn't mind making this kind of 'donation.' In his mind, he was innocent. He actually told me that he got the extra computer—he never thought it was a problem. I didn't fire him, but I explained to him that it was unethical to take such gifts."

Menon tells of another instance of "gray" employee misconduct. "When a person travels, she stays in different hotels depending on her level and position. If she is allowed to stay in a hotel at RMB300 [US$43] per night, she might go to a RMB100-a-night [US$14] hotel but produce an invoice for RMB300, then keep the difference for her own pocket. In the Chinese mindset, if the company is willing to pay RMB300 per night, what's wrong with keeping the difference? We have to explain to them that it is not correct behavior; that it has to do with the image of the organization. If the company pays for a business class ticket due to company image, you cannot fly economy and keep the difference. But many Chinese don't see this as a lack of integrity."

Our interviewees also stressed that Chinese staff are not the only group susceptible to loose ethics at work. Construction company founder Phillip Branham says the temptations to accept kickbacks impact both domestic and foreign hires, especially in the procurement field when buyers are constantly forming deals with suppliers. "When I first came to China, someone I knew of was skimming US$10,000 in cash from the company every month. He was a foreigner, an American."

Starting a Competing Business

As the previous case indicates, one of the most damaging types of corruption our entrepreneurs face occurs when former (or even current) employees set up directly competing businesses, using the knowledge, training, and contacts gained through the original employer. Simon Lichtenberg explains the feelings of frustration and betrayal: "By far, the worst thing for me is if my employees cheat me. I know my suppliers will try to cheat me, but I take my employees very seriously and I treat them well. We put a lot of money into their training and education."

Internal theft is even more serious in cases where valuable intellectual property (IP) is at stake. Software entrepreneur Eric Rongley faced a serious case several years ago at Bleum, when a team of employees working on a specific project hatched a plan to quit the company and take the project and the client with them to form their own company. The team members all planned to quit on the same day. "In the middle of their planning, we discovered the plot. We found out what these people were doing," says Rongley. "We fired half of them, but we kept half on temporarily, until the project was completed. If we had fired all of them, the impact to the customer would have been significant." This created an extremely awkward and negative environment. "I would

The worst thing for me is if my employees cheat me. I know my suppliers will try to cheat me, but I take my employees very seriously and I treat them well. We put a lot of money into their training and education."

Simon Lichtenberg
(Denmark), Founder and CEO, Trayton Group

have liked to fire them all immediately, but the customer also needed them. We fired the worst offenders first, but kept on the others—that way we worked out a transition plan with our customer."

WHEN YOUR STAFF BECOMES YOUR ENEMY

Danish furniture designer and manufacturer Simon Lichtenberg, a 15-year China hand, has much experience in dealing with untrustworthy employees in China. When asked to describe any bad experiences involving his own staff, he replied: "I could write a book! I have *plenty* of stories." Lichtenberg shared two incidents with *China Entrepreneur*:

We have a department that does the sampling, prototyping, and calculation for the new products—production of documentation, all that. The manager of this department was a very clever, skilled worker. He was one of the very first workers to join my factory. We trained him and he became a supervisor, workshop manager, and then plant manager. We sent him overseas for training. His wife was the supervisor of the sewing workshop. He had his limitations because of his lack of education, but he was a very good craftsman. He had worked here for eight years. One day, his wife suddenly left. He told me her health wasn't very good. After a while, I asked him, "How is your wife doing?"

"She's fine," he said. "She has started a small sewing workshop."

"Doing what?" I asked.

"She is doing curtains."

I knew then that I had to watch out, because all of our industry knowledge and trade secrets were in his department.

A couple of months later, I asked him again, "How is your wife's workshop doing?"

"Now she is also doing some cushions," he said.

Then, my alarm bells really went off. I said, "Right now, we go visit her." I took him by the hand and said, "Let's go see your wife's workshop."

In another case, Bleum's information security officer was using the company's resources to operate his own side business. "The moment I found out, he was fired," says Rongley. "It affected me a lot, because I counted on him as one of the people I trusted. He was a shareholder in the company, but the temptation to do his own business on the side was too much for him."

> It was five minutes from our factory. The place was a full-fledged sofa factory, more than 100 employed workers, doing exact copies of our products. He and his wife were running it. They had taken the drawings, everything from our company. They were even soliciting our customers. I was very, very disappointed.
>
> Lichtenberg recalled a second case of an unfaithful employee.
>
> Our financial manager was helping me with a project for a new factory in Jiashan, Zhejiang province. I was doing land negotiations with the government, and he was doing the paperwork and the day-to-day communication with them. He went to Jiashan quite often; in fact, he was there more often than I thought was needed. His work became less and less efficient. He was very busy in Jiashan, but there wasn't very much going on that required so much attention. So, I started fishing with the government guys in Jiashan. One day, one of the government guys said, "By the way, how is the new factory going?" I said, "Which factory?"
>
> I found out that my finance manager was using our resources to arrange his own deal behind my back. He'd acquired land for my company, but he also got his own piece of land not very far away, in the same district. He was building his own factory. He managed to get one of our suppliers to finance him. Imagine . . . he had been with me for *10 years*!
>
> According to Lichtenberg, 10 of his former employees have started their own sofa factories. Five of them were professional people who left on good terms. The other five were people who stole intellectual property in order to establish their own business. After these experiences, Lichtenberg now knows much better how to select people. "I can't say that I won't encounter this situation again, but I *can* say that if I was the way I am now five years ago, I would have avoided at least half of those cases."

Avoiding Government Corruption

Our interviewees offered the following advice for avoiding corruption when dealing with the Chinese bureaucratic system.

CASE STUDY

EMPLOYEE RELATIONS GONE WRONG

Retail display designer/manufacturer Susan Heffernan describes her first-hand experience of how employers can be taken advantage of by even their "best" employees. "In China, you need to be very careful about the personality of your key employees. It's the opposite mindset of employers in [Australia]. Back home, you want to hire people who are better than you—super-good at everything. Here, you have to be very careful about the personality of the people you hire, to make sure you can trust them. Everyone is an entrepreneur in China, which is completely different from the situation in Australia. In Australia, it's hard to get some employees to keep their motivation going past 4 p.m. on Fridays."

Heffernan says the work ethic is far better among employees in China. She warns, though, that some superstar staffers may be working hard not to build your business, but to start a *competing* business. One of her seemingly hardest-working employees—someone she had spent years training and sharing trade secrets with—secretly started a related furnishings business on the side. "At first, I was very disappointed and felt sick about it, because I'd given so much love and trust to that person," says Heffernan. "She thought what I was doing looked easy. She thought, 'Oh, I can do this. I can make all this money for me.'"

Another of our interviewees had similar experiences, and now takes precautions such as not teaching all responsibilities to any single employee. "I realized that you need to split up responsibilities and divide them among people. It's not the most efficient way, but it's harder for them to walk away if they don't have all the necessary information," he says. But even this method isn't secure," he warns, because employees often freely share information with each other. "I've become less naïve. I think that employees are only with you for the moment. If you can keep this mindset, you won't be disappointed and you won't be left in the lurch."

Strategy #1: Stay off the Slippery Slope

Import/export startup Juan Martinez advises new companies to try hard to avoid paying *hongbao* (red envelopes) and kickbacks; once you start, he says, it can be a slippery slope with no guarantee that the pay-outs will bring the results you are seeking. He explains: "The thing is, sometimes the rules in China are not so clear. You ask for the rules, and they will give you a piece of paper, but many details are not written down—details that you need to understand." He adds that while regulations are becoming clearer over time, especially in the urban centers, "some people still try to use [the lack of clarity] to find ways and get opportunities to get extra money." Martinez says that companies often come up against bureaucrats seeking *hongbao* when applying for a business license or other types of approval necessary to start or grow their business. "It is important that you don't follow this path," he says. "If you follow that path, you will be trapped and nobody will guarantee you anything at the end of the day."

Another entrepreneur gave similar advice, warning that once a company pays the first bribe, this can lead to more and more requests. "When I was applying for my first license, my company was approached for a payment of RMB2,000 [US$286]. My first thought was to pay the money and solve the problem. But another friend always said, 'Don't pay—otherwise, next time the problem will be bigger and bigger.' He fought so hard against it, and he was right. Now I realize that people never want just RMB1,000 or 2,000 [US$145–286]. When I talked to another person, they paid RMB2,000, and then RMB20,000 [US$2,860], and then RMB200,000 [US$28,580]. So, it became worse and worse."

Meal delivery services entrepreneur Mark Secchia agrees with the "don't start" policy. He has been able to expand Sherpa's steadily over nine years and has launched other businesses, while following a zero tolerance policy, but he says he has lost much time and met with many frustrations along the way: "At Sherpa's, we don't pay [*hongbao*]. We haven't paid, but we have had to spend so much time and

> *In China, you need to be very careful about the personality of your key employees. Back home [in Australia], you want to hire people who are better than you—super-good at everything. Here, you have to be very careful about the personality of the people you hire, to make sure you can trust them."*
>
> **Susan Heffernan** (Australia), Founder and Managing Director, Soozar

TIP Avoid using under-the-table practices. Once you begin paying officials, you may end up paying "extra fees" constantly, with no guarantee of effectiveness.

Investigate which agency, and even which officials, have the authority to give you the permits you need. Involve as many agencies as possible; when regulations are vague or unclear, play one agency against another.

energy discussing problems that could have been solved for a few hundred RMB."

Strategy #2: Involve Multiple Agencies

If more than one government agency is involved in the license approval process, Juan Martinez suggests playing one agency off the other by demonstrating to one how another agency is successfully moving your case forward. "Some people have tried to ask for money, but we always try to involve some other government organizations so that they can see that we are not alone."

Martinez also advises doing lots of due diligence to find out which government agencies, and even which officials, truly make decisions on your case. If your company is pressured into "giving gifts," he warns: "First, make sure there is really no other way to get the license." After all, paying a bribe is not a guarantee of success. "Remember that, even if you pay *hongbao*, nobody can guarantee that you will get what they have been promising. I know people who have this problem—they paid [the bribe], and then nothing happened."

Strategy #3: Give the Government "Face"

Another way to avoid extra expectations from officials is to win them over to your side from the start. Serviced offices provider Maggie Yu gives the following advice on winning over Chinese officials, and dissuading them from misusing their positions of power against your startup: "Taiwanese attitudes are a little different from Chinese ones. When we talk, we can be very polite. That can be very impressive to Chinese government officers. They feel we are *too* polite, sometimes. That's the biggest difference. You can use it here. If you are not polite to the government officers when you ask for something, they won't want to help you, even though they can. If you are very polite and very humble, they are more willing to help you." (*Note:* There are many more tips on developing the right attitude toward government officials in Chapter 1.)

Strategy #4: Hold Your Ground, Be Persistent

> **A humble and respectful attitude toward officials can be the best strategy for getting things done.**

Eric Rongley gives another example of how to beat corruption through persistence. His software company recently applied to receive government subsidies for which it was qualified after its software products were awarded the top quality rating of Level 5. However, Rongley found himself facing "a bit of goofing around" from bureaucrats. Before Bleum could receive the subsidy, he says, "We had to make sure we gave gifts to various people. If not, they would forever have been saying, 'First, we need to consider this, then we need to consider that.'" Even after the gifts were distributed, some officials were still dragging their heels. Rongley took direct action. "What finally made them pay [the subsidy] was that we had a press conference to announce that we had been awarded Level 5. We brought in the government officials and had pictures taken with them, holding our certificate. Then there wasn't really any plausible way for them to deny us the funding. So, they paid us."

Even though the process was frustrating, Rongley credits China for offering the subsidies to foreign invested companies in the first place. "There aren't many countries in the world where a foreigner is treated almost equally with the local people. In India, we weren't treated equally. In countries in Africa, and even in Europe, I don't know. So, I can congratulate China on that."

Strategy #5: Raise a Fuss

Several of our interviewees stressed that, if you or your company end up paying a fine or fees to a government entity, the fees often can be negotiated or bargained down. Import/export company founder Oto Petroski explains: "The funniest thing here is that when you get a penalty, you can go to the government and bargain over the fee. When I show my face, increase the volume of my voice and shout a little bit, a penalty of RMB100,000

TIP If you are sure you are in the right, defend your case by making as much noise as possible. Use your *guanxi*, use the media, and bring the case out into the open.

[US$14,300] becomes RMB20,000 [US$2,860]. This shows that there is no law, in the way that we understand the law. It is just a game."

Another case involved furniture entrepreneur Simon Lichtenberg. In the mid-2000s, it wasn't easy for him to find high-quality leather for his sofa factory. So, in 2004, when he found a qualified supplier in the town of Leshan, Sichuan province, Lichtenberg bought RMB37 million [US$5.3 million] worth of leather from him. However, RMB3 million [US$428,600] worth of the leather was of very low quality, so Lichtenberg withheld payment of that amount and returned that part of the merchandise.

He then heard nothing of the incident until, one day, two judges and two judicial police from Sichuan appeared in his Shanghai office with an order to freeze RMB3 million from his bank account and RMB4.2 million [US$600,000] of company assets. The four people had traveled more than 2,000 kilometers just to issue Lichtenberg with the order. The owner of the leather factory had managed to use his *guanxi* to present a claim in a local court where he could control the judge, and had paid for the travel, hotel, and more. "What can a foreign business owner do in that situation?" Lichtenberg asks. "He closed my bank accounts and wanted to take assets worth RMB7 million [US$1 million]. He thought by doing that, he could force me to pay, even though I was in the right and not liable to pay anything."

When you are confronted with dirty methods and corrupt courts, you have to fight back the same way, Lichtenberg believes. He decided to make as much noise as possible through as many of his own connections as possible. "I used a high-ranking military officer, the Danish Embassy, the party secretary of Sichuan province, and a High Court official, a very good friend of mine—four big potatoes putting tons of pressure on this Sichuan leather supplier. He thought it would be easy to get a stupid foreigner to pay up, but he came to the wrong foreigner." What happened in the end? Lichtenberg won. "The leather supplier ended up paying me RMB800,000 [US$114,300] in compensation."

Lichtenberg stresses that his experience cannot be extrapolated to the whole of China. "This case is a very good example of what happens in Western China, which is far behind Shanghai."

TIP Assess upfront whether corruption is a big factor in the sector and region where you plan to launch your business in China; then decide whether you should really launch.

Blocking B2B Corruption

A different set of strategies should be used to avoid business-to-business corruption than is appropriate when dealing with the government, our interviewees stressed. For one thing, entrepreneurs can freely choose their business partners, suppliers, vendors, and even customers. Here are some other key strategies shared with *China Entrepreneur*.

Strategy #1: Pick Battles You Can Win

Six-year China veteran consultant Steven Ganster first advises clients launching in the China market to research their market, and pick sectors in which it is feasible to operate with minimal corruption. "My advice is to be aware of where corruption is and what options exist to deal with it. Does it mean you really can't do business here? Understand the situation going in, so that you don't get blindsided here. Structure yourself so you are insulated from, or just don't participate in, certain markets," he says.

Ganster advises his clients that some sectors may not be worth the effort. "Besides having the right kind of people and the right governance—the more traditional things—you also need to assess upfront whether corruption is a big factor for your business here [in China]. If it is, you need to ask, 'Should we even *be* here?'" Ganster stresses: "There's a lot of paranoia among American companies. Since the passage of the Sarbanes Oxley Act, they are pretty religious about playing it safe."

TIP When possible, use anti-corruption legislation from your own country to support your position. Chinese businesses are beginning to understand the need for foreign businesspeople to abide by their home-country legislation.

Strategy #2: Play the "Foreign Card"

One method of staying away from corruption is simply to play the "foreign card"—explaining clearly and often that your firm must abide by home-country rules and regulations. This will likely cost your company some business and will slow your growth prospects, but it is often worthwhile in the long run. Rules such as Sarbanes Oxley are becoming known and understood in China, and can be recognized by Chinese as reasons why foreign companies must not engage in under-the-table deals.

Strategy #3: Cut out the Corrupt Middleman

Facing "pervasive" corruption in procurement operations for his newly opened Shanghai-based construction company, B & L Group founder Phillip Branham explains why he has decided not to use the method of choice for many foreign firms: hiring a consultant to act as go-between. Using a middleman often results in engaging in bribery and kickbacks along the supply chain, says Branham. "A lot of [foreign] companies have hired consultants. The consultants get paid and then arrange the necessary *hongbao* and kickbacks. The company doesn't even know how the things get done, because the consultants handle it."

> *A lot of [foreign] companies have hired consultants. The consultants get paid and then arrange the necessary* **hongbao** *and kickbacks. The company doesn't even know how the things get done, because the consultants handle it."*
>
> **Phillip Branham** (USA),
> Founder and President,
> B & L Group

But Branham advises against this, saying he took a tough stand against paying under the table after launching his company. With a concerted effort, he says foreign companies can use their foreignness to avoid paying out. "When I hire procurement people, I let them know that taking bribes isn't acceptable. I tell the vendors that if I even suspect that anything is happening, I will stop it."

Branham requires suppliers to sign a document stating that if any corruption issues are exposed, the agreement with the vendor will be terminated. "I explain this company policy to the vendors in front of my employees. I explain that the vendor shouldn't pay anybody in the company for the contract. If they *do* pay for the contract, I tell them I will both fire the employee and cancel my contract with the vendor." Asked whether this method will work in China, Branham says: "Even this kind of effort cannot get rid of 100% of corruption; it's pretty pervasive."

Another Western business owner agrees, advising large companies setting up in China to avoid going through middlemen as much as possible. During his time in China, he has found that clients who rely on service companies often end up paying more, because the middleman skims off any discounts offered to the client.

> **TIP** Make it clear upfront that corruption practices aren't accepted in your company. Explain to your suppliers that any attempt at corruption will result in cancelation of your contract with them.

Strategy #4: Create Internal Control Systems

Furniture manufacturer Simon Lichtenberg gives a first-hand account of how internal cheating works in a manufacturing company. "You buy 100 rolls of fabric, for example, and your purchasing guy takes 20 rolls and drives only 80 rolls to the warehouse. The guy at the warehouse writes down '100 rolls', and he splits [the 20 rolls] with the purchaser. This is a real story." Another scam involves the quality control controller accepting sub-par products. "The supplier says, 'If you let it go, I will give you something.'"

To fight such practices, Lichtenberg recommends setting up "control systems." First, his company has established an Internal Audit Department. Second, he has separated the sourcing and buying functions in his company. "The Sourcing Department finds the suppliers and fixes the price, and the Purchasing Department handles the actual buying—two completely different people in two different departments, to some extent competing, and keeping an eye on each other. We have also split the authority over Quality Control and Warehousing at a high level," Lichtenberg says. "If you really want to cheat, you need to convince Sourcing, Purchasing, Warehousing, and Quality Control. Without linking those four together, you can't do anything." Finally, another effective safeguard, he says, is job rotation—moving people to new positions before they can develop the *guanxi* necessary to begin cheating.

"

*When I hire procurement people, I let them know that taking bribes isn't acceptable. . . . I explain this company policy to the vendors in front of my employees. If they **do** pay for the contract, I will both fire the employee and cancel my contract with the vendor."*

Phillip Branham (USA), Founder and President, B & L Group

A strategy that Lichtenberg warns must be used with caution is anonymous internal reporting systems, where employees can write a letter denouncing misbehavior among their fellow employees. "The problem with this system is that it sometimes gets misused. You sometimes get fake stories. So, if you use this system, you have to punish fake stories as well as punish the perpetrators in the real stories."

Strategy #5: Dissuade the IPR Pirates

While IPR infringement is a fact of life for many business operators in China, our entrepreneurs offered battle-tested advice for surviving in this environment. One piece of advice to consider from the start: make your product less of a target for IP pirates by not pricing your goods too far above market rates. The wider your profit margin, the more likely that your product will be targeted by pirates. In fact, consultant Nicolas Musy suggests to some clients that, to avoid becoming a target of IP pirates, they reduce their profit margin in China a little. "For example, machinery made in Switzerland is very expensive. If you copy it here, you might cut the price to one-third or one-fourth, especially when you can get rid of some features that aren't needed here. If you make it here, compared to importing it, it's much cheaper. But if the foreign company comes to China and sells its equipment at a reasonable price, there is much less chance that a Chinese company will start copying it because the margin is much less. If the Chinese counterfeiters can only sell their products for half of your price instead of one-fifth, then they are less of a threat to you."

TIP Put internal control systems in place to halt corruption. Divide tasks among different departments such as Sourcing, Purchasing, and Quality Control.

Fighting Internal Corruption

Fighting corruption among your own employees is often the most difficult task, but *not* doing so can have the most devastating results for a startup. Our interviewees discussed how to dissuade and detect corruption among the employee ranks.

Strategy #1: Run a Tight Ship

At the most basic level, our entrepreneurs advised treating all employees—including the entry-level staff—strictly but fairly. Says Mark Pummell, "We are careful in small details, such as the way we manage our *ayi* [cleaning personnel] and the guards who lock up at night. I think it's about how we relate to people. They can make our life easy or very difficult. The security guards at night, for example; if they like you, they keep your place very safe. If not, they might loosen your locks. It happens."

At Sherpa's food delivery service, founder Mark Secchia says he controls employee corruption and theft by first establishing clear accounting systems and making it clear that any theft—of food or money—will be detected. "I will find out, at the end of the month, if a courier or the call center operators give some food for free or keep the money. In the database, I know who the courier for that order was and who the call center operator was—so I don't worry about these little things. It's self-regulating."

Logistics entrepreneur Jeffrey Bernstein stresses that fighting internal corruption must be made a regular part of business operations in China. "Staff training in ethics cannot be accomplished in a once-a-year annual training session, which some MNCs do in China, and then just check off the box. Fighting corrupt practices is the full-time job of the manager. He or she needs to be thinking about it every day, finding opportunities to talk to the staff about the right and wrong things to do, really leading by example. There is no alternative to being very involved. Not micro-managing, but having ethics at the forefront of your mind." Bernstein also warns foreign managers in China that, if something *smells* a little fishy, chances are high that it *is* fishy. He urges managers to investigate if any situation seems unusual. "Even though some staff might chafe when the manager 'snoops,' it is more accepted here because people know how big the problem of integrity is. The Chinese are very entrepreneurial, so they empathize with the boss in such a situation. If they were running the company, many of your staff members would investigate and snoop around."

> **TIP** For high value-added products, it may pay to adjust your margins in China. Counterfeiters will find it less tempting to copy you when the margins aren't so attractive.

> **TIP** If something *seems* fishy, it probably *is* fishy. Don't hesitate to investigate. Your employees expect and accept "snooping around" from the boss.

TIP To minimize IP risks, compartmentalize your technology and limit clients' and employees' access to it. In addition, put legal protections in place.

Strategy #2: Protect IPR against Insiders

Consultant Jan Borgonjon tells client companies that they can expect to lose technology through former employees to a certain extent. "Of course, you can try to limit the impact. First, you need to pay attention to the people you employ; then you have legal means; and finally, you could decide not to bring some new technology to China as a way to safeguard it. If there is some really key technology, don't transfer it to China. China might not be ready yet."

Another alternative is to "compartmentalize your technology," by limiting access to it among your employees or clients. Borgonjon admits, however, that this method isn't always feasible. "We know companies [in China] where there are no hard drives, no disks, and no USB ports on the computers; every piece of information that goes in and out has to be certified. You can have that kind of control."

Fellow consultant Nicolas Musy agrees: "This is the case for those areas where you may not have patents. A lot of people copy. If you don't have a patent for machinery, then there's nothing wrong with the copy, legally speaking. If you have a patent, you can actually act. In general, if you do things right, and you make sure to have certain precautions when you come to operate here, I think it's better to come to China than to stay at home. It's more risky *not* to come. You can always keep your key elements in Europe so that nobody in the China operation knows how to make it." Musy also recommends not sharing all aspects of key technology with any single staffer. "You can split that knowledge through the different functions of the company. Unless the whole group is going to leave, or the whole management team is going to leave, they are not able to build a new company. Usually, when you are making technology-intensive products, the required capital is high. It's capital intensive, so it's difficult for them as well."

Consultant Ruggero Jenna offers this advice: "Instead of focusing on bringing people to court [for IPR infringement], or getting the patent registration, IPR strategy should be based on planning what technology should be transferred here. Every product has core parts, the most advanced features; while other things are less crucial. So, if you want to produce something here, you can ship the core parts from your own country. You see it in many cases like the chip in the computer, or the engine in the car. It's impossible for the people to copy it from here. We can give this advice to our clients."

Strategy #3: Hire Young, Train Well

One challenge when hiring seasoned employees is that, the more experience they have, the greater the chance that they have learned unethical practices at their previous jobs. South African consultant Kobus van der Wath describes the pressures inherent in B2B transactions in China: "In business-to-business, whether you can win a deal or not depends on what you are willing to do—your willingness to compete by using under-the-table methods. You need to have a clear policy on that. If you hire a new person and that person used under-the-table methods in his previous job, he will assume that he can do it again. This is something that needs to be managed carefully." Brazilian entrepreneur Winston Ling agrees: "I decided not to hire older people; only young and inexperienced people. If you teach them from the beginning and you are consistent, they will do the ethical thing."

Consultant Jan Borgonjon stresses the importance of screening employees before hiring—not only for skills, but for the right ethics. "Any applicant who is going to have any level of responsibility in the company must go through roughly 10 interviews with me and other people in the firm. We have many people to judge the applicant. We select 50% based on personality—we look for a combination of honesty, integrity, and aggressiveness. It's not easy to find all these elements together in one person." He also stresses the need to check references and call previous employers—practices that are now catching on in China.

One warning: Good English skills don't necessarily mean a good understanding of Western values or ethics, says Bernstein. "There are so many organizations, especially large ones, that will hire a U.S.-educated Chinese manager and assume that, because he speaks English well, he has good American-style

> *If you hire a new person and that person used under-the-table methods in his previous job, he will assume that he can do it again. This is something that needs to be managed carefully."*
>
> **Kobus van der Wath** (South Africa), Founder and group Managing Director, The Beijing Axis

When you hire, don't assume that good English skills in a Chinese manager will translate into Western-standard ethics.

ethics. But when that manager returns to China, he might not act in ethical ways."

Conclusion

In this chapter, we have covered corruption and ethics at three levels: government, business-to-business, and internal employees. The gravity of corruption in China varies depending upon the nature of the business activity, some activities being more affected by corruption than others. Geographical location is another factor affecting the level of corruption; bigger cities and those on the coast are closer to international levels, while small cities and interior areas are more corrupt. A special problem is corrupt practices between companies and by unethical employees. These factors need to be considered when doing business in China. However, our entrepreneurs advised that they weren't deterred by corruption from starting their business or operating successfully in China. One key message is that while giving in and participating in corrupt practices can provide short-term advantages, once a company starts down the path of giving kickbacks and bribes, it is very difficult to stop such practices later. It is better to play the "foreign card" (claiming that under-the-table dealings are not allowed in your home country), and to grow slowly but ethically.

SUMMARY OF TIPS
ETHICS AND CORRUPTION

STRATEGIES FOR AVOIDING CORRUPTION

GOVERNMENT CORRUPTION

Strategy #1: Stay off the slippery slope
Avoid using under-the-table practices. Once you begin paying officials, you may end up paying "extra fees" constantly, with no guarantee of effectiveness.

Strategy #2: Involve multiple agencies
Investigate which agency, and even which officials, have the authority to give you the permits you require. Involve as many agencies as possible; when regulations are vague or unclear, play one agency against another.

Strategy #3: Give the government "face"
Sometimes a humble and respectful attitude can be the best strategy for getting things done.

Strategy #5: Raise a fuss
If you are sure you are in the right, defend your case by making as much noise as possible. Use your *guanxi*, use the media, and bring the case out into the open.

Strategy #4: Hold your ground, and be persistent
Don't give up when you face the first bureaucratic difficulty. If you give up easily, you will be seen as an easy target for further corruption.

B2B CORRUPTION

Strategy #1: Pick battles you can win
Assess upfront whether corruption is a big factor in the sector and region where you plan to launch your business in China; then decide whether you should really launch.

Strategy #3: Cut out the corrupt middleman
Make it clear upfront that corruption practices aren't accepted in your company. Explain to your suppliers that any attempt at corruption will result in cancelation of your contract with them.

Strategy #5: Dissuade IPR pirates
For high value-added products, it may pay to adjust your margins. Counterfeiters will find it less tempting to copy you when the margins aren't so attractive.

Strategy #2: Play the "foreign card"
When possible, use anti-corruption legislation from your own country to support the position. Chinese businesses are beginning to understand the need for foreign businesspeople to abide by their home-country legislation.

Strategy #4: Create internal control systems
Put internal control systems in place to halt corruption. Divide tasks among different departments such as Sourcing, Purchasing, Quality Control, and Warehousing, to make corruption difficult. Rotate people in and out of key positions regularly.

EMPLOYEE CORRUPTION

Strategy #1: Run a tight ship
If something seems fishy, it probably is fishy. Don't hesitate to investigate. Your employees expect and accept "snooping around" from the boss.

Strategy #3: Hire young, train well
When you hire, consider the candidate's honesty and personality. Find good candidates through your networks. Don't assume that good English skills in a Chinese manager will translate into Western-standard ethics.

Strategy #2: Protect IPR against insiders
To minimize IP risks, compartmentalize your technology and limit clients' and employees' access to it. In addition, put legal protection in place.

Chapter 7
Business Negotiations

"The finest negotiators in the world are the Chinese. No doubt about that. Negotiation in China is a lot more subtle than in India. In India, you say this and mean it, no hidden agenda—it's much simpler than in China. In China, there are layers and layers of hidden agendas, and you have to search to find what they really mean."

Prakash Menon (India), President, NIIT (China)

"You can't really say there is one Chinese way of negotiation because there are so many different cases: north China, south China, private companies, state owned. . . . They have very different ways to negotiate and different levels of predictability."

Jan Borgonjon (Belgium), President, InterChina Consulting

Introduction

In most business books, the chapter on negotiation ends at the point where both parties sign a contract or agreement—mission accomplished! Not so with this book, because in China, business negotiations are generally not finished when the contract is signed. As our 40 interviewees explained based on their first-hand experience, a contract or agreement signed with a Chinese business partner acts more as a "marker" showing the state of the partnership at a certain point in time. There is a clear understanding (at least from the Chinese side) that the terms of all business dealings will continue to evolve and shift as the partnership operates. In this way, a contract is more like the beginning of a new chapter of negotiations between partners, rather than a conclusion.

For many non-Chinese businesspeople, the idea of a loosely defined, evolving agreement clashes directly with the concept of a contract as used in most developed nations worldwide. This difference in thinking is one of the primary issues covered in this chapter.

In addition to sharing advice on adapting to the Chinese approach to contracts, in the pages that follow, our interviewees outline strategies for coping with other common challenges to business negotiations with Chinese buyers, sellers, partners, and customers. While our interviewees hailed from 25 different countries or provinces, and work in a full range of different industries, nearly all had struggled to adapt to Chinese-style business discussions. In fact, most of our interviewees had suffered through hundreds (even thousands) of business-related negotiations during their combined 500 years of work experience in China. Their advice on surviving in Chinese negotiations produces the basis of this chapter, which covers three main topics:

1. Pre-negotiation preparation
2. At the negotiation table: tactics and strategies
3. Post agreement: after the contract is signed

To set the stage for the advice shared below, we offer the following metaphor: if the two extremes in negotiation styles are represented by, on one end, a wrestling match (in which the stronger side simply uses force to beat the weaker side) and on the other end a waltz (in which the two sides carefully coordinate their movements), then Chinese-style negotiation is somewhere in the middle of the range. The martial art of *tai chi*—which can be described as a combination of dancing and wrestling—is an apt metaphor for the Chinese negotiation technique, because the process involves both strength and flexibility. *Tai chi* also invokes the principle of using your opponent's own force against himself (for example, tiring him out by encouraging him to struggle in a way that does not tire your side). The Chinese are masters in *tai chi;* in this chapter, we share advice from our interviewees on making you a master *tai chi* negotiator.

> *One of the worst mistakes for many [foreign] people, even smart investment bankers, is to be in a hurry. Sometimes, the Chinese counterpart gets you to agree on certain things because you are in a rush."*
>
> **Ruggero Jenna** (Italy), Managing Partner for Asia and Asia Pacific, Value Partners

Pre-negotiation Preparation

One of the first necessary steps upon entering into business discussions with a Chinese counterpart, according to our interviewees, is to accept the fact that the negotiation process will likely require more time, energy, and work than would be true back home or in other developed markets. In fact, most of our interviewees warn that negotiations with domestic Chinese suppliers, buyers, or other partners tend to become a convoluted process. The good news is that going through this long and difficult process often results in the formation of a partnership that can be stronger and more supportive than business partnerships formed elsewhere.

Rule #1: Be Prepared for a Long Journey

China-based business consultant Ruggero Jenna explains: "One of the worst mistakes for many [foreign] people, even smart investment bankers, is to be in a hurry. Sometimes, the Chinese

"

*When you
negotiate in China,
my advice is this:
you should prepare
for your meeting
like a German, sit
down like a
Chinese, and enjoy
[the process] like a
Mediterranean."*

Josep Giro (Spain),
Co-founder and Managing
Director, SBC &
Associates

counterpart gets you to agree on certain things because you are in a rush. You have to take your time. You have to manage your time. Sometimes, things aren't sorted out in the first meetings." Jenna advises thinking of the negotiation as a mystery to be solved, step by step, as you discover what your opponent really wants. "[The Chinese side] won't tell you what they want, so you have to find out what their ultimate goal is, and see if their goal is compatible with yours," he says. "Mutual understanding is really crucial."

After nine years of consulting work in China, Spanish consultant Josep Giro advises adopting a multicultural mindset to best handle business negotiations. "When you negotiate in China, my advice is this: you should prepare for your meeting like a German, sit down like a Chinese, and enjoy [the process] like a Mediterranean." He explains: "'Prepare like a German' means that you try to make things as clear as possible concerning your plan and your target." When sitting down at the negotiation table, he advises adopting a Chinese bargaining mindset— which can seem inefficient and meandering to non-Chinese. "'Sit down like a Chinese' means just sit down and talk. [Consider that] the contract is just a draft. Today, it can be like this; and tomorrow, it might be like that." He also advises expecting a fluid discussion with lots of changes, and retracing of ground that was already covered. "Westerners want to close one point and go to another, but the Chinese move from point to point and then back again. You should accept that."

Finally, Giro advises foreign businesspeople to learn to enjoy this convoluted process. "'Enjoy like a Mediterranean' means enjoy [the negotiating process] like a Latin person. The Chinese will tell you: 'We are negotiating; nothing is fixed and nothing is closed. We can come back to it later.' I use the same system. It's like martial arts. You need to use the energy of the opponent to use less effort [of your own]. It's the same." Part of the "Mediterranean" style that Giro recommends involves, he says, following your intuition about how the negotiation is really going, in order to avoid being cheated.

This loose negotiating mindset seems inefficient to many non-Chinese, but there is an upside to it: while partnerships with

Chinese counterparts typically get off to a slow start, when a successful business relationship does form, the bond is often stronger and more supportive than is the norm elsewhere. The bottom line: the laying of the foundation for a good partnership cannot be rushed or hastily built; however, once built up, that foundation can usually be depended upon by both sides.

American negotiation expert Gene Slusiewicz explains that, while initial negotiations can take longer in China than in the West, after a partnership begins operating, the waiting times for future agreements are typically slashed. Slusiewicz says that while it may take many months to work out an initial agreement to produce a precision part with a new Chinese partner, for example, by the time the company places a second order, the part may be completed in half the time. After the design is finalized, he can produce a tool within a dozen days in China — work that would take at least a month in the United States. "The negotiation takes longer, but once it kicks off, the work will be done faster. Things get done a whole lot faster in China, and the overhead is a lot lower."

Our interviewees advised accepting that the negotiation process will require both extra time and effort, and then following two steps: adopting the right mindset, and doing your homework. Shah Firoozi, founder and president of The PAC Group, explains: "First of all, the Chinese negotiation system isn't black and white; it uses gradual steps. Westerners are too black and white, and Chinese are too gray." He explains that many negotiations between Chinese and Westerners stumble because the two sides come to the discussion from different starting points. "The Chinese start [a business negotiation] by saying, 'Let's start with this and grow from here.' Westerners start by saying, 'This is what I want to achieve when I'm done.'"

On the Chinese side, Firoozi explains, the goal is rarely determined before the first negotiation; instead, they use the first meeting to judge how far they can push their opponent. "China has 5,000 years of trade and negotiation experience. Negotiation is a part of their culture." Firoozi explains that Chinese businesspeople expect that both sides will be aggressively testing the situation to see how much they can gain for

Westerners are too black and white, and Chinese are too gray. . . . The Chinese start [a business negotiation] by saying, 'Let's start with this and grow from here.' Westerners start by saying, 'This is what I want to achieve when I'm done.'"

Shah Firoozi (USA), Founder and President, The PAC Group

Prepare thoroughly before you begin negotiating. Research the other party's needs. Understand what they really want and decide what concessions you could make.

themselves. "It is still considered a part of [the Chinese negotiator's] responsibility to try and improve upon what's been offered—if you don't do that, you're not doing your job. Chinese people feel the personal responsibility to try and win better terms." On the other hand, the Chinese side will be expecting your side to seek better terms for yourself. "The same opportunity exists for you. If you get a request, you have the responsibility to bring a counter request. What can you give in return? My experience has been that, in China, you can't negotiate with 'yes' or 'no' answers."

Rule #2: Do Your Homework before the Negotiation Begins

China-based negotiation expert Gene Slusiewicz stresses that negotiating in China requires being much better prepared than would be needed in the U.S. or other developed markets. You must be crystal clear about the goals your side is trying to achieve, he says, while not letting your counterparts know these too early in the negotiating process. A process of discovering the true goals of each side is an expected part of the challenge; the Chinese side will likely make it very difficult initially for you to uncover their true goals.

Slusiewicz offers the following advice for when preparing to negotiate with a Chinese supplier: "You want to understand what you want to obtain from the negotiation, the final outcome. In any purchasing agreement, you have to balance many things: quality, technology, service, warranty, and price. Price is the last thing on my list that will be discussed and resolved."

Before the discussion, Slusiewicz advises holding a "stakeholder meeting" including all relevant voices—people from sales, quality, purchasing, and manufacturing. "You need to understand what your team needs. You also need to listen to the voice of the final customers. Is the customer very demanding or easy to please? What is critical to the customer: time, price, design, or something else? This will give you the key elements in the negotiation."

Next, Slusiewicz and his team spend time considering the other party's needs. "What is he [or she] going to ask for?" Slusiewicz suggests investigating by talking to other buyers who use that particular supplier, then drafting a list of the key points you expect him or her to ask for.

Last, Slusiewicz suggests taking control of the meeting schedule and the top-priority issues to address. "The final step is to have an agenda, otherwise the other side will run the meeting. Write down the key issues that are important for you, so that you won't forget them in the heat of the negotiation. You will then be prepared for the negotiation."

Business development and investment entrepreneur Aviel Zilber agrees that far more preparation is required for business negotiations in China than back home in Israel. Because the goal of the meeting is typically to gain the trust of the opponent, and to unearth his or her true (often unstated) goals, Zilber recommends having a kind of dress rehearsal to plan strategies for different possible scenarios: "Actually, you have to do the meeting before the meeting." Zilber also stresses that much work will need to be done as a follow-up after the meeting itself, and that most meetings are conducted mainly as a kind of goodwill gesture. "The follow-up can be more important than the meeting itself. The purpose of the meeting is for introductions, and sharing contacts and ideas. Chinese businesspeople don't make decisions during meetings."

"Know your opponent inside and out" is another key piece of advice offered by our seasoned China negotiators. Says consultant Ruggero Jenna: "Negotiations are very important [in China], as a lot of business terms get settled through negotiations. Don't be afraid of negotiations, and take your time." He adds that "pre-discussion" homework will include knowing as much as possible about the opponent's business—such as their profit margin, revenue, and business goals. "You need to know the margin structure and how much money they make on their products. We always develop a proposal based on our understanding of their numbers and their goals." Also critical, says Jenna, is to be extremely clear about the terms you hope to achieve. "The Chinese are smart negotiators. They know exactly

 Take control of the negotiation by preparing an agenda that covers the key issues you want to discuss. Otherwise, the other side will run the meeting, not you.

The follow-up can be more important than the meeting itself. The purpose of the meeting is for introductions, and sharing contacts and ideas. Chinese businesspeople don't make decisions during meetings."

Aviel Zilber (Israel), Chairman, Sheng Enterprises

"

There isn't one Chinese way of negotiating. . . . Each region in China has different characteristics— the Shanghainese have a way of negotiating, the Beijingnese have a way of negotiating, and people from Shandong have another way."

Jenny Hsui (Singapore), Co-founder and President, ChinaVest

what they want. So, we should know exactly what *we* want on the other side of the table. Otherwise, it's a problem."

Rule #3: Adapt Your Negotiation Style and Tactics

One important part of your preparation is to adapt your negotiation style, depending on which part of China your counterpart comes from. Our China veterans described several distinctly different regional negotiating styles. ChinaVest founding partner Jenny Hsui explains the basic regional differences she has noted after 30 years of doing business in China after leaving her native Singapore. "There isn't one Chinese way of negotiating. People write books about how you negotiate with the Chinese, but actually there isn't one style of negotiating. Each negotiation style is very specific to the area they come from. Each region in China has different characteristics—the Shanghainese have a way of negotiating, the Beijingnese have a way of negotiating, and people from Shandong have another way."

Our interviewees provided the following advice for working with business partners from northern, eastern, southern, and less developed regions in China.

Beijing and Northern China

A typical negotiation with northern Chinese, says Jenny Hsui, begins by first ascertaining whether the opponent is a trustworthy, decent, and worthwhile negotiating partner. "For northerners, the relationship is very important. They want to know that they will get along with you before they will agree to anything else. It isn't a straightforward transaction in that sense."

Hsui gives examples of typical "starting point" questions from a northerner preparing to negotiate with a potential new business partner. "The northerners—for instance, in Shandong— tend to start off with principles. They first establish that: we're going to cooperate on this and that, we're coming here in a friendly manner, we're not trying to take anything from you, right? And you are not going to take anything from me. Do we want to work toward the long term? Good." Only after they feel certain that their opponent shares the same basic principles and values, and can be trusted, will the negotiation begin, Hsui says. "After you establish good [shared] principles, then you can do business together." Next, northern Chinese will set out the main "big points," or shared goals, to keep in mind. "You establish the big points; maybe it's just five points, but you always have to think of these five points. [Northern Chinese] will fight like mad for the principles, and not pay so much attention to the details."

Hsui's business partner (and husband), ChinaVest co-founder Robert Theleen, adds this comment on the difference between northern and southern Chinese: "If you start with numbers in Beijing, [Chinese businesspeople will] think you are an idiot; they'll think you are unsophisticated. You must begin with the concepts and principles. On the other hand, in southern China, if you cannot quantify your ideas, then they don't take you seriously."

Turkish stone materials supplier Onder Oztunali makes a similar observation after his five years in China. "The Chinese are great negotiators, so you have to understand them. In every city, there is a different negotiating style," he says. "Beijingers aren't really price-focused. They want you to treat them with respect and dignity, and they want to really believe in you. I prefer the northern style, but most of my customers are southerners."

Shanghai and Eastern China

Many of our interviewees described businesspeople in Shanghai and the Yangtze River Delta as "tough negotiators" and "sticklers for detail." They also expressed confidence that an agreement signed in this region would be followed (in contrast to the situation elsewhere in China), partly because of the business culture in China's commercial center, and partly because the region has recently become so internationalized. A 25-year China veteran, Jan Borgonjon sums up the Shanghai experience in this way: "In Shanghai, you can be sure that you will have very tough negotiations, and that you can be very straightforward, very explicit. Normally, once you have a deal, you have a deal. Once something is signed, you know it will be implemented — in Shanghai and the whole east China region."

Jenny Hsui offers this advice concerning Shanghai residents: "The Shanghainese will beat you up on the details and won't care about establishing principles." She says that businesspeople in the Yangtze River Delta region care less about establishing shared values (as compared with their northern counterparts), get to the nitty gritty of the negotiation more quickly, and expect both sides to fight aggressively in order to win the best possible terms. "When negotiating with a Shanghainese, if they come up with an offer and you accept it without discussion, they are going to think they gave away too much. They will then renegotiate the whole thing," she says.

Consultant Josep Giro warns that Shanghainese business-people can be very fickle, tending toward short-term thinking: "In Shanghai, if you are successful, you are only successful today. Tomorrow, if you are not efficient, maybe you are out of the market."

Guangzhou and Southern China

In general, southern Chinese were described as the most difficult to work with in terms of giving misinformation and failing to follow agreement terms. Consultant Jan Borgonjon's advice is typical of the warnings about working with southern Chinese: "If you go to the south, you never know what you are going to get. In Canton [Guangzhou], it's very tricky. It's a complex, traditional environment, more suitable for Hong Kong and Taiwanese entrepreneurs, and quite difficult to navigate for Westerners and often also for Chinese from other parts of the country." He stresses that such warnings are "generalizations," and that experiences vary with individuals. Nevertheless, he says, the different styles found in the different regions of China are an important factor in negotiating situations.

Jenny Hsui also describes people from Guangdong province as "very numeric," adding that "the Cantonese are pure traders." Josep Giro agrees: "In Guangdong, it's all about money—like in the northeast of Spain."

Interior (Undeveloped) China

Adventurous pioneers seeking to establish enterprises in the less developed regions of China face even greater challenges, mainly because there may be a huge gap between international business standards and the business norms practiced in the undeveloped area in which you have chosen to invest. South African consultant and 13-year China veteran Kobus van der Wath offers this specific advice for those managing a business in the hinterlands: spend time learning everything possible about the potential partner's situation and appreciate that they may be lacking in resources, information, or basic business practices taken for granted in more developed markets. He tells of one first-hand experience: "We negotiated with some small SMEs in central China. They didn't have computers. How could they price? They didn't know the real numbers. In some cases, you have to help the Chinese side to understand some of the issues; some may be a little unsophisticated. Someone in the company might say, 'Let's do business,' but they don't know why we are cooperating. They don't understand what strategic thinking means." In such cases, you may need to explain fully to the Chinese side how your partnership will work. Don't assume that your partner has basic business knowledge or will stick to the standard practices that you employ.

Especially when working with partners from undeveloped regions of China, entrepreneurs are advised to take extra time to ensure that the Chinese side really understands the terms of the agreement. Says Jan Borgonjon: "If you negotiate something with the other person, but the other person hasn't really understood what he [or she] is signing, you will have problems. If he [or she] has really understood, there is less likelihood that they will breach the agreement. You have to make sure they have understood. It's not about the American way. It's not about drafting a contract and putting in some tricky things—'I got you!' You didn't get anybody in that case."

*Chinese are very skillful in making things look as they are not. Knowing this, helps in business a lot. When I'm negotiating, once I see that the Chinese side apparently isn't interested in something, I know that this is actually the thing they are **most** interested in."*

Oto Petroski
(Macedonia), Founder, Trading company

At the Negotiation Table: Tactics and Strategies

The most challenging aspect of the actual negotiation process, our interviewees explained, is that the Chinese side typically won't directly share the main goals they hope to achieve—at least not at first. For strategic reasons, they may prefer to conceal their truly critical goals in order not to lose bargaining power. Instead, they may present "decoy" goals in order to confuse their opponent. This creates a far more challenging scenario than is typical in developed markets, when both sides tend to be upfront about their desired outcome. In this section, our pioneers offer strategies for surviving China's "cat-and-mouse" negotiation process.

Rule #1: Know the Needs of the Other Side

Danish furniture entrepreneur Simon Lichtenberg explains the difference between European and Chinese negotiating methods: "First of all, the whole goal [in a negotiation with Chinese opponents] is to find out the real needs of the other side. You have to understand what the other guy needs and put yourself in his [or her] shoes to get the best possible deal." He gives an example of the trial-and-error method that one must use to determine the true goals of the Chinese side. "The classic example used is that of two sisters fighting over an orange. You have to determine how to make both of them happy. If you cut it in half, neither will be happy. Finally, you realize that one needs the peel in order to make a cake, while the other wants to eat the orange fruit because she is hungry. So you give the peel to one and the orange fruit to the other and they are both happy." A similar discovery process is often necessary in negotiations with Chinese, he says. "The challenge is to understand what the other side really needs. Maybe it's warehouse space, or maybe it's low price. Listening to what they are saying isn't enough. Discovering what the other person needs is the hard part."

Adding complexity to the process, Lichtenberg comments, is the Chinese side's possible attempt to pretend that one particular goal is important in order to sneak in the most important goal unnoticed. "One of the main mistakes [foreigners make] is that they don't know what the other side really needs or wants, or what their objectives are. The most obvious mistake is to believe what the other side is saying. You have to look deeper. It's much more complicated than that."

Trader Oto Petroski of Macedonia shares the following strategy for unearthing the true goals of a Chinese opponent: "Chinese are very skillful in making things look as they are not. Knowing this, helps in business a lot. When I'm negotiating, once I see that the Chinese side apparently isn't interested in something, I know that this is actually the thing they are *most* interested in. They know how to make a problem concerning something that isn't interesting or valuable. They make you waste time on unimportant questions; they try to make you hot, make you tired, try all kinds of tricks to make you lose concentration."

Another mistake that foreigners make, says Petroski, is to believe the Chinese side when they seem to be agreeing readily to give concessions. "Usually, when a foreign guest comes to a Chinese company, the Chinese [hosts] are very polite, so if you want this and that, they say, 'Fine, you get what you want.' But this isn't true. It doesn't work like that, because they cannot give you whatever you want. You can't take that at face value."

The underlying message from our interviewees is that international businesspeople who treat the negotiation process as a simple, straightforward exchange of information will end up confused and frustrated, because the Chinese side likely will be neither simple nor straightforward in their discussion. Consultant Kobus van der Wath explains: "One key issue for me is that you always get the sense that the [Chinese side] is hiding some information that may impact the final outcome. They are holding back some information, or they have some motives, or a set of facts, figures, or data that I don't know about. So, in a way, I'm negotiating blindly. I don't really know what they want to do. They do it on purpose." Van der Wath warns foreign clients to

> *Whereas in the West, people might come to a certain conclusion [in business negotiations] simply because it is the best decision for their company, in China, it is often more complex than that. . . . there is usually at least an element of personal gain involved."*
>
> **Jeffrey Bernstein** (USA), Founder and Managing Director, Emerge Logistics Shanghai

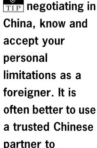

When negotiating in China, know and accept your personal limitations as a foreigner. It is often better to use a trusted Chinese partner to represent the company.

> *[The Chinese] feel better about a negotiation after having had a long struggle. Their thinking is that you will have respect and admiration for your adversary after a long battle.*
>
> **Gene Slusiewicz,**
> negotiation expert, The PAC Group

change their strategy when working with the Chinese. "Usually, foreign companies are transparent. You immediately understand their strategy, programs, process, and so on." But communicating in a straightforward way with Chinese opponents will be misunderstood, as they expect to have to play a complicated game of hide-and-seek to discover your true goals and motives.

Long-time China hand and logistics entrepreneur Jeffrey Bernstein also advises focusing the negotiation on seeking to identify the true goals or obstacles facing the opponent, considering that the items laid out openly are not the truly critical issues. "One piece of advice is: be patient. Second, try to understand the needs and the pressures on your counterpart. In many cases, it might seem like the counterpart is just stalling or causing problems. But there might be a good reason why the person has no ability to come to a decision. You really have to take the time to understand. In many cases, the counterpart may want you to dig deeper to learn why there is an obstacle. You will be expected to understand what they are hinting at."

Foreigners may misread, or not even notice, such evasive Chinese-style hints. Thus, Bernstein advises bringing China-savvy partners with you to all negotiations. "It is important to have a person you can trust reading the tea leaves for you, otherwise you may miss hints—and that could be very costly." Of course, he says, "it is important to ensure that the China-savvy partners' interests are in line with your own; otherwise, you might not be getting the full and correct story."

Entrepreneurs can also benefit from assuming that the chief decision-maker will have a personal stake in the negotiation outcome, says Bernstein. "Always assume that the person on the other side of the table has some kind of personal benefit lining the transaction somewhere. Not necessarily a kickback—maybe it's as innocent as seeking approval and recognition from their boss, or maybe they want a personal relationship to come out of it. Or it could be a financial benefit."

Bernstein advises that the concept of "success" in any negotiation is different for the Chinese than for the Americans and Europeans. "Whereas in the West, people might come to a certain conclusion [in business negotiations] simply because it is the best decision for their company, in China, it is often more complex than that. People don't just do something that is the right thing for the company. Instead, there is usually at least an element of personal gain involved, which isn't necessarily financial. It could be gaining face, or returning a favor to a friend or another third party who isn't directly related to the negotiation."

Finally, one has to be careful in identifying the real decision-maker among those on the Chinese side. "One mistake foreign negotiators make," Marjorie Woo says, "is to mis-identify the Chinese who can speak good English as the smarter, better educated, and more aggressive negotiator—that is often not true." The key people, Woo says, are usually in the background, or not present or not vocal in the negotiation. "They typically don't speak English and may have little relevant Western business knowledge, but they're the real decision-makers. So, once you think you've agreed on certain points, actually the person has to go back to confirm with the people in the background."

Gene Slusiewicz also warns that foreign businesspeople often don't get to talk directly with the real decision-maker on the Chinese side. Therefore, he advises: "Try to meet the person who has the decision-maker's ear. He [or she] is the person who tells the decision-maker, 'This is a good deal.'"

> *Americans want to have a two-hour meeting and to accomplish their goals and be done. But you don't get done in the first try [in China]; it might take three or four visits. It's like a slow dance in which both partners learn what the other side wants.*
>
> **Gene Slusiewicz,** negotiation expert, The PAC Group

Rule #2: Use a Skilled Negotiator

Choosing the right person to represent your company during the actual meeting can also be critical to success. American courier and call services company founder Mark Secchia says his secret to successful negotiations in China is to keep himself away from the discussion table. "I'm a terrible negotiator, and I know that. I have people around me who are much better negotiators than I am." In particular, he tells how he promoted his former CSR (Corporate Social Responsibility) manager to purchasing manager for both his meal delivery business and his newer export business. "She has a great personality and is an awesome negotiator."

"

Here, you have to build relations more slowly. . . . If you are not patient, or if you come for a short time and have to leave, it won't work. The Chinese work in a very sophisticated way."

Aviel Zilber (Israel), Chairman, Sheng Enterprises

Secchia asks others to negotiate for him because he finds that his American background still hinders him when facing Chinese opponents. "When I negotiate with Americans, I believe everything they say. But that doesn't work in China," he says. Although Secchia long ago learned to second-guess and double-check information shared during a negotiation in China, he still finds himself unskilled at the game of bluffing and exaggerating. "What makes me a poor negotiator in China is that I'm too emotional," he says. "When we buy plastics for a company, for instance, I know what the real production costs are: the labor rates, electricity rates, the taxes due. So, if, for example, the [potential supplier] lies to me straight off that their cost is RMB5,000 [US$715], and I know it's actually RMB1,700 [US$240], that makes me feel I've been cheated. By their standards, they're not lying—that's just the negotiation technique they use. But for me, it's so hard to believe anything once they have started negotiating with a lie. I'm just not comfortable with that negotiating style and so I'm not good at it." His advice: expect such tactics, stay cool, and if necessary, leave the discussion to someone on your team who is comfortable with such strategies.

Belgian consultant/entrepreneur Jan Borgonjon employs the same strategy: "I don't negotiate; it's my Chinese partners who negotiate. My advice is that when negotiating with Chinese, leave it to the Chinese. If you go to France, you work the French way. So, in China it's the same. Many of the so-called problems of China are problems of the foreign businesspeople who come here. You can't complain about something you should have known about." Dutch internet entrepreneur Marc van der Chijs admits a similar weakness: "I don't think, as a foreigner, that I negotiate well. It's a disadvantage because of the cultural background and the language." However, he says sometimes, he must do negotiations himself, as there are some things he can't delegate. Van der Chijs also warns that the negotiating process in China generally takes longer than in Europe, and that "face" can be a serious issue. "Embarrassing or offending your counterpart—even inadvertently—can be the end of the deal," he says.

Selecting the right negotiation team is also a top priority for consultant Kobus van der Wath. "You must overall make sure that you select teams, especially for negotiations, that understand the basics of *guanxi*, Taoism, and Buddhism, and that know about Chinese history and current news events. "All such cultural information may be referred to during the negotiation. If you don't know these things yourself, bring along Chinese colleagues who do."

Rule #3: Have a Heart-to-heart Talk

One feature of many negotiations, our interviewees said, is an offline, heart-to-heart talk between the two sides' top decision-makers. Advises veteran China entrepreneur Jenny Hsui: "What you want to do when you run into a problem is to reach the chief decision-maker and have a talk. I call it a 'walk in the woods.' You ask about his personal life, his family, his children, his friends, about the province he comes from." Only through this painstaking process—in which you must also share information and build trust—will true deal-breaking and deal-making issues emerge.

Shah Firoozi agrees that the most important discussions in many negotiation sessions take place away from the negotiating table, during the break periods. "I've seen many times that most negotiations don't take place in the meeting rooms, but in dining rooms, or outside. I can tell you a story: I don't smoke cigarettes, but I started smoking cigars so that I can also go out during the key part of the discussion—the smoking break. I started smoking these small cigars because I can't afford to miss those conversations."

Firoozi says the key point is to make a friendly connection with the other side. "It comes down to building connections—you need to connect with the people you are dealing with; you need to be sincere and genuine. Everybody knows that you are here to make a profit. There's no misconception about that. You need to understand that your counterpart also has the same objective."

> **When negotiations hit an obstacle and begin stalemating, try to arrange for an offline talk with the other side's decision-maker. Communicate and build trust in an informal setting.**

> **"**
> *Most negotiations don't take place in the meeting rooms, but in dining rooms, or outside. . . . I don't smoke cigarettes, but I started smoking cigars so that I can also go out during the. . . . smoking break. . . . can't afford to miss those conversations."*
>
> **Shah Firoozi** (USA), Founder and President, The PAC Group

Rule #4: Compromise and Trade

U.S. negotiation expert Gene Slusiewicz describes the negotiation process as a kind of detective case in which both sides strive to discover the other side's needs (critical goals) and desires (smaller goals), then begin compromising and making concessions in order to reach a conclusion. "You try to meet your key needs, wants, and desires. But you also must know the opponent's needs and priorities. Then you can say, 'I will trade you one need for a couple of desires.'"

Slusiewicz advises taking an almost mathematical approach to weighing the needs of both sides: "Before you go into a negotiation, you need to write down on a piece of paper

American vs. Chinese Negotiation Style

Based on 12 years spent working in China—first for a Fortune 500 company, then as an expert with The PAC Group—American businessman Gene Slusiewicz describes the key differences between U.S.-style and Chinese-style negotiations. "Americans emphasize timing—making decisions quickly. Americans don't like long negotiations; they are more into execution. They write down what they want, go for a compromise, and make things happen."

Such thinking is very different from the Chinese mindset, Slusiewicz says. "The Chinese are slow. They want to get to know the people. It's more about relationships. When they have the relationship, they have the trust." Slusiewicz says that the Chinese expect, and even want, a long negotiation process. "They feel better about negotiation after having had a long struggle. Their thinking is that you will have respect and admiration for your adversary after a long battle. If you have a long-fought battle, you will be more satisfied with the result."

Making the process more complicated is the tendency among the Chinese to conceal their most important goals so that their opponent is unaware of them. Slusiewicz gives several examples. In one recent negotiation, his opponent's unstated, but critical, goal was to help his daughter learn English. Another customer's hidden want was to receive job training in the United States. For these two Chinese partners, their personal goals were more important than the what are the supplier's needs and desires, and what is his strength and bargaining power." For example, if the supplier knows he is your top supplier and that it would be difficult for you to change suppliers, he realizes his advantage. On the other hand, if you can offer something that the supplier needs or wants, such as industry-specific training, then you have an advantage.

American leadership development training company founder Marjorie Woo warns that this slow, back-and-forth negotiation process is often frustrating, especially since the Chinese side may reconsider terms already agreed to. "You think they've agreed on some points and then you meet them the next day, and they start from zero. Initially, I got very frustrated and angry, since I'm

Make a list of your primary and secondary objectives. Try to do the same for the opposing side. Start compromising and trading concessions based on the list.

company-related goals. "They don't tell you directly; you have to find it out. These are the things you learn after a glass of beer and some cigarettes," says Slusiewicz. "Discussions at the table are formal, but very often, the actual deals are cut in-between meetings, in a casual conversation."

Slusiewicz sums up the East–West differences in this way: "The Americans want to have a two-hour meeting and to accomplish their goals and be done. But you don't get done in the first try [in China]; it might take three or four visits. It's like a slow dance in which both partners learn what the other side wants. You don't start negotiating until you know each other. The [Chinese side] won't just tell you what they want."

A typical meeting schedule; he says, is set this way: "You have an agenda before the meeting starts, but I learned from my Chinese colleagues that in the morning nothing gets accomplished except getting to know each other. Then you have a long, big lunch. Then we drag on and on. At about three or four o'clock, we start to trade concessions: I give you this if you give me that; I'll do this if you'll do that."

While the style may seem inefficient, Slusiewicz says the whole meeting offers a chance to learn valuable information about the other side. "Don't expect things to happen fast, but be attentive. Watch your opponents' body language and gauge their attitudes. Learn what you can about the people you negotiate with." Last, he warns Westerners not to become impatient and give away concessions easily. "When you negotiate, don't concede too soon. The [Chinese side] expect to negotiate for a long period of time."

Western-trained in my business dealings." Woo concludes that such backtracking doesn't show ill intention from the Chinese side, but more often indicates a degree of misunderstanding on both sides. Says Woo: "Over time, I began to realize that the

Israeli vs. Chinese Negotiation Style

Aviel Zilber offers this comparison of business negotiation styles in China and in his native Israel: "I love to negotiate. I love the game in it, and I love the challenge of finding a solution. Israelis are good negotiators." But even given his culture-based sporting spirit, Zilber still finds China to be a "difficult" environment in which to negotiate business terms. Why? "First of all, you have to be much more patient. It's not as open and upfront as the Western way of negotiation, certainly not the Israeli way. Israeli people are very straightforward and very down-to-earth. They don't ask about how is your day; they go to business directly. It's completely different in China."

Zilber describes business discussions in China as "one step forward and two steps back." Oftentimes, he must find an indirect way of initiating a relationship with a future Chinese business partner—for example, working through a third-party connection. Only then can the relationship take root, laying a foundation on which to eventually negotiate. "You have to understand that, here, you have to build relations more slowly. It's different and challenging. It's more psychological. If you are not patient, or if you come for a short time and have to leave, it won't work. The Chinese work in a very sophisticated way."

Zilber explains the Chinese "go slow" policy as follows: "I tell the [foreign side] they have to understand that, as much as they are suspicious of the Chinese side, the Chinese side is also suspicious of them. The Chinese side will always have a question mark about you: 'Will he deliver? Should we put our money on him?' Therefore, we have to be patient and do it step by step."

Aviel's business partner (and brother) Jordan Zilber comments on another factor that complicates business discussions in China: for the Chinese, words matter far less than actions. "Communication is a problem even when I am using a very good interpreter," he says. "In Israel, we are very straightforward. In China, when someone says, 'That is very interesting,' he could actually mean that he doesn't want to do business. You need to judge by their actions, not their words."

Moroccan vs. Chinese Negotiation Style

Moroccan exporter Aziz Mrabet feels very comfortable negotiating in China because his cultural background helps him to understand the way Chinese negotiate. "Chinese people are quite emotional, which is similar to Moroccans. When we negotiate prices with factories, we first have to make the [supplier] believe that we're going to work together to solve problems—the trust between us is the key to success. I also make them understand that the deal is beneficial to both of us. I promise that we're going to have more business in the future," he says.

"We don't do quick business. I like to negotiate with people based on forming emotional ties and with a long-term focus," he explains. "If you go into a shop to buy things in Morocco, people prepare a cup of tea for you and invite you to be seated. If you don't intend to buy, they'll still give you a cup of tea. Then, you may become friends somehow. That's the traditional way to do business in Morocco, which is quite similar to the approach here with my Chinese suppliers." In fact, like many Chinese companies, Mrabet doesn't use contracts with some of his suppliers; the relationship is based purely on trust.

Another similarity between his country and China is the tradition of bargaining. "Moroccans are good at bargaining, which is quite similar here in China," Mrabet says. However, he recommends not overdoing it: "You can't bargain *too* much—otherwise, you can make people angry as well. When Chinese people get angry, they don't usually show it—so you won't know they're angry until you receive your merchandise and the quality isn't up to your standards. Only then do you know that you have crossed the threshold of bargaining, and have squeezed the price too much."

The Chinese are not so experienced in our style of negotiation. Though sometimes they don't really understand, they show no objections in order not to offend you. Then we tend to assume that they've agreed, because they haven't objected. Finally, when they sign the letter of intent or memorandum of understanding, it's only a draft for them. Once the representatives sign the contracts, they go back and talk to their friends, colleagues, and boss. Then they make notes on the points where people have different opinions. Next day, when we meet again, the boss may say: 'I think perhaps we have to do it in a different way.' By doing this, they don't really mean to cheat you. They just don't have enough information to really know where they stand."

UNDERSTANDING YOUR OPPONENT'S MOTIVES

As an example of the difficulty foreign businesspeople face in determining their Chinese business partners' true motives, American business consultant Gene Slusiewicz shares this story from the many years he spent as an outsourcing manager in China for General Motors, and then with Delphi.

During Slusiewicz's time with GM, the company prepared to launch Buick brand cars in China in a joint venture with the state-owned SAIC (Shanghai Automotive Industry Corp.). Slusiewicz was responsible for sourcing "everything electrical in the car," including a US$200 computerized component called the ECM (engine control module), which he describes as "the brain of the engine."

At that time, the Chinese government required that cars built in China used 40% locally made components. Slusiewicz thought the ECM was an ideal candidate for localizing. But this effort soon ran into trouble, because choosing a Chinese supplier for the ECM required SAIC's approval. In his regular weekly meeting with SAIC, Slusiewicz explained that GM planned to search for this component locally, and that they had found a qualified supplier: Delphi. Slusiewicz had good reasons for recommending Delphi, he recalls. "The current supplier for that Buick engine in the United States was Delphi. The ECM was already developed by Delphi. Besides, Delphi had an operation in Suzhou that was capable of doing that part."

But to Slusiewicz's surprise, the Chinese managers of the joint venture disagreed. SAIC agreed to buy locally made ECMs, but only from Bosch UAES. Slusiewicz describes his confusion: "I knew Delphi would make [the ECM] faster and cheaper. It takes years of working together and testing to build an ECM for a specific engine. So, Bosch UAES couldn't do it, because it would take too long to make that part for that engine."

But the Chinese side held fast, insisting on either using Bosch UAES or importing Delphi-made ECMs from the United States. "The SAIC partner absolutely refused even to consider giving the contract to Delphi Suzhou [in China], even though it could save us

Finally, Woo advises giving concessions when necessary. "The other common characteristic is that Chinese people feel better when they get 51% profit and you get 49%. To them, 50% and 50% isn't winning. I think that we have to insist only on the

a million U.S. dollars, time, and would give us a nice localization percentage," says Slusiewicz. "We were flabbergasted; we couldn't understand the logic. We knew Bosch UAES couldn't do it, so we ended up importing this item from Delphi in the States. We paid a very high price, as there was 17% duty at the time."

It wasn't until years later, after Slusiewicz began working as a consultant with The PAC Group engineering firm in Shanghai, that he discovered the reasoning behind SAIC's decision. In 2007, he happened to meet the same SAIC representative, and he asked him why SAIC had refused to buy the ECM from Delphi Suzhou. "[The SAIC rep] told me he hadn't had a choice—the government had given a license to Bosch UAES to produce the ECM, and he couldn't go against that policy. Although personally, he understood the benefit of giving the contract to Delphi Suzhou, he couldn't do it." Thus the problem lay in the fact that the government had promised the contract to a company in Shanghai, while Delphi was based outside the Shanghai city limits, in Suzhou.

Why hadn't the SAIC representative told the GM side the true situation? "Because we didn't ask!" says Slusiewicz: "We were so adamant about getting quotes from everybody that [the SAIC side] didn't want to tell us to forget it and give the contract to Bosch UAES. We had to follow our normal policy at the time, to get the best supplier. [The Chinese side] didn't want us to think they weren't professionals, but they knew that at the end we had to either work with Bosch UAES or import the part."

The big lesson learned from this experience, says Slusiewicz, is that he and his team should have worked harder to understand the true reasons behind his Chinese partner's insistence on using Bosch UAES. He offers this tip for foreign managers: "Take detailed notes during the negotiation. When you find there is an unclear point or position, ask the other party to clarify it. You must try to see the other party's needs. Don't jump to conclusions, or tell the Chinese side they are irrational. There may be a good reason why they don't tell you. You have to discover it. Don't stop until you understand the other guy's needs."

Take detailed notes during the negotiation. If your Chinese counterpart takes a confusing position on any aspect of the deal, ask them to clarify. Don't stop asking for information until you understand all the reasons behind your opponent's decision.

things that are really important. Since 1% represents only a small amount of profit, we usually agree on that. We're clear that on certain things we can't compromise, but we're flexible on other points."

Rule #5: Expect Dramatic Outbursts

A feature of many Chinese-style negotiations is a fair amount of drama, such as planned displays of emotion, and even losing one's temper. Seasoned China hands say this should be accepted as part of the game of negotiating. Such scenes are generally forgotten after trust is established and a deal is struck. (Note, however, that losing one's temper with a staff member or colleague can cause them to lose face, and is not considered acceptable behavior.)

Italian consultant Ruggero Jenna describes a recent negotiation between a key client and Chinese suppliers. "We tried to fix points of agreement, but the Chinese came in with something new every day." Jenna says that, at certain points, his client had to show frustration, as a cue that the Chinese side had met his breaking point. "If you are showing your displeasure with some issue during the negotiation, you can shout or even break things. We sometimes walk away from the discussion table. In such cases, the Chinese side usually comes back to you with a concession. This is the way of negotiating in China."

Twenty-year China veteran Jenny Hsui agrees. The Singaporean consultant shares her own tactic, which she calls "banging the briefcase." When negotiations reach a critical point and she needs to signal to the other side that they are really asking for too much, in the middle of the meeting she snaps her briefcase shut, slams the top of it with her fist, and marches out of the meeting room. In most cases, the Chinese side eventually makes a concession in order to re-start the meeting and get the negotiations back on track.

While Western businesspeople may be uncomfortable in displaying such calculated emotional outbursts, Chinese negotiators consider this to be part of the game. One important factor is that such displays are planned, rather than a real loss of emotional control. Software entrepreneur Eric Rongley points out that bluffing and brinkmanship are common in Chinese negotiations, even at the level of bargaining for clothing in a street-market. "If you go to a marketplace [in China] to bargain with street vendor, you have to haggle and then walk away in disgust. Then the vendor calls you back because he sees that he has reached your limit. It's exhausting if you have to do it all the time."

Even after 11 years in China, American delivery service entrepreneur Mark Secchia is still uncomfortable with the "acting" employed in some negotiations. "The ability to be enemies one minute and best friends the following minute is very difficult for me to understand—that two people sitting across the table could be yelling and screaming at each other and then, 10 minutes later, walk to the elevator arm in arm. I can't emotionally go up and down that quickly. In Chinese negotiations, there are a lot of emotional ups and downs."

Entrepreneurs from cultures in which bargaining is accepted and normal, such as Turkey, tend to feel more comfortable with the theatrics of Chinese-style negotiating. Building materials supplier Onder Oztunali explains, "Actually, as a Turk, I really don't feel any difference between my country and other Asian countries because we are pretty Asian ourselves, even if we want to get into the EU. Turkish people are great negotiators as well. My mom is a great negotiator."

When negotiating on price, Oztunali says the discussion with Chinese opponents always includes a dispute over numbers. "The first lesson you learn is that the Chinese will never accept your first price—they will always say it is too expensive. But I always know that my prices actually are *not* too high, because I know the prices other guys are charging and I know the retail price for my product in China. I think, 'I am not going to listen to BS from this guy.'" By knowing the going wholesale and retail prices, Oztunali can set limits for the negotiation. "You have to set a limit, such as: 'I cannot sell below this price.' As long as it is a seller's market, and as long as they can still make 20% profit,

Learn to "bang the briefcase" when your opponent is asking for too much. This strategy, which involves walking out of the negotiation in disgust, sends a clear signal to the other side that you have reached your bottom line. Your Chinese counterpart will usually offer a concession to re-start the discussion.

💡 **A good** **TIP** **translator is critical for a good negotiation. An interpreter in China who is truly fluent in both languages and knowledgeable about your industry is rare and extremely valuable.**

buyers will be fine with that. They don't want to lose time—time is definitely money for them."

As a final tip, consultant Josep Giro advises foreign clients to hold back several key concessions, to offer at the very end, if needed. "When Spanish clients come to the negotiation table in China, I tell them, 'You need to have some weapons. When the Chinese side throws you something, you need to have a weapon in your hand.'"

Rule #6: Use a Good Translator

For foreign entrepreneurs who don't speak Chinese, a good translator is critical during negotiation. Ideally, that means finding someone fluent in the language and knowledgeable about your industry—often a tough match to make.

Says negotiations expert Gene Slusiewicz: "You can't have a general interpreter trying to interpret during a technical discussion. You need someone who really knows the technology, the engineering. You need to have some industry knowledge. You will have to pay for an interpreter with the right experience." Because the translator must know your business and must know the nuances of both languages being used, the value of a good translator is extremely high.

Says Slusiewicz: "There is value in using a translator who can translate the meaning *behind* a set of words or a comment—who can understand the body language—because what is meant may not match what is literally being said. If an interpreter can smooth things out, he or she is a kind of negotiator, too. That's very valuable." Slusiewicz's solution: when he finds a really qualified interpreter, he hires the person full-time.

Rule #7: Double-check the Agreement before You Sign

In some cases, contracts or agreements will be written in Chinese. If so, take the time and effort to have all the terms translated into English or your native language, warns French fashion wholesaler Valerie Touya. She describes a recent case in which she unknowingly signed a contract (written in Chinese) with a clothing retailer that included terms she had verbally rejected. In her original contract with the retailer, Touya had agreed to a 50:50 split of all profits from the sale of garments she had supplied. When the first contract with that retailer expired, Touya insisted on the same terms for the second contract. "The Chinese side agreed verbally, but after I signed, I found out that the terms in the contract were not 50:50 but 60:40 in his favor." Touya describes her frustration: "I couldn't read the contract; it was in Chinese! I sent an email to the retailer saying, 'This is not fair. You have abused me. Our agreement is to a 50:50 split.'" The issue ended in a dispute.

Gene Slusiewicz has had similar experiences. "We have to watch Chinese companies, because they sometimes make changes to the terms and they don't bother to tell you. They might not even do it on purpose. They think that an alternative material has the same effect and don't think it matters." His solution is to make it very clear that no changes to the terms are acceptable without discussion. "They need to be informed that they are not allowed to change *anything* without my prior approval."

 Have a trusted Chinese speaker double-check the final agreement. The document that is legally binding in China is the Chinese one, not a version written in another language.

Post-agreement: After the Contract is Signed

The major difference between Chinese and non-Chinese negotiators is that, in China, the signed contract is considered as just one step in a continuing and fluid process of working together as partners. It is understood by the Chinese side that the contract spells out guidelines, but that these terms can and will still be discussed as the partnership operates. Marjorie Woo explains the differences between the East and the West: "Negotiating with Westerners means you discuss with them and sometimes you argue with them; then, once you reach an agreement, you sign the contract. After that, for the most part, you follow the contract."

TIME PRESSURE AS A DEAL CLOSING METHOD

Several of our interviewees explained how they use time pressure to help close a deal in China. Import/export entrepreneur Oto Petroski shares one of his strategies for reaching a conclusion: "My power weapon is that I start the negotiation at 15 minutes to noon. If you don't give the Chinese lunch at noon, they completely lose their mind. I don't allow them to stand up until we've closed the deal. If I schedule the meeting for between 12 and 2 p.m., the negotiation happens quickly and efficiently. But if you go in at 9 a.m., you will lose all day. They will ask 10 questions before lunch; then they want to make *ganbei* [toasting with liquor] during lunch; and then after lunch, in the negotiation, they want to kill you. This is my experience in doing negotiation."

American negotiations expert Gene Slusiewicz also favors using the tactic of time constraints. He describes a recent case where he kept the discussions going with a potential supplier until just before they were due to catch their train. The supplier sought a $3 price increase per unit—more than doubling their original price—because subcomponent prices had gone up. "The supplier brought in seven people to negotiate against me and my colleague," recalls Slusiewicz. "We stayed there and held the line from morning till night. I knew they had to catch the 9 p.m. train, the last train out of the city, but we stayed in that hot little room all day long."

During the day, Slusiewicz made a few concessions—agreeing to help the supplier find a cheaper subcomponent supplier, and agreeing to a modest price increase, "but not the $3 increase they requested." Then came crunch time. "At 10 minutes to 9, when they were leaving to catch their train, they said: 'OK, if you find an alternative supplier for us, we will agree.' We used this tactic against them and it worked. In the end, we agreed to a 17% price increase instead of 100%, and they met our timing goal. But we had to negotiate all day long, from 8.30 a.m. to 9 p.m., holding our line."

The process is quite different in China, however. Woo says: "With Chinese business partners, once you develop the relationship and sign a contract, they will stay with you longer than without one, because they consider signing a contract as forming a closer personal relationship, rather than conducting a business transaction. This is the good side." Therefore, if the partnership is good—like a good marriage—both sides will adapt to new situations in ways that continue the success of both sides. If the partnership is bad—like a bad marriage—the tendency to re-negotiate contract terms can be extremely frustrating to the foreign side, who believed the deal was done when the contract was signed.

Rule #1: The Contract is a Formality

Meal delivery entrepreneur Mark Secchia has come to consider contracts as more of a formality than a useful document. "In our business, contracts are meaningless. It's a piece of paper that I sign; but in the end, it's about having a good relationship, not a contract." Far more valuable than reviewing and updating the contract, he says, is for his team to maintain frequent, open communication with the restaurants he supplies with Sherpa's delivery service. Secchia sends employees to each restaurant regularly to check in. "These restaurants stay with us not because of the contracts, because contracts can expire or can be broken. In our policy, we say that our managers have to visit each restaurant every two months, and each time they go, they can spend RMB200 [US$28] eating there. They don't take free meals. We want the restaurants to see us spending money in their establishments. We work with 140 restaurants, and we have to visit them every two or three months and pay RMB200 each. That's almost RMB100,000 [US$14,300] that we are spending per year just to keep the relationship strong."

Import and distribution entrepreneur Winston Ling says he de-emphasizes the importance of contracts for his China-based business deals. "The value of a contract in China is just the value of the paper. I used to be accustomed to working with a contract. When I arrived here, I spent so much time on contracts. In the end, what matters is trust. The Chinese aren't accustomed to working with contracts. After the contract is signed, they forget everything. I still do contracts, but I don't pay much attention to them anymore."

> *[Chinese businesses people] consider signing a contract as forming a closer personal relationship, rather than conducting a business transaction."*
>
> **Marjorie Woo** (USA), Founder and Chairwoman, Leadership Management International (China)

TIP Think of the contract as an intention by both parties to work together. In the end, trust and a good relationship are worth more than any document.

Rule #2: Adapt the Contract Terms to Prevailing Business Conditions

Investment entrepreneur Aviel Zilber offers further insight into the differences in mindset: "Westerners like to respect contracts, but they look all the time at the contract to see whether they are able to do something that isn't according to the spirit of the contract. In Chinese culture, the contract reflects what happened on the day of the signature, according to what was going on at that time. The Chinese don't think it's a big deal to change the agreement terms according to how conditions change. It's part of their business culture, and you have to know this in advance." This flexible mindset makes it more critical to maintain good relations so that both sides can work together through evolving terms. Says Zilber: "It's much more difficult and challenging, because it's not about reading the words on the contract but about maintaining a win-win situation. Only if you are able to work with your partner, are you able to say: 'I want to change [the terms] because the conditions have changed.'"

Consultant Jan Borgonjon says that his clients who come from cultures in which business relationships are valued over written terms tend to understand the Chinese mindset faster. "Southern Europeans have fewer problems in accepting this. You see more problems with Anglo-Saxons and Northern Europeans."

Our veteran China hands conceded that there is some logic in the Chinese concept of contracts, especially since business conditions in China change frequently and drastically. Says Gene Slusiewicz: "Even if you sign a contract, there are always opportunities to ask for something else. For instance, the government may change the duties, making it cheaper to import—in that case, you can ask for a price reduction." He says there is more willingness on both sides to alter the terms as conditions in China change. "Of course, you can say, 'This is the agreement and this is your signature. You have to do it the way we agreed.' But what is the use of that if the supplier goes bankrupt?"

China veteran and ChinaVest founder Robert Theleen also advises foreign businesspeople that if they want the terms of a contract to be implemented, they must work hard *after* the signing to make it a living, breathing part of the business operations. Too often, he says, the contract is signed and then forgotten and ignored as the business evolves. He explains: "Westerners, especially Americans, negotiate these 50-page contracts, and when the contract is signed, the American says, 'OK,

THE RETURN OF THE SOFA LEGS

Danish furniture business owner Simon Lichtenberg urges foreign entrepreneurs in China to screen their suppliers and other business partners carefully. "I have been cheated many times," he says. "But when you have a bad experience, you can only blame yourself for not understanding what the other guy really wanted."

Lichtenberg shares this anecdote, which illustrates the thinking of many smaller, less worldly Chinese suppliers:

In one case, we ordered sofa legs finished by a small factory. They dry the wood, they glue them together, they stain them, they put in the screws, and they send them to our factory. When a shipment came in with thousands of sofa legs, 400 of them were bad. We, of course, said: "Send them back, and make sure they are good next time."

The next shipment comes in and there are still 400 bad ones, and 200 of the bad ones are from the ones that we already sent back once! This is very typical. Foreigners will say: "How can the supplier be so stupid? They are trying to cheat us!" But the Chinese supplier's thinking is different. He thinks, "Out of the 200 bad ones that we sent back again, if their quality control guys are a little sleepy, maybe 30 of them will get accepted." So, they get an extra 30 legs through the system at no cost—that's a good deal. It's very simple. They are not bad people, but they are using very practical, short-term thinking. It definitely doesn't help to think that they are cheaters; they just think in the short-term. This is a typical [Chinese] mindset that foreigners don't understand.

"

The Chinese don't think it's a big deal to change the agreement terms according to how conditions change. It's part of their business culture, and you have to know this in advance."

Aviel Zilber (Israel), Chairman, Sheng Enterprises

let's get on with business.' But if you put the contract away, if you don't go and implement the key stipulated points immediately, the Chinese will assume that the contract has disappeared because you are not enforcing it." Theleen warns that once the Chinese side has the impression that the contract is being ignored, then it is "almost impossible" to revive and implement the terms. He explains: "When you want to bring the contract back, then it's very difficult—if not impossible—because the contract is now seen as separate from the running of the business."

A common mistake among Western businesspeople, Theleen adds, is to adopt a complacent attitude after the contract is signed. "The Western view would be to say, 'The contract governs the business.' Nonsense—it's only a frame of reference," he says. "After [signing], unless you constantly implement the agreement, the business is going to be run as it evolves." In other words, if any of the terms aren't actually followed, and the situation is allowed to continue, the Chinese side will consider the entire contract to be non-binding. To avoid that scenario, Theleen advises monitoring the operational terms and referring often to the contract.

Conclusion

Conducting a successful negotiation in China is not an easy endeavor. The Chinese are master negotiators. They expect long, convoluted negotiations with hide-and-seek tactics and changing of terms—even on the points that had previously been agreed upon. Chinese-style business negotiations use a loose, open process that can be confusing and frustrating for foreigners. Furthermore, the negotiation process frequently doesn't end with the signing of the contract. In the mind of the Chinese, if business conditions change, agreements must change. On the positive side, those companies that successfully form an agreement to do business stand a high chance of developing a strong, supportive, and long-lasting partnership.

SUMMARY OF TIPS

BUSINESS NEGOTIATIONS

USEFUL RULES AND TACTICS

Pre-negotiation Preparation

Rule #1: Be prepared for a long journey—Be prepared for a long negotiation process with Chinese opponents. If you are in a hurry, your Chinese counterpart will use your urgency to extract more concessions from you.

Rule #3: Adapt your negotiation style and tactics—Be ready to adapt your negotiation style and tactics, depending on which part of the country your Chinese counterpart is from. Business practices vary in the north, east, and south. In the undeveloped regions, expect to educate your partner on standard international business practices.

Rule #2: Do your homework before the negotiation begins—Prepare thoroughly before you begin negotiating. Be very clear about what you *must* achieve and what extras you *hope* to achieve.

Research the other party's needs. Understand what they may ask for and what concessions you could make.

Take control of the negotiation by preparing an agenda that covers the key issues you want to discuss. Otherwise, the other side will run the meeting, not you.

At the Negotiation Table

Rule #1: Know the needs of the other side—Put yourself in the other side's shoes; try to understand what they really need. Usually, they won't tell you directly.

Expect to play a complicated game of hide-and-seek. The Chinese often conceal information, motives, and facts that can impact on the final outcome of the negotiation. Foreign negotiators who are completely transparent will be misunderstood and be suspected of hiding something.

Be attentive to hints. Chinese businesspeople are sometimes evasive and ambiguous. You need to observe their behavior and try to understand the reasons behind it.

Rule #2: Use a skilled negotiator—Know and accept your personal limitations as a foreigner. It is often better to use a trusted Chinese partner to represent the company.

At the Negotiation Table (*cont'd*)

Rule #3: Have a heart-to-heart talk—When negotiations hit an obstacle and begin stalemating, try to arrange for an offline talk with the other side's decision-maker. Communicate and build trust in an informal setting.

Rule #5: Expect dramatic outbursts—Learn to "bang the briefcase" when your opponent reaches your breaking point by asking for too much. This strategy, which involves walking out of the negotiation in disgust, sends a clear signal that the other side has reached your bottom line. Your Chinese counterpart will usually get the message and offer a concession in order to keep the discussion moving forward.

When negotiating price, know the current market rates and set clear limits for yourself. Walk away from any agreement you don't consider fair or feasible.

Rule #7: Double-check the agreement before you sign—Have someone double-check the final agreement, especially if it is written in Chinese. In the end, the document that is legally binding in China is the Chinese one, not one written in another language.

Rule #4: Compromise and trade—Make a list of your primary and secondary objectives. Try to do the same for the opposing side. Start compromising and trading based on the list.

Take detailed notes during the negotiation. If your Chinese counterpart takes a confusing position on any aspect of the deal, ask them to clarify. Don't stop asking for information until you understand all the reasons behind your opponent's decision.

Rule #6: Use a good translator—A good translator is critical for a good negotiation. An interpreter in China who is truly fluent in both languages and knowledgeable about your industry is rare and extremely valuable.

After the Contract is Signed

Rule #1: The contract is a formality—Think of the contract as an intention by both parties to work together. In the end, trust and a good relationship are worth more than any document.

Rule #2: Adapt the contract terms to prevailing business conditions—Expect the Chinese to renegotiate the agreement after it has been accepted and signed by both parties. In the Chinese mind, if business conditions change, agreements have to adapt.

WESTERN VS. CHINESE NEGOTATION STYLE

Chinese won't tell you directly what they think; you have to find it out. Casual conversations held after hours and in-between the formal discussions can provide critical information necessary to finalize a deal.

When you negotiate, don't concede too soon. The Chinese side expects to negotiate over a long period of time and will respect a counterpart who remains calm and controlled.

Chapter 8
Living in China:
A Survival Kit

"If you have a Monday-to-Friday, 9-to-5 kind of thinking, forget about doing business in China. We get phone calls on Saturday and Sunday, or six o'clock on Monday morning. It's really 24 hours. We work hard and play hard."

Mark Pummell (UK), Founder and CEO, ChinArt, Sinapse and Music Pavillion

"China is more of a civilization, than a country. You can't be neutral about it; you either love it or hate it."

Josep Giro (Spain), Co-founder and Managing Director, SBC & Associates

Introduction

Even in China, and even for entrepreneurs, life cannot be all work and no play. Ultimately, success as an investor or manager in China requires creating a positive and sustainable life for yourself—and your family—outside of work.

In this chapter, we look at how foreign entrepreneurs have adjusted their lives, and the lives of their spouses and families, in order not just to work successfully, but also to live happily, in China. The chapter covers five main topics:

1. Clearing the language hurdle
2. Hardships of life in China
3. The Struggle for work–life balance
4. Foreign businesswomen in China
5. The good life, China-style

Since the 40 entrepreneurs profiled in this book hail from 25 different home countries or provinces outside mainland China, it is not surprising that their answers varied widely when asked, "What do you find difficult about living in China?" That is, except for one area: nearly all of them shared a common challenge in grappling to overcome the language barrier. Thus, we start this chapter with the challenge most commonly faced by non-Chinese businesspeople living and working in China.

Clearing the Language Hurdle

Of the 40 entrepreneurs interviewed for this book, only six were native speakers of Mandarin Chinese (being ethnically Chinese), the national language of China. While each of the non-native Chinese speakers faced a language barrier, they differed in the importance they placed on overcoming it.

Just how critical is the mastery of Mandarin to operating a business in China? In answering this question, our interviewees fell into two camps, arguing either that learning Mandarin is not critical or that it is "essential."

The key differential for foreign managers is whether they themselves must communicate directly with their Chinese clients, partners, and employees, or whether they can delegate Mandarin-language communication to a key staffer.

The "Mandarin is Not Essential" Camp

Among those with the viewpoint that "Mandarin is nice to know but not essential" is Swiss consultant Nicolas Musy. According to research conducted by his firm on 111 Swiss companies operating in China, the results of which were published in 2006, Chinese-language skills were not rated as a top priority. "Interestingly, language ability ranked very low among the success factors in our research; ranking in the 38th position among 47 success factors." American consultant-entrepreneur Steven Ganster agrees: "Do [foreign] entrepreneurs have to speak Chinese? I don't think so. I'm not fluent in Chinese, but I have people whom I trust do that."

Italian consultant Ruggero Jenna tells his foreign clients that Chinese-language skills do help in China, but he says the importance varies depending on the business and the role of the foreign manager in a company's operations. "The importance of Chinese skills depends on what you want to do. When you speak Chinese, it does make a difference in doing business." If the foreign executive must work directly with Chinese-speaking suppliers or customers, then language skills are a significant advantage: "If you are talking about starting up a manufacturing venture, for example, then speaking Chinese means a lot. Especially when you deal with production and need to really negotiate with Chinese companies." But if your clients are mainly English-speaking multinational companies, he says, then Mandarin skills are less critical.

In his consulting business, Chinese-language skills are not a make-or-break necessity, Jenna says. "In my own case, speaking Mandarin is not that important because what I have to do is to

> *I study Chinese every day, but my Chinese isn't very good. Does it prevent me from operating here? No, but I need to cover my weaknesses. I do that by having very good staff."*
>
> **Kobus van der Wath** (South Africa), Founder and Group Managing Director, The Beijing Axis

build a team. Our key people must speak both Chinese and English because we have to deal with our clients, who are typically multinationals."

Lack of Chinese-language skills also hasn't stopped consultant Kobus van der Wath from building a successful business in China. As he explains: "I study Chinese every day, but my Chinese isn't very good. Does it prevent me from operating here? No, but I need to cover my weaknesses. I do that by having very good staff." He warns fellow expatriates that being sensitive to Chinese cultural differences is more important than learning the language.

Even those international businesspeople that had mastered Mandarin recommended leaning on the local staff for help with some aspects of professional — and even personal — life in China. For example, U.S. executive Mark Secchia says he regrets not having asked his staff for help when he purchased real estate. Says Secchia: "Buying an apartment in China was one of the worst experiences in my life. We had a property agent and we gave the down payment and three months later, we got nothing for it. The bank took advantage of us and the property agent took advantage of us. I didn't ask any of my staff for help. If I had asked my staff to help me, I wouldn't have had so many problems."

The "Mandarin is Essential" Camp

Among those executives who would argue that achieving a working level of Mandarin is critical for business success in China is Israeli business developer Aviel Zilber: "I speak Chinese, but it's not good enough. My life is here now. I don't think it's right to live in a country without being able to speak the language."

Among those of our interviewees who were struggling to master Chinese, most had a similar modus operandi to that of American Mark Secchia: make an effort, show your sincerity, but accept your limitations. "Our managers speak English, so we communicate in English. But still, you must be able to speak

Chinese in order to form successful relationships. For instance, how can I prove to my staff that I'm committed to them if I don't speak Chinese? The message I send [by not learning Chinese] is that I'm going to leave China next month." While Secchia has mastered a conversational speaking level in Mandarin, he relies on key staff for assistance with reading and writing in Chinese.

Having committed several years to studying the Chinese language, Moroccan businessman Aziz Mrabet explains the clear benefits for his work in China: "If you can speak Chinese, it definitely helps you to understand the culture better, to understand the subtleties that are crucial in doing business in China. You can still do business without speaking Chinese because so many people speak English here. But if you have a good command of Chinese, it definitely helps you to negotiate with the Chinese. Since you're a foreigner, some Chinese may take advantage of you using the language. Thus, I usually conduct negotiations in Chinese."

Most of our entrepreneurs said they wished they had more time to study Chinese. Internet businessman Marc van der Chijs's viewpoint is typical: "I planned to study Chinese for a year. I believe that one year is the minimum for language learning, but I finally quit my study to run the business. I regret that my Chinese isn't perfect now. I'm able to communicate with most Chinese people, but I'm still far below fluent."

Adding an element of frustration to the already tough task of mastering Mandarin, several of our interviewees stressed that learning to speak Chinese won't overcome communication problems. Many misunderstandings between local and foreign businesspeople are caused not by lack of language skill, but by misreading the Chinese communication style. Business communications in China tend to be conducted in an indirect and roundabout way, leaving both sides to solve a puzzle. This communication style can be exhausting and frustrating for foreigners, especially those used to direct business talk.

Macedonian trader Oto Petroski explains: "The Chinese are masters of confusing communications." He says that when he began working with China from the Macedonian capital of

> *If you can speak Chinese, it definitely helps you to understand the culture better. If you have a good command of Chinese, it definitely helps you to negotiate with the Chinese. Since you're a foreigner, some Chinese may take advantage of you using the language. Thus, I usually conduct negotiations in Chinese."*
>
> **Aziz Mrabet** (Morocco), Managing Director, Impact Promotional Concepts

TIP Speaking Chinese shows your commitment to China; it will help you to better understand the culture; and it will be very useful when negotiating with domestic partners.

Skopje, his first Chinese client began asking questions about the terms of the business deal. Petroski noticed that the client seemed to ask many questions about the same topics. "Back then, I didn't know Chinese well, so I didn't know why [my client] had to ask the same question many times. But now I know." Petroski explains that when Chinese do business with each other, they often share only part of the information, leaving the other side to work out the full details. "[My client] had experienced many tricky business situations, so he felt he had to constantly ask and confirm whether I was saying one thing but meaning another thing," recalls Petroski.

This cat-and-mouse style of communication can be extremely frustrating for newcomers. "In my culture in Macedonia, we speak very concisely, very clearly," says Petroski. "If anyone asks the same question several times, we consider them to be stupid. But in China, I have to ask 10 times for the same information. When I ask about registration of the company, I ask once and get an answer. Then I come from another side and ask again the same question. Then slowly, I get the answer, piece by piece."

Hardships of Life in China

Despite their diverse backgrounds and cultures, and disregarding individual yearnings for such things as their favorite food from home (Philadelphia cheese steaks, for example) or hometown traditions (Catholic services), when interviewed for this chapter, our 40 foreign businesspeople identified several aspects of life in China that they all considered to be hardships. The most frequently cited of these were:

- Distance from nature
- Driving woes
- Lack of community
- High cost of expat living

We consider each of these in turn.

Trouble with Translators

Working with translators is a fact of life for foreign business executives in China—even the most accomplished Mandarin-speaking expats need a true linguistic expert for some types of negotiation. Thus, our 40 interviewees offered the following advice on finding and using translators.

Danish furniture business owner Simon Lichtenberg warns of the challenges of finding a qualified interpreter in China: "If you use a foreign translator, he may not understand the Chinese well; if it's a Chinese translator, he may not catch the English nuances." His solution has been to develop his own Chinese skills to the level where he is fluent. "You get so much closer by speaking Chinese. I do everything in Chinese. I speak Chinese to my son."

Brazilian distribution entrepreneur Winston Ling comments that it was only after his Mandarin skills improved that he began to recognize mistranslations. "Learning the language helps. I just started to speak it a year and a half ago. Before that, I had to have an interpreter all the time." He tells of an instance when he hired a translator for a business deal. "I used a PhD student to translate many of the presentations I gave—I did it in English, and she translated into Chinese. At the beginning, I didn't speak Chinese. Some years later, when my Chinese was okay, we did a presentation in Suzhou and I asked her to come along. While I was presenting, I realized that she wasn't saying this and that. She was summarizing way too much, but I didn't know that in the early years."

Gaining the ability to assess the quality of translations is only possible for those who can invest years of study into speaking fluent Chinese. For those who need to rely totally on a translator, consultant/entrepreneur Nicolas Musy advises finding a translator who not only has excellent language skills but, more importantly, is also committed to understanding and helping you and your company. "My Chinese partner supported me as an interpreter in the beginning. He's not a professional interpreter, actually, but you need to have a person that is more than just an interpreter. You need a person who not only understands what you want to do and what you want to say, but also what it means in the circumstances, and who can also give you his opinion and advice."

China Hardship #1: Distance from Nature

I miss my sports. I miss being able to get in my car and just drive someplace. I miss blue skies and sunshine, and I don't like the pollution [in China]."

Phillip Branham (USA), Founder and President, B & L Group

Many of our interviewees from the West said that the main challenge in enjoying life outside of work had to do with handling China's crowds, pollution, and the distance from nature. (Most of our interviewees live and work in the megacities of Shanghai, Beijing, and Guangzhou.)

Swiss consultant Nicolas Musy voiced a common sentiment when asked what he finds most difficult about living in Shanghai: "It's the lack of countryside that is frustrating; that and the noise." American software entrepreneur Eric Rongley said: "I miss driving my BMW around on good roads without many people on them." British entrepreneur Mark Pummell concurs: "I really miss fishing; I like to go fishing in the countryside where there is fresh air."

U.S. citizen and construction entrepreneur Phillip Branham, who owns a home in Hawaii, says: "I miss my sports. I miss being able to get in my car and just drive someplace. I miss blue skies and sunshine, and I don't like the pollution." After 11 years in China, he says: "I'm still not used to crowds." He also misses having access to U.S. sports programs on television, as well as live sporting events. "In the U.S., you take it for granted that you can turn on the TV and watch sports in English, or that you can watch sports in person." For the sports-minded, he says "quality of life is obviously better in the U.S." than in China.

Food and beverage delivery business founder Mark Secchia also hankers to escape the city life, and admits to feeling home-sick for America: "Shanghai isn't the world's most beautiful city. When I was in Michigan, I liked to fish, to be outdoors, and breathe fresh air. You don't get that here." Still, like many of our interviewees, Secchia believes the business benefits outweigh the disadvantages: "The business environment here is so awesome, that makes me so much happier."

Our entrepreneurs did mention missing specific creature comforts, although those based in China's megacities said that many of these comforts of home could now be found in China—albeit at a price. Phillip Branham measures progress in this area by the current ease of finding his favorite fast food: "You can get good pizza [in Shanghai] now, and you couldn't when I first came."

"Bad pollution" was the second most frequently named hardship among our interviewees. Even after 15 years spent living in the Middle Kingdom, Spanish consultant/entrepreneur Josep Giro is still sometimes bothered by China's pollution and by the lack of certain comforts from home. "Last time I was in Spain, the sky was blue, the weather was nice, and the food was good. Sometimes, I say, 'What am I doing here [in China]?' Shanghai is cold in the winter, hot in the summer, and very polluted," he says. "That is why many Spanish companies have trouble sending and keeping people [expatriates] in China."

Although our Asian entrepreneurs in China tended to suffer less from homesickness than the Westerners, many of them also wished to escape from China's crowds, pollution, and fast pace of life. Taiwan-born serviced office provider Maggie Yu explains: "I miss Taiwan very much. I really miss the countryside in Taiwan—there, we have small hotels with hot springs, and the people are very friendly."

Escaping the crowds and pollution by moving out of the cities and into suburban or rural areas is generally not a viable option for foreign businesspeople in China. First, most entrepreneurs will likely need to live in one of China's larger urban areas in order to find the infrastructure, and the access to customers and clients, necessary for their business. Second, those who do end up in a less-developed area—for example, in order to establish manufacturing operations—are not likely to find an idyllic rural setting. Much of the Chinese "countryside" available for investing is also crowded, polluted, and poorly planned. In addition, foreign startups will find primitive infrastructure, a less-educated workforce, and limited access to international media, imported products, and Western-style restaurants. In other words, locating your operations in the Chinese countryside is generally not the answer to homesickness for the great outdoors.

Generally, our interviewees who hailed from elsewhere in Asia or from other congested urban areas had less trouble in adjusting to China's big-city hassles. Their twinges of homesickness came instead from missing specific elements of life back home. For most entrepreneurs, traveling outside of China satisfies such cravings.

> *Last time I was in Spain, the sky was blue, the weather was nice, and the food was good. Sometimes, I say, 'What am I doing here [in China]?'*

Josep Giro (Spain), Co-founder and Managing Director, SBC & Associates

Recently, I was almost involved in an accident with a car that entered a ring road and drove in the wrong direction. And that driver shouted at me, asking me where I got my license! It's unbelievable."

Onder Oztunali
(Turkey), Founder of
Globe Stone Corp.

Another hardship—one that cannot be overcome by spending a long weekend at a resort in Thailand, and which impacts on many foreigners on a daily basis—is the challenges associated with driving (or even being driven) in China.

China Hardship #2: Driving Woes

Most businesspeople in China—and all the entrepreneurs we interviewed—must drive regularly in the course of doing business. For those working in the less developed areas of China, that means struggling along poorly constructed, and very often overcrowded, roadways. Roads in the larger cities may be better, but the problem of overcrowding remains. Either way, China's notoriously worsening traffic (the nation is adding more than a million cars per year to its domestic streets) is a key source of stress and frustration.

Taiwanese food service entrepreneur Michael Yang offers a graphic description of the demands and dangers of driving in China. "In Hong Kong, Taiwan, and Singapore, traffic is very good now. Years ago, it was probably just like China is now; but over the years, people got more educated and they now know how to follow the rules. But in China, there is still a long way to go—drivers don't follow the rules. They don't care about red lights. Sometimes, I have to sound the horn and yell at them, because they are endangering my life."

Driving is "the biggest frustration in China" for Turkish building materials supplier Onder Oztunali. In fact, the dangers of driving have impacted on life in one of his favorite cities in China: "Xiamen is one of the most beautiful places in China. Very clean, very nice—but unfortunately, that's not the whole picture. The way people drive in a country tells me a bit about how they do business. In Xiamen, if there are only two cars on the road, the other car will try to get in front of you even if there is no car in front of him. Driving in Xiamen is crazy; traffic rules don't exist. Cars never stop when entering a main highway or a faster-speed ring road—or any crossings, for that matter. They drive across at the same speed regardless of whose right of way it might be. Recently, I was almost involved in an accident with a car that entered a ring road and drove in the wrong direction. That driver shouted at *me*, asking me where I got *my* license! It's unbelievable."

Many of our interviewees told of losing their temper while driving in China. Macedonian import/export company founder Oto Petroski shared a typical anecdote: "I had a case when a taxi driver drove around me like crazy—passing from left, then the right. He cut me off three times. Then suddenly, I became Chinese. I drove in front and cut *him* off. I pulled him out of the car and asked him, 'What do you want? Do you want to kill me, or to kill yourself?'"

Others among our long-time China hands were more philosophical and accepting of the challenges of the roadways. Israeli entrepreneur Aviel Zilber downplayed the difficulties of driving on China's roads. "I drive in Israel. Driving in Israel is also crazy. The rules here make sense to me. I understand very much what they do on the road. It's not as bad in Israel, but I understand it here."

Some veteran China drivers, including American entrepreneur Mark Secchia, claim to recognize, and even appreciate, an underlying logic behind the appearance of chaos. "When foreigners look at the traffic, they say, 'How can they drive like this?'" he says. "But it's a controlled form of chaos." Secchia says there *are* rules, though they are unspoken and unwritten. For example, when driving down a rural street in China, he tends to stay close to the middle of the road, while allowing enough space for oncoming traffic to pass by. "The guy driving toward me will do the same thing; he also goes to the middle of the road. So, we are communicating. As long as we both leave enough room to pass each other, it's okay." While he acknowledges that drivers do "the exact opposite in the States"—meaning that they crowd over to each side to give a wide berth—Secchia says the system in China usually works. "When foreigners come here, they say, 'Oh, my God, he's going to hit us!' Actually, he isn't. He's communicating with you. He is saying: 'This is how much space I need,' and you do the same thing with him." Secchia says that business negotiations in China are conducted in much the same way as these *Rambo*-like driving methods.

❝

When driving, the Chinese have a pragmatic point of view: 'Go forward as fast as possible without endangering anybody. Know the rules, but if you can get around them, fine.' There are actually not that many accidents when you consider how people drive."

Simon Lichtenberg
(Denmark), Founder and
CEO, Trayton Group

Danish furniture business owner Simon Lichtenberg agrees: "When driving, the Chinese have a pragmatic point of view: 'Go forward as fast as possible without endangering anybody. Know the rules, but if you can get around them, fine.' There are actually not that many accidents when you consider how people drive."

At a far end of the spectrum is 25-year China veteran consultant Jan Borgonjon who claims not only to drive like a domestic Chinese, but also to find driving in China an enjoyable leisure activity. Says Borgonjon: "I've been driving in China since 1988. For me, driving in China is relaxing. When I go to Europe, I get quite nervous. I'm used to driving in China." Asked if he is frustrated by traffic rules that either are unclear or are disregarded, he responds: "There *are* rules. They are not written down, but I know them instinctively. One is: the bigger you are, the more power you have—until you have a traffic accident. Then, it's exactly the other way around; the one who is the weakest wins, and gets more compensation. What else? You go with the flow, expect the unexpected, and always have your hand on the horn."

Several of our interviewees drew a comparison between China's chaotic roadways and the nation's confusing, but somehow functional, business practices. Oto Petroski explains the (slightly tongue-in-cheek) insights into the Chinese mindset that he gained through driving: "If you want to understand the Chinese, their mindset, you have to drive. When you drive, you discover the nature of Chinese behavior. Why? When the Chinese drive, they cannot wear a mask; they can't pretend. In the acting of driving, they show their life philosophy clearly, which is: 'Try to abuse any position you have in your favor, no matter what the price—even if you are in danger of killing yourself in the process.'"

💡 Driving in
TIP China can be
compared to
doing business in
China: the rules
are followed when
necessary, but
ignored whenever
possible.

Mark Secchia agrees that Chinese driving behavior serves as an apt metaphor for Chinese business behavior, but he describes the situation in a more sympathetic light. "The rules of driving in China are like the rules of doing business," he says. "You can't say that the Chinese government is corrupt. They just work differently within their system. I don't look at it as corruption; it's just a different system."

China Hardship #3: Lack of Community

Among the negative aspects of expatriate life in China, our interviewees mentioned the stress of living as an outsider. For example, when asked how his non-working life is different in China than in his native Netherlands, businessman Olaf Litjens says he lacks a sense of community and belonging. "I'm Catholic. In Holland, that means that you go to a Catholic school, Catholic church, and the Catholic social club. I'm from a small village where everyone knows each other. Here [in China], you are on your own; people come and go every three years. Because of that, as an expatriate, you are not integrated with the place you live."

Because of the high demands of working life in China, most international businesspeople tend to form friendships with fellow expatriates, based either on work or, if married and with children, on family connections. Before they had a child, social life in China for entrepreneur Susan Heffernan and her husband, a Dutch businessman, revolved mainly around their work. "My friends in China were basically in the same business I am—architectural designers, furniture suppliers, maybe even competitors. That's the way it is. Even if they are your competitors, they are the same kind of person, so it is natural to become friends." Except for a few close Chinese friends, Heffernan says that most of her friends in China are foreigners—a natural phenomenon, since friendship is easiest among people with similar "cultures and values."

Bridging the culture–values gap in order to form strong friendships with Chinese people requires a significant "stretch," agrees Spanish businessman Josep Giro: "If you have an open mind, it's very easy to make [casual] friendships with the Chinese. I say hello to people when I take the lift in my apartment, and my neighbors become my friends. But to form *real* friendships is different, and more difficult." Giro says that one of the most off-putting differences, from a Western viewpoint, is the tendency among the Chinese to hide their emotions and feelings. "Western people are more extroverted and outgoing. It doesn't mean that Chinese people don't feel

CASE STUDY

THE CAR ACCIDENT

To illustrate the trials and tribulations of driving in China, import/export entrepreneur Oto Petroski shares this anecdote about an incident that occurred while he was on a visit to Shandong Province:

Recently, I was driving at around 8 p.m. along a village highway in Shandong [Province]. Suddenly, the highway was closed for reconstruction, so I moved into the other lane. It was four lanes on a village highway full of trucks and motorbikes, all driving slowly and carefully. I drove a little bit too slowly, and the truck in front of me went ahead 50 meters, creating a small gap in the chain of traffic. In the minds of the local villagers, that gap meant "open space"—a chance to cross the highway! It was night, and suddenly in front of me in the darkness I see 20 or 30 bikes trying to cross the highway in a big group. They had sensed a gap in the traffic and they all jumped in. I was driving only 25 miles an hour. I braked, but the car skidded for 10 meters. So, after a big bang, I see a Chinese bike-rider flying in the air. I was driving slowly, and I tried to stop, but I still hit him.

When I opened my car door, several of the riders took one look at me and ran away. Another rider was lying on the road and making noises, but it was very suspicious. I saw that the bicycle was perfectly okay. I hadn't hit him. Then I saw the worst case—the man I had directly hit, who had flown a few meters through the air. When I went over to him, he also jumped to his feet, and I thanked God that he was okay. He had some blood in his mouth, but he was moving around.

After I saw that everyone was okay, I took out my camera and shot photos of everything. I was perfectly sure that I wasn't in the wrong. I don't think I would have been considered guilty by the laws of any country. Then I waited for the police, along with the two Chinese who had been hurt.

When the police came, they told me to get into their car for my safety. Maybe some village people would attack me, they said. They were trying to scare me, so I said: "Chinese people aren't like that." Then we all went to the police station and waited for local government officials from a bigger city to arrive. By now, it was 10 p.m.

When the big boss finally came, he asked me two questions that I will never forget. First, "What were you, a foreigner, doing on this highway at this time?" His meaning was that, if I hadn't been there, there wouldn't have been an accident. So, immediately, I was guilty. I said, "I was there because your highway is under construction. I was following the driving directions."

His second question was: "Why did you stop the car?" His meaning now was that a problem existed *only because I had stopped*. If I had run away, there would have been no problem, no case. Since I *did* stop, I had created a problem, which he had to solve!

Then a drama began. For the next hour, relatives of the two men who had been slightly hurt, as well as other village people, came to the police station to cry and point to the scratches the men had received in the accident.

In the end, the situation was resolved in a typical Chinese way: they asked for money. Money in China fixes everything. The men asked for RMB8,000 [US$1,140] as compensation for them being scratched after jumping in front of my car.

I feel very unhappy about bargaining with poor people in this kind of situation, but it's the usual way of dealing with a car accident. Everyone bargains. So I offered them RMB3,000 [US$430]. The chief of police said, "Okay, RMB3,000." Then he spoke with the Chinese side, and there was more crying and wailing. Then he came back to me, and said: "RMB3,000 is not enough!" From his point of view, the poor Chinese villagers must get more money, otherwise he would lose face because he isn't protecting his fellow Chinese. Then he tried to scare me by saying they would take my car, and this and that.

If I had only been in China for a month, I would have been scared. But now, I know the game. Whoever has more nerves and more time, will win. So, I started to enjoy the game.

I insisted on calling my embassy and insisted on calling another police officer to make a record and take measurements. Then I said, "I want to go to court." This is a big problem in China, if a foreigner goes to court. When I said that, I knew right away that my position was strong. In addition, the chief of police wanted very much to solve the problem immediately, so it wouldn't escalate. If it escalates, he has a problem. So, for both of those reasons, my position was strong.

We finished negotiating after two hours, back and forth—offering this money, that money, this money, that money—and finally, we settled on RMB5,000 [US$715]. Then they took my fingerprints and I paid the money. In the end, we all kissed and hugged each other—including the wounded people, the police chief, and the party secretary of the village. Then they asked, "Can we all go to eat somewhere?" They were very happy with me. This is a typical case in rural China.

emotions, but they don't show them that much. It's a cultural habit."

Even those foreign businesspeople with broad and diverse social networks described experiencing difficulty in forming real friendships with local Chinese. After 13 years in China, Iranian-born American entrepreneur Shah Firoozi says his social circles span many demographics. Among Chinese communities, he says it is easiest for foreigners in China to befriend either "returnees" (Chinese who had studied and/or worked in developed nations) or those from Taiwan, Singapore, or Hong Kong. "The most difficult group to make friends with is local Chinese," says Firoozi, explaining that the cultural divide—in terms of language, customs, and mindset—remains large.

Others among our expatriate interviewees said that their lives were so busy and harried, it was easier to socialize with those from a similar background and culture and with compatible leisure habits. Italian consultant Ruggero Jenna is typical in his thinking on the relative challenges of forming a strong friendship with Chinese nationals versus fellow expats: "It's not easy to make really close Chinese friends. It's much easier to become friends with other expatriates—they invite you out, you invite them out."

Artificial Society

While socializing with fellow expats is often easier logistically, there are also drawbacks to restricting one's non-work life to the foreign community. Several of our interviewees stressed that expatriate social circles can be quite superficial and artificial. China veteran Olaf Litjens says that some mid-level managers get carried away by the relative wealth they suddenly—and often temporarily—enjoy as expats in China. In many cases, he says, American or European managers whose packages back home didn't include expatriate-type perks experience a radical change in lifestyle when they arrive in China. Suddenly, they are provided with a large house, paid vacations, several domestic helpers, and a driver. For some managers, the expat lifestyle encourages snobbery. Says Litjens: "I get very upset when I

> *Western people are more extroverted and outgoing. It doesn't mean that Chinese people don't feel emotions, but they don't show them that much. It's a cultural habit."*
>
> **Josep Giro** (Spain), Co-founder and Managing Director, SBC & Associates

TIP Foreign businesspeople, must work to form true friendships with Chinese nationals. There are language, social, and cultural divides that many expatriates find difficult to bridge.

hear people complaining about their domestic help in China when they didn't have this kind of perk in Europe."

Another hardship for international businesspeople who are committed to a long stay in China is that most fellow expats are on short-term assignments. This makes forming strong friendships challenging. Eleven-year China veteran Phillip Branham says this is one aspect of his host country that makes him miss life back in the United States. "You can make friends here, but people are more transient. You wind up knowing a lot of people, but you don't make really, really good friends. They are here today, gone tomorrow, which doesn't happen quite that much in the U.S."

Crossing the Cultural Divide

Among our interviewees who had successfully scaled the cultural barriers and penetrated into Chinese social circles, their most common entry point was through a Chinese spouse. Israeli Aviel Zilber, whose wife is Chinese, is one example. In describing his social life, he said: "My wife is very much my friend. I don't really have other close Chinese friends. It takes time to build friendships [in China] because of the difference in culture and languages. But my wife's friends are becoming my friends little by little. We go out together and travel together."

Further along on the integration trail was Dutch internet entrepreneur Marc van der Chijs, who says: "I've been in China for many years and my wife, who is Chinese, has a lot of friends. So, my friends in China are now mainly Chinese. My Chinese business partner is really my best friend."

Japanese consultant Hiroshi Shoda also finds it possible to make Chinese friends, with some effort. "Most of the time, the Japanese in China socialize with other Japanese. But really, it's not difficult to make Chinese friends. I have Chinese friends here."

After six years in China, Brazilian business owner Winston Ling, who is ethnically Chinese but culturally Latin American, says he mingles within several diverse social circles: "I hang out

You can make friends here, but people are more transient. You wind up knowing a lot of people, but you don't make really, really good friends. They are here today, gone tomorrow, which doesn't happen quite that much in the U.S."

Phillip Branham (USA), Founder and President, B & L Group

For most expat managers, social life revolves around work and the community in which they live. Foreigners who speak Chinese and/or have a Chinese spouse tend to enter the Chinese social circles.

As an expat [new to China], I wasted a lot of money. My first apartment cost US$6,000 a month. Why would you pay that for an apartment? Now I live across the street and have two gardens. I pay less than US$2,000 a month. I think a lot of expats just waste money."

Eric Rongley (USA), Founder and CEO, Bleum

with all different types of people. I don't only deal with the Brazilians or Americans. I have local Chinese friends, and also friends from Taiwan and Hong Kong."

Sports and sports clubs can be a logical channel for breaking down cultural divides, comments American real estate entrepreneur Bruce Robertson: "I play tennis a lot. I have a group of Chinese to play tennis with. We gained a lot of social life that way and also by going to concerts or the theater together. It's not too difficult for me to make Chinese friends, except for the language problem. Most of my Chinese friends are bilingual." One factor impacting on East–West friendships is that relatively few Chinese aged over 40 speak English. Says Robertson: "Because of that, I have a lot of younger friends."

One factor that impacts on the social lives of foreign managers and business owners even more than cultural and language issues, however, is time. Belgian entrepreneur–consultant Jan Borgonjon sums up the experience of many international business managers in China with this comment: "I think it's quite easy to make Chinese friends. I speak Chinese, so that helps. But basically, I only have business friends. The problem with most people doing business in China is that you don't have much time for social life outside of work."

China Hardship #4: High Cost of Expat Living

Another hardship identified by our 40 entrepreneurial expatriates is the high cost of expat living in China. While it is safe to say that all foreigners in China suffer from the high cost of imported items—paying several times the costs paid back home for their favorite shampoo, chocolate, or wine—the degree to which high costs bothered our interviewees fluctuated widely.

At one end of the spectrum are businessmen such as U.S. software company founder Eric Rongley, who lives comfortably in China without spending at an expat rate. "[High costs are] not much of an issue for me," he says, explaining that he is "not a very vain person", and thus, doesn't choose to spend money on status symbols. Rongley originally came to China on an expat package paid by a U.S. company. When he quit that company to start his own business, he drastically cut his living expenses. "As an expat, I wasted a lot of money. My first apartment cost US$6,000 a month. Why would you pay that for an apartment? Now, I live across the street and have two gardens. I pay less than US$2,000 a month. I think a lot of expats just waste money."

The primary factor in determining the cost-of-living expenses of foreign businesspeople is the size of their family. As a single man, Rongley's expenses are a fraction of those of a married man with children. Rongley himself says he "thinks carefully" when hiring a foreigner with children, because expenses then rise exponentially.

The largest single reason for the high cost of expat families is international school fees. The going rate at most international schools in Shanghai and Beijing is US$20,000 per child, per year, from kindergarten up to the start of high school (see the box below). For companies bringing in an expat manager with a partner and, say, three children, expenses can be expected to soar. On top of the minimum of US$60,000 the company must pay annually for school tuition (additional fees are incurred for buses, uniforms, books, and other services), the apartment or house may cost US$10,000 per month. When other family-oriented perks—home leave airfares, babysitters, and car and driver—are factored in, the package alone can match the expat's salary. Companies can easily pay US$200,000 per annum for an expat manager and family's expenses, in addition to the salary.

By contrast, a young, single foreign manager footing his or her own bills in Shanghai, for example, could keep living expenses as low as US$8,000 per annum (US$700 per month) by renting an older, Chinese-style apartment, eating at streetside restaurants selling Chinese cuisine, and traveling by subway or motorcycle.

China's urban centers, such as Shanghai, offer a full spectrum of housing and schooling. Foreigners can lead a very expensive expatriate lifestyle, or can "go local" for around one-tenth the cost.

The Struggle for Work–Life Balance

Necessity for Long Hours

When questioned about their after-work life, most of our interviewees responded along the lines of: *"What* after-work life?" While entrepreneurs around the world work notoriously long hours and face the continual stress of never being truly "off work," the pace in China, our interviewees agreed, is generally more intense than in their home countries.

Schooling for Foreign Children

For foreign entrepreneurs with families, the question of how to educate their children is a complex cultural, academic, and financial one.

The good news, in terms of educational options, is that many of China's urban centers now boast top-quality expatriate-oriented schools, enabling parents to choose to have their children educated in English, French, German, Korean, Japanese, or another language. Iranian-born American Shah Firoozi, who sent his four children through an international school in Shanghai, is very satisfied with the education they have received in China. "The quality of international education has improved quite a bit. I think my children have graduated from one of the best high schools in the world."

Another satisfied parent is Korean financial investment entrepreneur Chun In Kyu. "My kids are in an international school in Shanghai. All the courses are in Chinese and English. They have adapted very well in China and are very happy here. When my sons don't behave well, I say, 'If you don't listen to me, I will send you back to Korea.' They then listen to me. They really like their lives in Shanghai."

The bad news is that most of these schools charge fees of around US$20,000 per annum for grade school, and US$24,000 for junior high and high school. For a family with two or three children, the fees quickly become astronomical. In fact, for Macedonian trading company founder Oto Petroski, sky-high school fees were one reason he moved his wife and two children to the U.S. while continuing to operate

Real estate entrepreneur Bruce Robertson explained how life differs in Shanghai from what he had been used to back home in the U.S.: "Here, in China, it's 24/7. Tonight is Saturday night. I worked all day today, and I'll be working tomorrow again, meeting with clients. This wouldn't happen in the U.S." Robertson explained that, in China, business meetings are often set up for Saturday and Sunday. "In the U.S., no one would propose to customers or clients that we work all weekend; it would be considered impolite, insulting, boorish. Here, if an opportunity to do something productive arises, everybody jumps at it."

Another entrepreneur who works all hours is internet business pioneer Ken Carroll, partly because he can so easily check

his business from China. Says Petroski: "I am not a manager in General Motors. I can't pay US$20,000 for one year of school."

International schools aren't the only option for parents to consider, however. First, children who learn Chinese fluently can test into China's private domestic primary or secondary schools, where school fees are typically one-third to half that of an international school. A word of warning regarding traditional Chinese schools, however: they tend to be extremely demanding in terms of memorization and competitive testing, and are heavily focused on preparing students for the Chinese entrance exams into junior high and high school. Reports of seven-year-olds studying for more than 12 hours a day, skipping gym class and music class to do homework, and not sleeping well because of weekly exam pressure, are not uncommon.

Two new, and increasingly popular alternatives, are Chinese-owned "experimental schools" or private schools with a "foreign track." These two options cater to students who don't hold a Chinese passport, and can therefore be spared the mandatory education curriculum (and its focus on entrance exam preparation). While these programs vary widely in their curricula, facilities, and quality of teachers, most offer a mix of Chinese and Western teaching styles plus a bilingual environment, and a greater emphasis on sports, art, theater, and other electives than is found in traditional Chinese schools. Fees at such schools are usually slightly more than the Chinese private schools, but still significantly (30–50%) less than at expatriate schools.

Home schooling is another option followed by some international families.

Here, in China, it's 24/7. Tonight is Saturday night. I worked all day today, and I'll be working tomorrow again, meeting with clients. This wouldn't happen in the U.S."

Bruce Robertson
(USA), President, Asia Pacific Real Estate

Try to make your China offices as comfortable as possible. You will probably spend more time there than at home.

on his business online. "In the morning, the first thing I do after I wake up is work on the computer in bed. The last thing I do at night, after my wife and daughter go to bed, is to check [online] to see who was 'in the store.' My wife thinks I'm crazy."

With the click of a mouse, Carroll can check how many users are logged on to his language-learning websites, and he can read the real-time online comments uploaded by users. Operating a Web 2.0-type business, where customers are online and viewable, makes maintaining "off hours" difficult, since the website is being used continuously around the globe.

One way to create some balance between work and leisure is to build your social life around your work. Says entertainment and counseling entrepreneur Mark Pummell, "We enjoy our work—the work is fun. A lot of times, we do business with our friends. The model in Shanghai is business-to-business friendship. You socialize a lot with people who you do business with, but not in a formal way. We do business with our friends and they join us for drinks. We enjoy our work a lot."

How does he balance this full-on work pace with fatherhood? Says Pummell: "I go home to play with my son until he falls asleep, then I go back to work or go out. If you want to do business in China, you've got to live within your businesses. This is our model. We don't literally live here [in the business offices], but almost. We try to make it a very nice workplace, with a nice bar. We can eat there. I think this model is very good."

The Personal Toll

Others among our entrepreneur interviewees said they were struggling with an overwhelming workload, which was causing frustration, stress, and exhaustion. Consultant Ruggero Jenna, who has a strong desire to live and work in China, describes his situation: "I enjoy China as a country. I'm interested in understanding the Chinese culture and the Chinese people. The weak part about life here is the fact that I'm working too much. I want to spend some more time with my family and my kids, which is a sacrifice for me. I would also like to have some time for myself, because I'm really working too long hours now. I need to sort it out."

Mother of three children (with a fourth on the way at the time of the interviews for *China Entrepreneur*), French fashion wholesaler/retailer Valerie Touya describes her work–life imbalance. "I am working 24 hours a day now because I have three stores and six employees. My costs are high, so I am myself working every day." In addition, during the time when she met with the authors, her retail shop in Suzhou was "not working out"—a situation that was demanding much of her personal time. "It is hard for me. It is new, but right now, I'm not balancing work and life very well."

Most difficult to handle, she says, is the constant stress of being the main decision-maker in a young and unstable business venture. "There is always this pressure—the pressure to make the right decision. You are always wondering, 'Is this a good decision? Is a fashion show the right way to attract customers?' I studied for my EMBA at China Europe International Business School [in China] to avoid making mistakes, but in China, there is no recipe. You have to make decisions alone." The solution, she says, is to rely on other China experts in making decisions. "I rely more and more on other people's specialties."

Our interviewees conceded that the working pace of an entrepreneur in China could cause problems at home. Entrepreneur Susan Heffernan considers herself lucky that her husband "understands the pressure" of her business. "My husband is general manager of a big company. He also has to work very hard. If you have a partner who isn't at the same stage as you, it will be horrible." She says the couple share the same lifestyle of coming home at around 7 p.m., then working at the computer until midnight to get ready for the next day. "If you have a partner who doesn't understand, he would leave straight away."

Heffernan says that being able to relax in China is more difficult than in her native Australia. "It's not the same as it is back home. You can't just take your dog out for a walk after work and meet other people in the park and pull out some chardonnay and organize a barbeque. Lately, I really miss that."

> *There is always this pressure—the pressure to make the right decision. . . . I studied an EMBA at China Europe International Business School [in China] to avoid making mistakes, but in China, there is no recipe. You have to make decisions alone."*
>
> **Valerie Touya** (France), Founder, Curiosity Fashion Store

She says that while she knows that sports clubs such as softball or basketball clubs exist in Shanghai, she hasn't yet made the effort to find them. "I've been running my own business for more than four years, and I don't have that much of an after-work life. It's pretty sad." Instead, she makes it to yoga class, goes to the gym, or meets friends for lunch or dinner whenever she can. But most weekends involve at least some time for work: "When you have your own business, you don't get peeved that you have to work on the weekend. It's normal."

The few entrepreneurs we interviewed who didn't complain of a work–life imbalance said they try to leave their weekends free. Mexican trading company founder Juan Martinez, whose wife is Chinese, is one example. "On the weekend, my wife and I try to disconnect ourselves from work. We turn off our mobile phones or don't answer them. We don't turn on the computer. If we work all the time, we think it's not healthy." Much of his off-work time is spent with his wife's relatives. "On weekends, we visit my wife's family a lot. Her sister and husband and their two kids come over and we take the kids to the zoo, museums, and the aquarium. We are getting some training for our future kids. We are Catholics and we go to mass at St. Ignatius Xujiahui's Cathedral [in Shanghai]. We also sometimes meet friends and classmates for dinner."

Health Issues

The one interviewee who clearly claimed to have achieved a healthy and satisfying work–life balance had suffered a stress-related ailment and subsequently changed her lifestyle. Serviced office facilities owner Maggie Yu explains how she got caught up in a workaholic lifestyle during her first years in China. "Shanghai is a very dynamic, exciting city. On the flip side, however, it can be difficult to keep up with the pace, and that may produce a certain amount of anxiety. The fast-paced life-style is one of the things that people have to adapt to here. Expatriates may find that business entertainment plays a much bigger part in their working life than they are used to in their own country, and that can be tough. Late nights spent socializing with business associates can take a toll on your health, but this is an expected part of doing business in China. After the first few years of adapting to the lifestyle and culture here, I have now achieved a better balance in my life."

Yu's primary method of calming and balancing her life, she says, has been through studying Buddhism, taking yoga classes, eating well, getting more sleep, and traveling every other month for relaxation. "When I made this change, I stopped taking medicine, and my gastric problem was cured completely within a month. It's amazing."

> *Late nights spent socializing with business associates can take a toll on your health, but this is an expected part of doing business in China."*
>
> **Maggie Yu** (Taiwan), Founder and Managing Director, Asian BizCenter & Consulting

Foreign Businesswomen in China

In any culture worldwide, businesswomen face specific challenges. To try and understand how China compares as an environment for foreign female managers, we included seven women among the 40 entrepreneurs interviewed. Hailing from Taiwan, Australia, Singapore, France, Canada, and the United States, these women represent a range of industries from furniture wholesaling and fashion retailing to consulting, silk flower manufacturing, and banking.

We asked our businesswomen interviewees for their thoughts on two topics of particular interest to expatriate businesswomen in China:

- Gender discrimination
- Balancing work and children

Gender Discrimination

One of the most welcome findings of this book is that none of the women entrepreneurs we interviewed reported experiencing gender discrimination themselves, or having women friends or colleagues who had been discriminated against on this basis. Singaporean co-founder of ChinaVest, Jenny Hsui, who has worked

"

Since 1978, I've spent 80% of my time in China. As a woman, I've never encountered serious discrimination here. If there was a slight bias in the beginning, it changed as I proved myself."

Jenny Hsui (Singapore), Co-founder and President, ChinaVest

"

Here, in China, women are definitely treated more equally than they are in Australia. It's still a relatively sexist society in Australia."

Susan Heffernan (Australia), Founder and Managing Director, Soozar

in China for 30 years, said: "Since 1978, I've spent 80% of my time in China. As a woman, I've never encountered serious discrimination here. If there was a slight bias in the beginning, it changed as I proved myself."

Hsui and our other interviewees attribute this openness to China's historical circumstances. "I came to China to do business in 1978, which was at the end of the Cultural Revolution. At that time, everybody wore gray and blue. All the women wore pants, rather than skirts. In a way, I suppose that women had more power then than they have now, because there was no obvious difference between the genders."

Hsui says, "What really surprised me was that, in the late 1980s, I found great discrimination outside China. The phenomenon isn't obvious—usually it's hidden—but you can sense it." Today, Hsui says, gender discrimination is obvious in developed countries such as Japan. "It's not easy for Japanese society to accept women entrepreneurs," she says. In Taiwan, she has found that women face some discrimination when starting a business; while in the U.S., women frequently are paid less than men for similar work and still find it difficult to speak out when men run their company.

By contrast, Hsui says, women in today's China find a supportive environment. Even though women tend to be "more feminine" today than they were during the Cultural Revolution, they generally continue to be treated as equals in the workplace. "Today, I don't feel any discrimination as a woman doing business in China. In terms of doing business, it's not harder for women; there aren't many barriers," she says.

Business owner Susan Heffernan finds the environment for businesswomen more favorable in China than in her native Australia. "Here, in China, women are definitely treated more equally than they are in Australia. It's still a relatively sexist society in Australia." Serviced offices supplier Maggie Yu also finds the lack of gender discrimination in China refreshing: "Women in China enjoy more equality than women in other Asian countries."

All our interviewees, and especially the six female entrepreneurs profiled, see the business environment for women—both expatriates and locals—in China as quite vibrant. Maggie Yu describes the environment in Shanghai for businesswomen as "welcoming."

"I've seen many successful women entrepreneurs here in Shanghai. Some of these women are only in their thirties, or even younger."

Being female can even be a plus, according to some of our interviewees. Canadian floor tiling entrepreneur Chee-Chin Wu, who works in mainland China, Hong Kong, Canada, the U.S., and Europe, puts it this way: "As a woman entrepreneur, I don't find there is any discrimination in the international business world. Sometimes, a woman's soft approach can be more successful in business than a man's approach." She adds that, during her time as president of the Shanghai Rotary Club from 2006 to 2007, she met encouraging reactions. "Some of the European clubs are restricted to men only, so many people were a little surprised — in a positive way — that there was a woman in the Rotary Club, and that the president was a woman."

American cultural training company founder Marjorie Woo agrees that China can offer businesswomen a gender advantage. "For me, my gender didn't have any negative impact on business. There's an interesting phenomenon in China: women have more leverage than men when doing business. For one thing, male clients tend to give you more time of day if you want to make a pitch; and women tend to have easier access to decision-makers in business." Woo, who has business ties in the U.S. and throughout Asia, says that the proportion of women entrepreneurs in the general population is far higher in China than elsewhere, mainly because it is easier for women to start businesses there.

"Women are more powerful in China," says Taiwan-born entrepreneur Wendy Tai, owner of an interior decoration manufacturing business. "I think being a woman here is an advantage. [Business leaders] show more respect to women in China than in other places like Taiwan." Tai says that women in Taiwan still suffer under the gender-discriminatory laws that were influenced by the 50 years the island spent under Japanese control (which period ended in 1945). For example, in Taiwan, she says, a married woman who owns property cannot sell it without her husband's permission, whereas a married man faces no such restrictions.

Another advantage for women entrepreneurs, says Susan Heffernan, is that Chinese government officials are sometimes slightly more lenient toward females. "It is especially obvious

> **China is a relatively egalitarian society, in terms of gender, as a consequence of its communist past.**

You have the support from your extended family, and you can have all the domestic support—such as drivers and ayis [nanny or domestic helper]—needed to make life much easier."

Marjorie Woo (USA), Founder and chairwoman, Leadership Management International (China)

when you tackle things at the government level. If you are a woman, they seem to be more lenient toward you."

Balancing Work and Children

Another very clear benefit for businesswomen with children in China is the relatively high level of childcare support that is available, compared with other countries. China's one-child policy means that most working women have only one baby to look after (although the policy has been relaxed slightly in recent years). Unlike in some other countries, a working woman's right to have that child is carefully protected. Once a woman is pregnant, China's labor laws provide extra protections against losing her job—in fact, it is extremely difficult to fire a pregnant woman or new mother. In addition, women are guaranteed four months of paid maternity leave after the baby arrives, and may take longer leave in the event of a difficult pregnancy, twins, or other complications.

Working mothers in China also benefit from the extremely low cost of live-in domestic help. At an average rate of RMB8–10 [US$1.40] per hour in Shanghai, and less than this outside the main cities, nearly everyone (even graduate students) can afford to hire domestic help. Families with a young child can often easily afford to employ a full-time, live-in nanny/housekeeper. The nanny will often work long hours and weekends, and will handle a range of chores—from shopping to cooking and cleaning, and even helping the child with his or her homework. Many working couples also have access to four doting grandparents for their single child. All this accessible assistance with mothering alleviates a major source of stress for working mothers.

"You have the support from your extended family, and you can have all the domestic support—such as drivers and ayis [nanny or domestic helper]—needed to make life much easier," says Marjorie Woo.

Business founder Mark Secchia and his wife, both Americans, fully appreciate the domestic perks available in China. "Raising kids is cheaper here. I can keep my kids here until they are six years old and have an *ayi* to take care of them for a couple of hundred U.S. dollars a month. My friends back home pay more than a thousand dollars a month for eight hours of childcare a day. Here, the *ayi* can watch the kids for 16 hours a day for one-fifth of the price."

Susan Heffernan, who became a first-time mother in late 2007, is also taking full advantage of the domestic help available in China. "Support here is more affordable, which definitely makes life much easier." In fact, Heffernan says her work–life balance improved after becoming a mother. "Before I had the baby, my life wasn't in balance. I often worked overtime. Since the baby, I try to keep some balance."

In fact, support for working mothers in China goes so far that our interviewees described a problem that may be unique to this country: working women are expected to work long hours and to leave the childcare to others. Says mother of four and entrepreneur Valerie Touya: "Chinese women don't try to achieve work–life balance." She says that, while many Western mothers insist on spending time on raising and educating their children themselves, many Chinese women pass these tasks nearly completely over to grandparents or nannies. "I try to balance my life, but Chinese women don't have the same thinking. Their parents educate and raise the child, and they just devote their time to their professional life. I always try not to work on Saturdays and Sundays—aside from the period when I first launched the business—but Chinese business-women who are mothers will work every weekend as well." Touya now limits her work time, in order to build in mothering time. "When I am with my kids, I don't have my mobile phone with me. Saturdays and Sundays are dedicated to the kids."

> **TIP** Many Chinese working mothers enjoy low-cost, 24/7 domestic help provided by nannies or grandparents.

The Good Life, China-style

When asked if, overall, they were happy living in China, most of our interviewees gave clearly positive responses. American Eric Rongley voiced a representative viewpoint: "I find life in the

REVERSE CULTURE SHOCK FOR AN EXPAT WORKING MOM

During her stay in China from 2001 to 2008, French businesswoman Valerie Touya made full use of the amenities the country offers to working women. While raising her three children (aged nine, seven, and five by the end of her stay in China) and becoming pregnant with a fourth in 2007, she completed an EMBA, then launched and sold a successful fashion retailing business. "One good thing is that in China, you have a lot of domestic help. In France, you don't have people to help—so it is easier here," she says.

Touya found that she was able to use her time far more efficiently in China than in Europe. Living in Suzhou (an industrial city located two hours from Shanghai) with her husband, who was offered an expat package, she had the use of a driver and a full-time nanny for her children. "With a driver, all that commuting time can be work time," she says. At home, the ayi took care of the shopping, cooking, and cleaning, so Touya was free to focus on her children.

Without such help, Touya says, she wouldn't have been able to launch her business, Curiosity Concept Stores, which initially required regular overtime work. "Here in China, you have a lot of ways to increase your productivity as a working mom. I don't spend time shopping for food. For me, a single hour is very important. I can do many other things in an hour if I don't have to shop."

When Touya's husband was relocated back to France in 2008, she decided to sell her business and return to life as a working mother in France. How did she feel about leaving? On the positive side, she said, she expected to find a slower pace of working life back home. "In Europe, they don't say you are a bad mother if you have a career. Still, in France, you work just 35 hours a week. Also, in France, you have eight weeks of holiday a year—so there is so much more time available to spend with your kids."

On the downside, Touya says, she will have to live without the domestic help she has grown accustomed to in China. "I will lose all this—the ayi, the driver. In Europe, you have to make sure you're really well organized. I told my husband, I want to live not more than 500 meters from the kids' school. I don't want to lose time commuting. In one day, I can work seven to eight hours, but if I have to spend two hours in traffic, I lose too much time."

By the time she and her family left Suzhou, Touya had already started a new clothing retail company in France, also focused on import/export with China.

United States rather boring, to tell you the truth. It's addictive to constantly stay in a different culture. Something surprising happens all the time, and that makes life interesting." Rongley, who lived and worked in India and traveled in Asia for several years before setting up his own business in China, describes an unsuccessful stint back in the U.S. several years ago: "Between India and Shanghai, my former company brought me back to Richmond, Virginia for six months, to learn the business and build the company network. I tell you, if it'd been longer, I would have gotten a gun and shot myself. Everyone goes home at 5.30, the wife has dinner on the table at 6.30, and everyone goes to bed at 10 o'clock. They then wake up the next day and do the same thing over again. Here, each day is different from the one before."

Mexican entrepreneur Juan Martinez also says he has built a happy and fulfilling life in China. "Both my wife and I enjoy our lives here a lot. Many famous people come to Shanghai for concerts, operas, sports, so we have opportunities to go to cultural events. Shanghai also has a good nightlife, good restaurants. It's much more international than Leon Guanajuato [in Mexico], where I am from! Living in Shanghai, we feel . . . wow!"

After seven years in China, Martinez says he has finally convinced his family back home that he is living a good life. "My parents have been to China and they enjoyed it very much. They came to China for the first time 15 or 20 years ago, so my mother had very different idea about it because of that trip. She said, 'Oh, my poor son is in China!' When she came a few years ago, she could feel that now it is a completely new world, a new country. Now she wants to come and stay with us here. Before, she really had misconceptions about China—it was all rice fields, and so on. Similar to Americans who still think that all Mexicans wear big hats."

Many of our long-time China hands now consider China as their home, especially those with Chinese spouses. A typical example is Israeli entrepreneur Aviel Zilber: "I have a big family in Israel and I do business in Israel, but my central life now is in China. I bought an apartment and I have a wife here and a dog. I enjoy life here very much. There are moments of frustration, but in general, it's very good."

> *It's addictive to constantly stay in a different culture. Something surprising happens all the time, and that makes life interesting."*
>
> **Eric Rongley** (USA), Founder and CEO, Bleum

Korean Chun In Kyu also has crafted a good life for himself and his family. "Living in China is very convenient. I'm very

China as Experienced by the Spouse and Children

One potentially serious challenge for foreign entrepreneurs bringing a foreign spouse or partner to China is how well she or he will adapt. Oftentimes, it is harder for a "trailing" partner or for children to find their way in China's challenging environment.

Some businesspeople choose to leave their spouses and families in their home country. Italian consultant Ruggero Jenna explains why he and his wife opted for this arrangement. "It's a bit odd, but my wife and two children are in Milan. I spend one week a month in Italy. My wife and children come here for school holidays. We try to maximize the time we spend together." Why not move the family to China? "We have discussed moving the family here, but my wife is reluctant. We haven't made the final decision yet. She has the perception that it is difficult to live here. I personally enjoy the Italian community here, which is big enough. I think it can be enjoyable."

It took Shah Firoozi three years to convince his wife to move full-time to China, rather than raising their four children partly in China and partly in their home in Michigan. But since she made the move, she and the children have been happy in China, he says. "We love to live here and we know a lot of families that live here." The children did struggle to fit into their new school and new community at first, he says. "At the beginning, it was very difficult for the children. They had no friends here; it was difficult for them to make friends quickly and they didn't know Chinese. But by the third year, half of my children's friends were in China and they were becoming very comfortable with their Chinese language."

It can be more difficult for "trailing" spouses to adapt, than for the children. Our interviewees offered the following advice: encourage the spouse to find an occupation—either paid or volunteer—or a line of study.

Korean investment advisor Chun In Kyu's family is a good example of full integration. His children attend an international school and his wife, also Korean, is using her time in China to study medicine, with the aim of becoming a doctor. While Chun's wife enjoys the advantage of speaking Chinese (thus allowing her to study with a Chinese medical school), spouses can also find study programs where Chinese isn't required—

satisfied. My family is here with me: my wife, two sons and my mother—five family members. We are all happy here."

from weekend classes in Chinese language or painting, to full business degree programs taught in English or other international languages.

Consultant Steven Ganster explains that his wife, who counsels troubled children, returned to her native US recently when the couple bought a home in Chicago. She is finding America more restrictive than China in terms of her career, Ganster says. "When my wife was here full-time, she counseled a Taiwanese family who had very traditional parents with a girl in an American school. She found her work exciting and challenging. Meanwhile in the suburbs in the U.S., she is blocked doing the same stuff. We loved it in Shanghai. She and I want to come back here full-time."

Spanish consultant Josep Giro strongly recommends that businesses that are considering bringing an expat to China spend time and effort making sure the spouse and family can adapt well. "If you bring somebody to China, it will be very expensive. If a person comes here, the commitment should be at least for five years; otherwise, it's not fruitful." Given the high level of commitment required, he stresses that the spouse must adapt well to China or the assignment will fail. "You must interview the spouse. You need to know what kind of person she or he is. You need to evaluate if this person will have a good life here." He stresses that providing "hardware," such as a nice home and a health club membership, isn't enough to ensure that families are happy in China. "Software," such as social life and a sense of purpose, are also critical to the happiness of the trailing spouse. As Giro puts it, "If you offer the [Spanish] wife a nice house but she doesn't speak English, how can she communicate with other expats? If there are no Spanish-speaking people around, how can she find out where to buy things, what to do?" Giro adds that spouses who don't learn English or Chinese often suffer from isolation, as their children and the working spouse will be using English or Chinese all day. "A Spanish wife will suffer because her children will go to a school where they will speak English or Chinese, and when they come home, they will speak English or Chinese. It can be very hard for the wife." The solution, he says, is to urge the trailing spouse to use the time in China well—to study Chinese or even English, or to find volunteer work or a part-time or full-time job. Those spouses who treat their relocation to China as an adventure and an opportunity tend to do well.

Single Life

A thriving nightlife and active dating scene in China are alluring facts of life for single foreigners—especially men. Even married expatriate men, warns import/export company founder Oto Petroski, tend to attract attention from the opposite sex, whether they intend to or not. "If you are single, male and work in a highly paid job, China is like a paradise. You cannot walk 100 meters here without some girl smiling at you, and telling you how handsome you are. If you enjoy such things, you will have a great time. But living here with a family is something else."

Single foreign women generally report a less thriving social life, since there seems to be a larger cultural divide between Chinese men and foreign women than there is between Chinese women and foreign men. However, the number of cases of expat women forming relationships with Chinese men or foreign partners in China is increasing.

The **TIP** **adaptation of the spouse and kids can be a critical success factor for a foreign entrepreneur in China.**

Conclusion

The main challenges foreign entrepreneurs face in creating an enjoyable life in China outside of work are the language barrier and the cultural distance from home. There may also be frustrations arising from China's crowded living conditions, pollution, the difficulty of accessing nature, the clogged roadways and long commuting times, the lack of a sense of belonging and community, and the high cost of expat living. Despite these hardships, in most cases, foreign entrepreneurs find their rewards in the dynamic business environment in China. For the same reason, it may be more difficult for a trailing spouse and children to adapt to China. Success for a non-working spouse depends on finding a sense of purpose and a social life in China. A good solution can be for the spouse to use her or his time in China to study, to explore China, or to find work or volunteering opportunities.

For working women, China offers a friendlier environment than is often the case in other countries. The seven women entrepreneurs interviewed for this book described China as an egalitarian business environment, in part because of the effects of the Cultural Revolution. In fact, women are strongly encouraged to work, women bosses are not uncommon, and working mothers have access to full-time domestic support through inexpensive nannies.

SUMMARY OF TIPS
LIVING IN CHINA

CHINESE LANGUAGE

Fluency in Chinese isn't necessary in order to be successful in China. Although it is sometimes awkward, many international businesspeople use competent staff to cover for their linguistic weakness.

Speaking Chinese conveys several advantages: it will show your commitment to China; it will help you to better understand the culture; and it will be very useful when negotiating with domestic partners.

CHINA HARDSHIPS

For many expatriates, China's dynamic business environment compensates for its crowds, pollution, and the lack of access to nature.

Driving in China can be compared to doing business in China: the rules are followed when necessary, but ignored whenever possible.

Foreign businesspeople must work to form true friendships with local Chinese. There are language, social, and cultural divides that many expatriates find difficult to bridge.

WORK–LIFE BALANCE

Try to make your China offices as comfortable as possible. You will probably spend more time there than at home.

Long working hours, and the pressure of making all key decisions oneself, can tax your health. You must disconnect and relax outside of work.

FOREIGN BUSINESSWOMEN IN CHINA

China is a relatively egalitarian society, in terms of gender, as a consequence of its communist past.

Many Chinese working mothers enjoy low-cost, 24/7 domestic help provided by nannies or grandparents.

The adaptation of the spouse and kids can be a critical success factor for foreign entrepreneurs, whose spouse is not Chinese. Spouses can find opportunities for study or work in China.

CHINA HARDSHIPS

For most expat managers, social life revolves around work and the community in which they live. Foreigners who speak Chinese and/or have a Chinese spouse tend to have wider social circles among the Chinese.

FOREIGN BUSINESSWOMEN IN CHINA (*cont'd*)

China's urban centers offer a full spectrum of options for housing and schooling. Foreigners can lead either a very expensive expatriate lifestyle or can "go local" for around one-tenth the cost.

Chapter 9
Are You Ready for China?

Necessary Traits and Expertise

"To do business in China, you have to really want to be here. Otherwise, you will just get tired or frustrated. Even if you want to be here, you'll get tired! On top of the traits you have as an entrepreneur, you have to have a genuine affection for China."

Steven Ganster (USA), Founder and Managing Director, Technomic Asia

Introduction

In warning students of the hardships of entrepreneurship, business school professors around the world like to quote sobering statistics on the challenges of launching a business, such as the "theory of thirds," which holds that among all new business startups in their first year of operation, one-third turn a profit, one-third break even, and one-third fail.

For expatriate business pioneers dreaming of starting a venture in China, the odds are stacked even further against success. Many promising ideas never even make it to the stage of applying for a business license, because so many daunting obstacles—cultural, social, financial, legal, logistical, and bureaucratic—must first be overcome.

Yet, despite all the odds, thousands of international entrepreneurs have started business ventures in China. Each of the 40 such adventurers we interviewed has successfully launched a business in China, and many of these are flourishing. What elements, then, separate those who succeed from those who don't? The key "ingredients" necessary in a foreign entrepreneur in China are the subject of this chapter.

Long-time China consultant Josep Giro summarizes the layers of challenges that foreign entrepreneurs must be ready to face when launching a business in the Middle Kingdom. "[Foreign-owned] companies fail for several reasons. The first reason is that companies adopt the wrong business model. The second reason is internal problems. The third reason is that China isn't an easy country for a business venture. You have all the world's competitors here, and you are operating in a very different culture. It's also a challenge to find the right management. It takes a lot of resources."

In this chapter, our interviewees share the necessary personal characteristics, professional background, and preparation needed to launch a business in China. The chapter covers five main topics:

1. Must-have traits for China entrepreneurs
2. Prerequisite expertise

3. Tools for surviving the tough times
4. Endgames
5. China's future

Must-have Traits for China Entrepreneurs

No matter how brilliant a businessperson is back in his or her home country, there is no guarantee of success in China. The chaotic business atmosphere, the language barrier and cultural differences, the constantly changing regulatory and business environment, the fierce competition, the lack of human resources, and rapid shifts in domestic consumer expectations all combine to create an extremely dynamic, but also extremely challenging, situation.

For all these reasons, whenever consultant Josep Giro meets Westerners who are eager to work in China, he offers them some simple advice: visit China before you decide to relocate. "I tell them, 'Just take a plane and come here. Don't waste your time thinking about it until you have come to China.'" Only after a would-be entrepreneur has visited and gained a sense of whether he or she can live and work in China, does it make sense to consider actually making the move. "Planning to move to China before you have visited the place is a waste of time," Giro says. On the other hand, he believes that those with a truly entrepreneurial spirit will likely catch China fever once they arrive. "If you are really a businessperson, you will be seduced by what you see in China."

Must-have Trait #1: Sense of Adventure

The first quality our interviewees agreed was a necessary ingredient in a successful expat entrepreneur in China is a sense of adventure. Danish furniture entrepreneur Simon Lichtenberg says, "There are multiple business opportunities [in China], but it depends on how adventurous you are. The opportunities for new businesses here are so many because there are so many

Surviving in the Middle Kingdom requires a sense of adventure and a genuine affection for China.

things that are not here yet. A seriously good sandwich shop in Nanjing, maybe it's not there yet. Go and open one!"

Consulting startup Steven Ganster agrees: "To do business here, and to live here, you need a sense of adventure, as well as an interest in and genuine affection for China. As an entrepreneur, you can't be too risk averse."

Describing working in China as "a great adventure," Israeli-born business developer Jordan Zilber explains the sense of enthusiasm needed in order to succeed. "Coming to China was extremely exciting from a cultural point of view. Chinese people are very open and warm. If you know the language,

CASE STUDY

TURNING RISK INTO OPPORTUNITY

Taking a risk, both professionally and personally, may sound exciting or even glamorous, but our interviewees share harrowing tales of facing extremely difficult personal decisions during their time in China—sometimes risking their personal safety for the sake of their business. Dutch businessman, and 24-year China veteran, Olaf Litjens describes one of the three times when he and his business partner faced imminent bankruptcy in China: "In the first 10 years, we represented [European] companies who wanted to sell agriculture and food-processing equipment in China. We acted as an agent, so we got a commission for the equipment we sold. In 1988, we did the first big deal—selling equipment to a pharmaceutical factory in Mudan Jiang [in Heilongjiang province]. The funny thing was that we didn't get paid our commission before the Tiananmen Square incident happened [in June 1989]. Afterward, we were the only foreigners who had no money to buy a ticket out of China."

But Litjens says being "stuck" in China without a ticket home later turned out to have been a benefit. "Martin [Litjen's partner] asked me, 'Are you afraid?' We looked at CNN. I said, 'A little uncomfortable.' Martin asked, 'Do you think the Chinese are afraid?' I said, 'They must be afraid, but it's an opportunity.'"

Litjens had an idea for turning the confusion of that time into a business benefit: "I figured that if our Chinese customers were worried about the future of their businesses, and if they had money to spend, they would likely rather buy equipment than hold on to their cash. I told my partner, 'Imagine if you have money and you have things can be perfect. I am traveling a lot in China. I enjoy it. If you are not open-minded, don't come to China."

For Japanese entrepreneur Fumito Suzuki, choosing to start his accounting company in China meant rejecting a stable, financially secure life in his home country. "If I wanted to make money, I would work for large companies in Japan. I chose to work on my own because I like to take risk. These are precious experiences in my life. . . . Actually, few Japanese people will think of starting a business on their own. They are used to serving big companies their whole life."

---

approvals to purchase equipment, but you don't know what will happen. In that case, you would want to spend the money. Let's call these guys.'

"So we called the [Chinese client] on the Monday after Tiananmen and asked, 'Do you want to have lunch?' They said, 'Where are you?' We said, 'China. This is an internal affair, nothing to do with us. We are committed to our business.'"

The strategy of staying in China worked well. "The Chinese really liked the fact that we were still there," says Litjens. "We got a lot of business in the two months after the Tiananmen Square incident, which helped us to survive over the next two years. Otherwise, we could have been in bankruptcy for sure."

Still, the decision was a risky one, Litjens remembers. "During the six weeks before Tiananmen, the atmosphere was like a big party. It was chaos. That night [before the incident], you could feel that something was going to happen. Most people were killed in front of Minzu Hotel, where we stayed. I myself could have been in trouble, but I wasn't.

"We moved to the Shangri-La Hotel because we could watch CNN there. In the end, there were six people in the whole hotel. It was a very uncomfortable feeling. The foreign staff of the hotel were gone, and there were only four other guests."

Looking back now, Litjens is sure that he and his partner made the right decision in terms of his career in China. "The good thing is: every time you are forced to make a change, something better comes out of it. The character for crisis in Chinese is a combination of 'threat' and 'opportunity.' You can be scared in the face of danger, or you can say: 'Let's look for the opportunity and grab it.'"

Must-have Trait #2: Passion and Commitment

"

There are multiple business opportunities [in China], but it depends on how adventurous you are. The opportunities for new businesses here are so many because there are so many things that are not here yet. A seriously good sandwich shop in Nanjing, maybe it's not there yet. Go and open one!"

Simon Lichtenberg
(Denmark), Founder and CEO, Trayton Group

The personal characteristics our interviewees named as the second-most necessary in China are passion and commitment. Italian consultant Ruggero Jenna, who has seen hundreds of foreign businesspeople struggle to succeed in the Middle Kingdom during his four years of working in China, explains: "When you talk about entrepreneurs, 90% of the final result depends on the qualities of the person. I think energy is one necessary quality. Persistence is another one. . . . They should be willing to sacrifice themselves. . . . this is a prerequisite. They must be serious about it."

Import/export entrepreneur Juan Martinez explains the personal commitment he has made in launching his China-based business: "First, you need to be 100% convinced of what you are going to do and be sure you want to do this business in China. You cannot have any doubts. You can't be thinking, 'Maybe I could try to do this, or that.' No, you have to be totally committed."

In his case, Martinez began by studying for his MBA in China (at the China Europe International Business School in Shanghai). "I have been doing this step by step. I have been anchored to China. I got my MBA in China, and I studied the Chinese language. Then I married my wife from China. If you don't have this full commitment, after two or three years, you might say, 'It's too much, I feel tired,'" he says. "I think if you come to China, you have to come to stay. You have to accept that you're going to stay in China for as long as it takes to make your business successful—maybe even never go back to your home country. You need to have real roots in China."

American construction startup Phillip Branham advises Westerners launching a business venture in China as follows: "You need to have passion. You need the expertise in your area, or to be able to get the expertise, but you also really need to have the passion for it. You have to be thrilled about the idea. You can't do it half-heartedly."

Irish internet language site founder Ken Carroll offers similar advice: "What drove us was a passion to do something. I still have the same passion. I see that there is something wrong with the existing business models, and I think I can do it better."

Demonstrating your passion for the business by working hard can be a key method of winning the support of employees, customers, and clients, especially in China, adds U.S. software entrepreneur Eric Rongley. Asked to identify the qualities needed in a successful entrepreneur in China, Rongley responded: "You'd better be bright and hardworking, first of all. Chinese are very competitive. If you are not bright and hardworking, you'll have problems. Your staff needs to respect your intelligence and your vision, and they need to see that you work at least as hard as they do. I think a lot of expats have the going-home-at-5:30 mentality. That will get entrepreneurs in trouble here."

A 24/7 work mentality is familiar to entrepreneur Marc van der Chijs, who co-founded the video downloading site Tudou (similar to YouTube). He explains his work ethic in China this way: "Never give up. You can succeed in China if you continue. Eventually, you'll be successful and you'll see the light." He warns new China-based entrepreneurs to expect to work harder than they did back home. "It'll be much tougher. You have to work harder, because Chinese people work hard. Before I came to China, it would be very unusual to get a phone call from somebody at midnight. Now I keep my cell phone on all the time and I'm available 24 hours a day. I also check my emails anywhere and at any time. It's very different from the situation in Europe. In Europe, people rest on weekends. To me, now, work goes on. Persistence is really important."

Wendy Tai, a manufacturer of high-end interior decorations, moved to eastern China from her native Taiwan in 1989. After two decades in China, Tai agrees that succeeding there requires a full personal commitment. She warns that some of her Taiwanese peers wrongly consider China to be an easy win. Instead, she recommends putting your best effort into China business ventures. Her specific advice to newcomers to China: "First, do only what is legal; never do things that are against the law. Second, you have to start your business on your own. Don't just put your money in it, or attract others to help and then walk away. Third,

You'd better be bright and hardworking, first of all. The Chinese are very competitive. Your staff need to respect your intelligence and your vision, and they need to see that you work at least as hard as they do."

Eric Rongley (USA), Founder and CEO, Bleum

 Making a business fly in China requires passion for the venture and a serious commitment to China. Be ready to work 24/7.

you have to be confident and have a clear mindset. Many Taiwanese think they can easily make money in the mainland—which is totally wrong. Instead, they have to perform at their best to make it here."

TAKING THE PLUNGE

At the age of 29, after three years of working in China for a multinational, Dutch internet businessman Marc van der Chijs decided to start his own company. His motivation is fairly typical of our interviewees, based largely on a belief that he could do things better than the current market practices. Van der Chijs explains: "During 1999 to 2002, I was a financial controller in charge of South Korea, Hong Kong, and Macau. In 2002, there was a turning point. I had to make the decision whether to renew my contract—doing the same thing for another three years—or to go back to the company headquarters in Germany." He did neither. "I saw many opportunities in China. I wanted to take a risk and to become an entrepreneur. I also wanted to prove I could do my own thing. . . . I quit my job without really knowing what was going to happen."

His first venture was a consulting company that focused mainly on helping foreign trading companies to become active in China. Van der Chijs remembers those early days: "I bought a small apartment and a bicycle. Perhaps I was the first foreigner to live in my all-Chinese neighborhood. Whenever I went to a local restaurant, people knew me."

After six months, "business was booming." Van der Chijs spent all of his time either working or studying Mandarin. After a time, his business grew to the point where he had to drop the language classes, which he regrets.

Today, Van der Chijs has launched three successful businesses, including China's biggest video-sharing website, Tudou. His latest venture is focused on online gaming. Despite the early days being "extremely hard," he says he made the right choice in launching his own venture in China. "I love China, and I thought my future was here in China. I'll never regret becoming an entrepreneur. It's true that I am busier than before. Now I work 24 hours a day, and there are a lot more risks and stresses than with my previous job, but it's worthwhile in order to run my own business."

Must-have Trait #3: Persistence and a Thick Skin

Our seasoned China entrepreneurs were unanimous in warning: be prepared to fail. Nearly all of our interviewees had met with serious setbacks in China, and several had weathered near or even total bankruptcy. All agreed that perseverance and a thick skin are needed to survive.

Veteran businessman Olaf Litjens explains the attitude he has adopted after 28 years and a series of business adventures in China. "All the things you do, teach you something and are important in coming to the next step—so if you make the wrong judgment, that's part of the learning process. I don't regret the decisions I have made. They were all part of the process of becoming a more knowledgeable person and building a better company."

Building materials supplier Onder Oztunali describes the thick skin he has developed, especially in working with Chinese customers. "Take nothing personally; it's only about money! Chinese customers will hammer you all the time. But as long as you know that, you'll be prepared for it."

Real estate businessman Bruce Robertson warns China start-ups to be patient and expect setbacks. "Don't be down on yourself, or on the Chinese, when you meet an obstacle that is causing you problems. Recognize that the system isn't going to function [in China] as it does where you come from. You've just got to be really creative and innovative." To avoid total frustration, he recommends spending time working and studying in China before launching your business. "Expect to spend one or two years before you've worked through these Chinese riddles. If you find success after two years, that's quick. It depends on how fast your trigger is."

After five years in China, Canadian Chinese flooring supplier Chee-Chin Wu gives this advice on surviving tough times: "Try to be both persistent and consistent. Don't keep changing directions. Determination does talk. In fact, many entrepreneurs have tasted failure many times before they reached success. It's

> *Expect to spend one or two years before you've worked through these Chinese riddles. If you find success after two years, that's quick. It depends on how fast your trigger is."*
>
> **Bruce Robertson**
> (USA), President, Asia Pacific Real Estate

TIP You need determination and a thick skin to survive the first years. Don't give up when you encounter the initial obstacles.

partially wrong to say they're lucky. Actually, opportunity flies up in the air and whoever catches it is the winner." In particular, she advises targeting only those opportunities you feel sure will bring a worthwhile reward. Finally, she stresses the importance of winning the government over to supporting your project. "In China, the government can also offer you good support with the whole infrastructure."

CASE STUDY

ROCKY BEGINNINGS

Taiwanese interior decoration manufacturer Wendy Tai shared her story of risking her family business by moving it to China where, initially, it almost failed. "My family ran a business in silk flower manufacturing for 10 years in Taiwan. But in the 1980s, there was a big change in the exchange rate between the New Taiwan Dollar and the U.S. dollar—it went from 40:1 to 22:1. We mainly exported to the U.S., so we couldn't stay in Taiwan anymore. We couldn't afford to pay our employees." The family closed the company operations and moved to Xiamen, in China, in 1989.

"We signed the contract on June 1, 1989, just before the Tiananmen Square demonstration on June 4. It was quite risky to make such a decision at that time; we didn't know whether China would collapse or not. That was one of the most difficult decisions I've ever made. At that time, we were the only people staying in our hotel [in Xiamen]. The entire hotel staff was serving just two of us."

Tai persevered and launched the business. "We started a whole new business in Xiamen. We hired new people. I needed to teach the workers from scratch about how to make artificial flowers and petals. I worked almost 24 hours a day, seven days a week during that period." Her efforts soon paid off. "Although I was exhausted, we made a lot of money from the flower-making business. It was partially because of the exchange rate—the Renminbi to the U.S. dollar was 10:1—and also because the salaries of the workers in mainland China were one-tenth those in Taiwan." Twenty years later, the family has benefited greatly from its move to China, despite the rough start. Says Tai: "We've grown a lot and our business has boomed."

Prerequisite Expertise

No newcomer succeeds in China without learning the ropes and adapting to the local environment. Consultant Josep Giro tells his clients to expect a steep learning curve at first. "When

CASH-FLOW TROUBLES

Food service distribution entrepreneur Mark Secchia tells of the hard times he endured when cash-flow problems struck his young company. He describes the low point in his business as "the time when I gained about 40 pounds and started losing my hair"—a period soon after launching when he counted on money coming in faster than was possible. "We thought we would be profitable in six months, but it took us 18 months. I ran out of money. I couldn't pay my staff, couldn't pay the bills. I couldn't sleep at night. That's when I gained weight, from 170 pounds to 210. I still haven't lost it yet. It was the most miserable time in my life. It was all about staff. If I couldn't pay them and they were going to quit, we would be finished."

For several weeks, prospects looked very dim for the company. "I had about 20 employees at that time. Not only would I lose my staff, but also it's a personal failure. A lot of restaurant partners were personal contacts from my previous job. I also owed friends and family US$15,000. And [it would have been a failure] for my résumé, for my life. . . . Because of all those things together, it was very difficult."

How did he survive? Secchia first tried some creative goodwill building among his staff. "When we knew we were running out of money, we tried this: we paid everyone early one month. We knew that we had enough money that month, but that we may not have it the next month. So, in the 18th month of the company's existence, when we were going to run out of money, we gave everyone their salary 15 days early. That way, the next month when we paid them 15 days late, it wouldn't seem like such a big thing. We did that and it was really close. I looked at my watch every day, waiting to see how much money came in the door. It got really, really close. Fortunately, we made it through."

The big lesson: be conservative regarding cash flow. Says Secchia, "When you look at any business plan, if the owners say they are going to be profitable in two years, double that time. I had a lot of people come to me with small business plans; none of them were ever profitable as quickly as they thought they would be."

"

First, you have to have some kind of experience in your industry. Then you need a relationship with the first client, which really reduces the risk and the ramp-up time. Third, even if you have a good initial business idea, you need real experience in China. Get some real experience — even if you have to work for pennies to get it."

Jeffrey Bernstein
(USA), Founder and
Managing Director,
Emerge Logistics
Shanghai

you come to China and do the wrong things, you cannot blame China. You need to learn from your mistakes. China will help you to improve yourself as a human being and as a company." The two areas of knowledge needed before anyone should plan to launch a business in China are, not surprisingly:

- Industry expertise
- China-specific expertise

Industry Expertise

Our entrepreneurs agreed that success in launching a venture in China depends first upon gaining a clear area of business expertise. American logistics entrepreneur Jeffrey Bernstein offers this advice: "First, you have to have some kind of experience in your industry. Then you need a relationship with the first client, which really reduces the risk and the ramp-up time. Third, even if you have a good initial business idea, you need real experience in China. Get some real experience—even if you have to work for pennies to get it."

Moroccan gift item supplier Aziz Mrabet warns fellow entrepreneurs that the opportunities in China have narrowed. Today, success is much easier for those coming to China with sought-after skills or expertise in the current government-promoted value-added fields. "Six or seven years ago, there were so many opportunities here in China. However, now the situation is changing and trading is becoming tougher as more Chinese are getting into it." Today, he says, the opportunities for foreigners are declining. "If you come to China without any expertise or any network, it's going to be very tough. The situation will be better if you are a doctor or engineer, or have acquired some other valuable or unique skills."

China-specific Expertise

Consultants Jan Borgonjon and Steven Ganster warn that expertise back home is only the first step in adapting a business to China. "Even now, people still come to China thinking they can use their entrepreneurial instincts that worked so well in Belgium or Germany and do the same thing in China," Borgonjon says. "Well, it's not going to work, because the rules are different." Borgonjon adds that learning what rules make a business successful in China is easier now than in years past. "The rules are quite well known." He stresses that newcomers can now seek information on their industries from consultants, banks, embassies, lawyers, accountants, and other companies. "The rules of the game are very different in China, but anybody who really wants to know can find out."

> **TIP** The number of business opportunities for foreign entrepreneurs is shrinking as competition from Chinese entrepreneurs grows.

Of course, one of the most critical types of China-specific expertise is mastering the Mandarin language. (The importance of learning Chinese, as well as tips for surviving in business without Mandarin fluency, were covered in detail in Chapter 8.)

In terms of learning to understand Chinese business culture, our interviewees warn newcomers or first-time entrepreneurs to plan to invest time and effort in getting up to speed. "You must do your due diligence and understand exactly what it's going to take to succeed," says construction entrepreneur Phillip Branham. He points out that, even after having worked for MNCs in China, he still deliberated before launching his own business in 2005. "I've been in the [construction] industry for a long time, but I still took several months to think before setting up my own business in China. I spent a lot of money investigating it, and I still changed my business plan several times."

> **TIP** Prepare to see a different China every year, as the economy expands and society adapts.

Many of our interviewees advised committing to a period of living in China and learning the ropes, before venturing into a business. Leadership training entrepreneur Marjorie Woo put it this way: "Come to China and do your research. Get involved in the international chambers, and read up [on China]. More importantly, come to China with an open mind. Whatever notions you have about China, leave your assumptions at home. Even after you get here, you can expect to see a different country every year."

Plan to spend several years simply learning to adapt, advises internet businessman Marc van der Chijs. "If you really want to do business in China, live here for a few years first. During that time, you can develop your *guanxi* [business/social network].

TIP **Talk to other entrepreneurs with experience in China. Learn from their mistakes and achievements.**

You also need a year to understand China and to gauge whether or not your plan is feasible here. If you don't want to do the experiment, you're doomed to fail."

Another point raised by our veteran entrepreneurs is that work experience gained elsewhere in Asia cannot be a substitute for working in China. Macedonian trader Oto Petroski explains, based on his personal experience: "For my first six months here, I wasn't working, I was mostly scanning the situation. No matter that I had lots of experience with Taiwanese and Singaporeans. This was China, and it was very different from Taiwan and Singapore."

Similar advice was offered by Scottish entrepreneur Jonathan Di Rollo: "Take your time building networks and getting prepared, and keep looking for when the time is right. Don't make your move too soon. For me, it has taken six years." He began in China as a student, then worked for two companies before laying the foundations for his publishing company. "You need at least five or six years to gain a deep understanding of China—its culture, the language."

Investment advisor Chun In Kyu also warns his fellow Korean clients to expect a learning period when they first arrive in China. "It's not possible for foreign companies to succeed immediately as soon as they come to China. They have to go through a hard period of two or three years, and they have to pay their dues. It's not good if they expect to succeed as soon as they come to China. They have to learn for some time first."

A final word of advice voiced by our interviewees is that, no matter how much effort a foreign businessperson puts into learning about Chinese culture, the work is never finished. Despite having launched a highly successful furniture business, 15-year China veteran Simon Lichtenberg explains his humble attitude toward understanding China: "I have two pieces of advice for entrepreneurs. One is: Listen. Listen to your employees, listen to the customer, listen to the supplier, listen to the Chinese and try to understand what they are really saying, what they really want, or what they are really doing. *Listen.* My second bit of advice is: Remember that China is very, very big. Don't think that you know China because you know Shanghai or

Beijing. China is way beyond that, and there are so many opportunities and differences. Don't look at China from wherever you sit in China. It's much bigger than that."

Tools for Surviving the Tough Times

Since all China entrepreneurs face critical points in the course of launching their businesses, we asked our interviewees what had pulled them through the worst of times. They identified the following four survival tools:

1. Find the right people
2. Have focus and vision
3. Be adaptable
4. Control your costs

Survival Tool #1: Find the Right People

The single most repeated survival strategy heard from our 40 China entrepreneurs was: find the right people to work with, especially local employees or trusted partners.

Finding local experts you can trust and rely upon is a necessary short cut if you wish to understand the Chinese and survive in business in China, said many of our interviewees. Business development entrepreneur Jordan Zilber explains the frustration that many foreign businesspeople feel at their relative lack of understanding of China, even after many years spent trying to get to know the country and its people. "I have already been six years in Shanghai, but I still know so little. The path to understanding is so long. The best way to do business in China is to find a Chinese partner in every field of industry you want to explore. I share my revenue with them, but it saves me a lot of mistakes. The partner has connections, experience, and knowledge—all very important."

Zilber gives an example of how local partners can help. "You have to be open to discovering why things are different here, and how to adjust to the Chinese ways. For example, some [foreigners] will say that the Chinese are not polite. But that's not the case; they just have a different type of politeness than we do and you have to learn to understand it."

Spending time and energy on building up local relationships has been critical to the success of Irish entrepreneur Ken Carroll. "You really need to understand a lot about China and be very lucky to connect with local people who really understand you. You need to have great connections and great relationships."

Consultant Jan Borgonjon emphasizes to his clients the importance of hiring the best possible local Chinese employees, and practices what he preaches in his own business. "Choosing the right people is very difficult for foreigners who have been here for only a few years. It took me more than 10 years to be able to assess people more-or-less correctly. Now I feel comfortable. If I choose somebody, in most cases I know what to expect. I also know who else's judgment I can trust."

Working with the right foreign partner can also be a huge help in times of crisis. A case in point is entrepreneur Olaf Litjens, who says he has survived more than 20 years spent in China—and several near failures of his businesses—mainly because he has the right business partner, a fellow expat from The Netherlands. "I started in China with my classmate and we are still in business and we are still friends, which is exceptional. Three times, we lost all the money we had and we are still friends. I think it has to do with an attitude. We believe it is useful to share when you are successful and also when you are not successful. Then you are not alone."

Internet entrepreneur Marc van der Chijs says it is important to develop an instinct about people, though he concedes that this is a skill that takes time and experience. "It doesn't always work. Normally for me, though, I can tell after two minutes whether I can work with this person or not. Since I've worked with so many different Chinese people for quite a long time, I'm able to recognize their characters."

Survival Tool #2: Have Focus and Vision

Another critical survival tool that our interviewees said helped them get through the bad times is a clear direction and strategy. Many of our entrepreneurs warned about the danger of being overwhelmed by the scope and size of China as a business environment. "You have to have a very clear vision, but that's more easily said than done," says consultant Jan Borgonjon. "There seem to be a lot of opportunities; but then, amid all those opportunities, you have to find one clear vision and stick to it. Then, of course, you have to be patient and persevere."

China veteran Olaf Litjens agrees: "The most important thing is that you are focused. This country is too big, and there are too many opportunities, or what look like opportunities. If you want to do everything, you will achieve nothing. Try to do one thing." He advises fellow entrepreneurs to "keep it simple" and to remember, "You aren't Chinese, and never *will* be Chinese" (so, rely on local experts when needed). Finally, he says, "Don't give up. If you have an idea and you stick to it, anything can be done here."

Fashion retailer Valerie Touya says there are two big mistakes that foreign businesspeople make in China. "The first mistake is total lack of preparation. For instance, a European meets a Chinese guy with connections in some Chinese city and starts sending him information about starting a business—something the European would never do anywhere else. Typical mistake! You don't invest based on the "opportunity of the moment"; you invest on the basis of a clear idea of what this market is, the challenges it will present, and the resources you will require." Too often, Touya says, foreign businesspeople take big risks because they rush into a China business deal thinking they are grabbing a limited time opportunity.

The second common mistake, Touya says, is not collecting enough information on your business venture. The good news is that there is no reason these days to suffer from this mistake, she says. "There are no more secrets about China. How many foreign companies are in China? A few hundred thousand or more? There's enough experience accumulated here now, and

TIP A critical skill is to attract the right Chinese employees to your business, a skill developed only after years of experience in China. Or hire a China-savvy HR director who can handle hiring.

Don't invest in China based on the "opportunity of the moment"; invest based on a clear business plan, and an understanding of the challenges.

TIP

there is no need to repeat the mistakes of others. You can learn a lot from the information out there, so learn it. Invest the time and understand the market. If you're not willing to commit the resources, stay where you are."

Survival Tool #3: Be Adaptable

While arguing that focus is important, our interviewees warned against becoming rigid, as the China business environment is in constant flux. Business development and investment strategist Aviel Zilber explains the need for both vision and a humble, open-minded attitude: "As an entrepreneur, you have to have vision and the ability to learn and to struggle. You also need to be humble; to know that you don't know everything."

Don't skip the due diligence you would conduct back home.

TIP

British psychotherapist and arts entrepreneur Mark Pummell explains the need for both skills in this way: "Entrepreneurs are a different type of animal, a different kind of person, from company men. In my opinion, you must be very hardworking and very driven. You must have a bit of vision, but you also cannot become obsessed with the small details." He explains how he uses this attitude in running his businesses: "My job, as the boss of the company, is not to get obsessed and is not to get stuck, but to adapt to changes and move quickly. I need to evaluate the business and do whatever we need to do to keep the whole animal running. . . . You have to make lots and lots and lots of decisions, thousands of micro decisions every day. For me, it's like the TV series *Prison Break*. It's like a maze; it's very complicated and you must find the way."

Tracking China's volatile business environment is crucial to success, says Taiwanese serviced office supplier Maggie Yu. "Laws and regulations are changing all the time, as a result of China's rapid economic growth. This means that systems and government policies are constantly being reformed. Due to inexperience and the complexity of some issues, it's understandable that the government adopts some temporary measures and makes adjustments to others from time to time. In some cases, there are discrepancies in their interpretation and implementation by different levels of government, which adds to the confusion. Therefore, it's vital that companies have ongoing communication with the relevant government authorities in order to stay up to date with all the regulatory changes."

> **Be humble.**
> TIP **Be aware that you don't know everything about the business situation in China.**

Survival Tool #4: Control Your Costs

Finally, many of our interviewees said that weathering the bad times requires controlling costs and focusing on profitability. "What drives your business is having a little bit of a shortage of resources. By having a shortage, you keep yourself resourceful

CASE STUDY

SUDDEN REGULATORY CHANGES

Frustration due to sudden changes in China's operating environment was a commonly experienced hardship among our 40 entrepreneurs. Real estate entrepreneur Bruce Robertson warns of a typical problem: "You really have to be good at dealing with unexpected government regulation that comes down." The most difficult situation his China-based company faced occurred after he took out a loan in order to purchase 75 apartments to be rented to teachers at an international school in Shanghai. "We took the contract [for the apartments] to the Bank of China, and said: 'Give us a 10-year loan. We'll pay it off every month using our payment from the school.' It was a normal deal. But then in the middle of construction of the apartments, the government decided that Chinese banks could no longer lend to developers for more than one year." Even though Robertson's loan had been signed several years before (the company was half-way through the life of the loan), the bank suddenly froze the loan.

Robertson describes his panic at the time. "If you are an entrepreneur, you're not a big global real estate company; what are you going to do? How are you going to keep your contractor from just walking off the job?" In the end, after much scrambling, he came up with a creative solution: get the bank to give the loan to the school that employed the teachers. But that result came about only after four months of struggle.

‟

*If you don't make money in year one, you're **never** going to make money in China. It is very, very important that you don't get carried away by the **China** thing. The **money** has to be there."*

Jan Borgonjon
(Belgium), President,
InterChina Consulting

and innovative. It keeps you focused and efficient," says field-marketing entrepreneur Olaf Litjens.

Based on his 15 years of helping foreign businesspeople to operate in China, consultant Jan Borgonjon advises clients to set a goal of short-term profit, since a long lead time before turning a profit is risky in China: "As an entrepreneur, you must have a very clear long-term vision, but you also have to make sure that in the short term you make money. If you don't make money in year one or year two, you're *never* going to make money in China. It is very, very important that you don't get carried away by the *China* dream. The *money* has to be there."

Endgames

One aspect of success as an entrepreneur anywhere—and especially in China—is to have a clear idea of the end goal for your venture. The adage that "you can't get to where you want to be unless you know where you want to be" is especially true in the vast and complex China market. As American startup Mark Secchia puts it: "An entrepreneur must always have an exit strategy somewhere in the back of his mind. It's not that you want to leave, or to quit your business. You have to think about the end, when you start something; otherwise, you're going to end up in a bad place."

Our 40 interviewees had specific end goals for their companies in China. These ran the gamut from growing the business in China, to expanding internationally, to selling the business and returning home.

Business Goal #1: Conquer China

Most of our interviewees focused their business goals simply on growing the business within China. Steven Ganster is typical in his plans to keep his consulting company and entrepreneurial projects China-focused: "I personally don't have any desire to conquer another world. China is big enough for me to go forward. That's our business; we're not going anywhere else."

South African consultant Kobus van der Wath also intends to focus on growing his China business into the foreseeable future. "I will stay in China for many years. I have no plan to retire; I have a mission and agenda to deliver. My engagement to China is a long-term one. I plan to venture again into new businesses; I see opportunities in many areas. This is a vast country with an 11% economic growth rate every year. This dynamism is a huge opportunity for business. I never regretted coming here, but only that I didn't do it earlier."

Business Goal #2: IPO, or Build and Sell?

American businessman Mark Secchia's end goal for his delivery service company in China is an IPO. "Our ultimate goal would be going public. We have to be present in 10 to 15 cities and get to 200 or 300 employees, and earning revenue of RMB15 million [US$2.14 million] per month—something like that. We can go public and increase the management team, their salaries. . . . That will be our long-term future goal."

Others plan to build up their company, and then sell it. Software entrepreneur Eric Rongley explains his professional and personal goals with Bleum: "I expect to be here [in China] for five to 10 years. The goal is to build Bleum into a billion-dollars-per-year company." The plan may or may not involve an IPO, he says. "The goal is to build a billion-dollar company so that I can move to the [U.S. West] Coast and hang out for the rest of my life. I suspect that once I get married and have kids, at least by the time they enter high school, I'll want to go back to the States."

Internet startup Ken Carroll is now attracting purchasing offers from potential buyers in the U.S. and Europe. "We have a lot of options. I like to stay lean and hungry; mean and lean. But at some point, we will make a decision whether we are going to stay here. It's great, it's fun; and we'll see what happens."

Create an exit strategy, whether you want to remain in China or to sell out and return home.

Susan Heffernan is another whose mid-term goal is to make her company sellable. "People want to buy small companies like mine. I have the expertise; I can do things much faster than they can, and I have the team already supporting it. I had [buyers] talk to me in the past, but I didn't have the legal status then, so I wasn't able to sell the company. Now I do."

Another type of exit plan is to keep the business, but turn operations over to a new top executive. After six years of running her business in China, Marjorie Woo is already planning to license her leadership training business to a successor. "I have a succession plan in process," she says, explaining that her potential successor is a Chinese PhD who was one of her clients. He is now joining the company with the goal of learning the business in order to take it over.

Italian consultant Ruggero Jenna has a similar exit plan: "My goal is that the company here grows, and is able to sustain itself without me. So, I have to create the necessary Chinese leadership that can take care of the business and run it independently. The office has to be able to work without me. That's my major goal. We will see."

China's Future

No matter how well your business is executed in China, if the domestic economy fails or if political turmoil erupts, your China-based venture may be at risk. With this danger in mind, we asked our interviewees—both entrepreneurs and representatives of major international business associations (see the Appendix to the book)—this question: Will China remain a viable environment for launching a business? Their responses ranged across the spectrum, from pessimism to optimism.

Voices of Caution

Among those investors who were cautious in their predictions was Macedonian importer Oto Petroski. Pointing to China's weak spot as a recipient of foreign direct investment, he explains:

"China is losing its advantage because labor isn't so cheap and living is no longer so cheap, in Shanghai especially. My clients are already remarking that China is not as attractive as before." For his China-based trading business, Petroski takes a short-term view. "Nothing is forever. I can't say that I will be in China 10 years from now. Probably I will stay for the next three years. You have to have the attitude that whatever you make in China can just disappear at any time."

Also cautious is Danish furniture entrepreneur Simon Lichtenberg. "China has been very, very focused, high energy, moving for the last 20 years. But the economic model right now isn't sustainable, because it's driven by exports and by investments in fixed assets. Too much money is being spent on infrastructure, which doesn't guarantee a return. Also, if something happens suddenly to the U.S. economy, then China could be hurt very badly. China needs to boost its internal consumer economy." Another factor that impacts on Lichtenberg's business is China's rising labor costs. "China's labor cost is no longer competitive. Bangladesh, India, and Vietnam are much cheaper than China for labor now."

Other interviewees noted potential areas of concern but were generally optimistic about China's future. Among these were Israeli businessman Aviel Zilber, who observes several economic and social difficulties from his vantage point in Shanghai. "The main challenge China is facing is the inequality; the gap between the poor and the rich." One factor operating in China's favor, Zilber believes, is that the Chinese government is aware of the rising threats to competitiveness. "If they don't solve it, it'll be a big problem. But the Chinese government knows about the problem very well; government leaders have been talking for two years about social harmony. They know they should direct a lot of attention to the underdeveloped parts of China," says Zilber. He points out that the Chinese government can be very efficient and effective: "Not being a democratic regime has its advantages, because you don't always have to think about the next elections. China's leaders are planning for the long term." Overall, Zilber is "more positive than negative about the future of China." He explains his thinking: "What is happening in China now has already been happening for 25 years—during a

> " "
>
> *China has been very, very focused, high energy, and moving for the last 20 years. But the economic model right now isn't sustainable, because it's driven by exports and by investments in fixed assets.*
>
> **Simon Lichtenberg**
> (Denmark), Founder and CEO, Trayton Group

"

China will continue to grow during the next 10 to 15 years. As for the dark clouds, so far I see challenges, such as limited resources and pollution, but I don't see any really critical issues arising."

Marjorie Woo (USA),
Founder and Chairwoman,
Leadership Management International (China)

whole generation. It's a challenge to manage a country with 1.3 billion people, but I think they are doing a good job."

A similar cautiously optimistic view is expressed by Dutch internet entrepreneur Marc van der Chijs: "On one hand, I think that China will continue to grow. On the other hand, they have to take drastic measures to control pollution." He also commends the Chinese government on its ability to act efficiently. "The good thing for China is that the government can make decisions quickly. For example, if the government wants to say that nobody can drive a car from tomorrow, they'll do it! In China, the government is able to interfere if necessary. Furthermore, efficiency here is higher than in Europe. I don't see political risks here in China. In general, Chinese people are happy about the government."

American leadership consultant Marjorie Woo is also conservatively bullish about the future of China. "China will continue to grow during the next 10 to 15 years," "As to the dark clouds, so far, I see challenges, such as limited resources and pollution, but I don't see any really critical issues arising."

Confidence in the Top Leadership

Among the more unreservedly optimistic entrepreneurs we interviewed, one key reason for their confidence in China's future as an investment destination was their belief in the top levels of the central government—a sentiment that surprised us authors. The thinking of Brazilian trading company owner Winston Ling is typical: "I'm optimistic about China. In general, the Chinese government is doing more right things than other governments in all the other countries. You go to other countries to see what the government is doing. The Chinese government is doing well by comparison."

South African consultant Kobus van der Wath agrees. "China is on an unstoppable trajectory. Unless we face some tragic events, China will continue its rapid development." Van der Wath advises recognizing the potential threats to stability, but not being unduly concerned. "China will encounter a crisis at some point," he says, but he believes the bad times won't be devastating. "We are unlikely to have social unrest, pension fund problems, state bank collapses, environmental meltdown, political deadlock or crisis, and currency instability—all at once."

Van der Wath points to the outbreak of the SARS epidemic in China—a health scare that came and went without any lasting impact. "I have this theory that China keeps rolling onward. An example of this is SARS in 2003. I was wearing a [protective] face-mask like everyone in Beijing. I was also scared and didn't know what would happen. FDI dropped to zero in one month—no new JVs, no new contracts, no foreigners coming, and no people on the streets. I went to the airport in Beijing, there was only me, no one else. It was everyone's view that SARS would kill China. But two months later, it was business as usual."

Boosting Van der Wath's confidence is the fact that, in recent years, China's top leadership have set aggressively pro-business policies. "Chinese policies are very pragmatic," he says. "They have moved from ideology to pragmatism. Deng Xiaoping set a new trend, Jiang Zemin has done the same, and Hu Jintao is doing the same. If you look at the young leaders, a lot of them have a PhD from overseas."

The government's ongoing economic development plans, especially the series of "five-year plans," was another reason for confidence, our interviewees said. Indian academic consultant Prakash Menon explains: "The Chinese leadership puts a lot of emphasis on economic progress. So, I'm very optimistic about China, because China's leaders want to get things done with care, and they don't want to interfere too much with economic progress." Menon does recommend, however, that the government address two key issues: the wealth divide between rich and poor, and the education system. "The Chinese educational system needs a big reform. It shouldn't be just about passing exams; instead, people really need to understand how to compete in today's world."

The past decade has changed the mindset of 25-year China veteran Jan Borgonjon: "I haven't always been that positive

> **"**
> *The Chinese leadership puts a lot of emphasis on economic progress. So, I'm very optimistic about China, because China's leaders want to get things done with care, and they don't want to interfere too much with economic progress."*
>
> **Prakash Menon** (India), President, NIIT (China)

about the future of China. If you had asked me 10 years ago, I would have been more preoccupied. But now, many issues are going in the right direction, and you have a relatively competent government that is moving in the right direction. So, I don't see big, imminent risk factors. We are quite positive about the future."

Changing Opportunities

Several of our interviewees cautioned that the period of the best business opportunities in China may, in some cases, already have passed. One such business pioneer is Taiwanese food and beverage entrepreneur Michael Yang. "Several years ago, I read an article in which the CEO of an international company said, 'Doing business in China is very risky, but if you don't come to China to do business, you will bear more risks.' I agree. Of course, you should come to China to do business. But it's more difficult now than 10 years ago for foreign entrepreneurs to start a business here. The environment is now more mature. Ten years ago, it was better here; but even now, you still have a lot of opportunities." He adds another reason for optimism: "During the short term, contrary to what everybody thinks, I don't think costs will go up. I expect that costs for food will remain basically the same, at least in Euro terms."

Swiss consultant-entrepreneur Nicolas Musy agrees that China's business environment is changing, but says that there are plenty of new opportunities still emerging. "There are always possibilities for unexpected things to happen, but I think China will continue to see high growth levels, as before. This will last for another 20 years, minimum." Musy advises incoming China investors to look to emerging sectors. "The other thing that will happen in the next 10 years is that China will become a technological innovation power. Scientific research will reach global standards, focusing first on applied research. In 10 years, Chinese companies will be capable of innovation research at low costs. That will be the biggest challenge Europe will face."

Bullish on China

Others among our China hands were frankly bullish on China as a business environment. China veteran Olaf Litjens, despite a series of near bankruptcies among several of his China ventures, summarized his outlook for China as follows: "There is no better place for business in the world," he says. He and his partner started their field marketing business around five years ago and were immediately successful. "Can you tell me of another country where, within five years in a new industry, you can work with Gillette, Unilever, Mars, P&G . . . ? If I had started the business in Europe, none of these companies would work with me." If you can start here and if you do it right, there is an incredible opportunity. It is a fascinating country. It's unbelievable, considering the history, to realize how innovative you can be now.

When asked what advice he would give to a fellow Korean national relocating to China, financial investment startup Chun In Kyu says he would "strongly recommend them to start a business in China." The reasons? "First, the Chinese market is very big and is developing very fast. Everybody can tell this. The most important thing is that Korea also went through the developing phase. Thirty years ago, Korea was very poor. Now that China is developing, most Koreans have recent similar experience. People from America, Europe, or Japan have forgotten the developing period in their home countries, so Koreans are really competitive in this regard." He adds that China and Korea "share a lot of cultural similarities", which offers Korean entrepreneurs an advantage.

Many of our interviewees voiced their belief that now is the time to be in China, and urged fellow entrepreneurs to ride the wave while it lasts. Calling China a "great place to start a business," project management entrepreneur Shah Firoozi says the country now offers "lots of opportunities." He adds: "I don't say that everyone will succeed. Many companies fail, and many expat families fail, too. But still, we are predominantly proponents of coming to China." Firoozi explains why he is generally bullish on China. "During the past 10 years, the

> *Can you tell me of another country where, within five years in a new industry, you can work with Gillette, Unilever, Mars, P&G . . . ? If I had started the business in Europe, none of these companies would work with me."*

Olaf Litjens
(Netherlands), Founder and CEO, Unisono Fieldmarketing (Shanghai)

growth and transformation in China has created a unique environment that likely will not be repeated elsewhere in the world."

Spanish consultant Josep Giro expresses his optimistic outlook this way: "I don't plan to leave unless the government throws me out. Living here is exciting. First, the coastal cities were developed; now we are developing the second- and third-tier cities. There are no limitations because China is challenging the world now, and is complementing the world. China is now a very big player—everyone must take China into consideration. This will only increase in the future."

Perhaps the most telling "bullish" statement comes from American real estate executive Bruce Robertson. Asked what he would say to a fellow Western entrepreneur contemplating heading to China, he replied: "I would say that you are going to be part of one of the greatest business revolutions in the history of mankind. So many things beyond your imagination will occur, but you can achieve your goal. I'm very positive about that. You will probably be successful. Do it!"

Conclusion

As one of our entrepreneurs told us: "Don't think twice. Come to China and explore the place for business opportunities." Despite the many challenges that may stand in the way of being successful in China, our interviewees all spoke of their satisfaction in starting something new. The results of their efforts compensated for all the sleepless nights and long working hours, they said. Our entrepreneurs all agreed that, while it wasn't easy to be successful in China, they had no regrets about embarking on the adventure.

This last chapter has distilled the combined 500 years of experience our entrepreneur interviewees have amassed in China. Hopefully, their insights will help you to avoid repeating some of their mistakes and increase your chances of making your China venture a success.

SUMMARY OF TIPS
NECESSARY TRAITS AND EXPERTISE

MUST-HAVE TRAITS

Must-have trait #1: Sense of adventure Surviving in the Middle Kingdom requires a sense of adventure and a genuine affection for China.

Must-have trait #2: Passion and commitment Making a business fly in China requires passion for the venture and a serious commitment to China. Be ready to work 24/7.

Must-have trait #3: Persistence and a thick skin You need determination and a thick skin to survive the first years. Don't give up when you encounter the initial obstacles. Expect difficulties to occur.

PREREQUISITE EXPERTISE

Industry expertise: The number of business opportunities for foreign entrepreneurs is shrinking as competition from Chinese entrepreneurs grows. To succeed, you need to be innovative, and to contribute knowledge and skills still lacking among the domestic players.

Talk to other entrepreneurs with experience in China. Learn from their mistakes and achievements. International work experience is useful, but it cannot directly prepare you for China's unique work environment.

China-specific expertise: Commit to a period of time in China to learn the ropes before launching your venture. Prepare to see a different China every year, as the economy continues to expand and society adapts.

TOOLS FOR SURVIVING THE TOUGH TIMES

Survival tool #1: Find the right people A critical skill is to attract the right Chinese employees to your business, a skill developed only after years of experience in China. Or, hire a China-savvy HR director who can handle hiring.

Survival tool #2: Have focus and vision Don't invest in China based on the "opportunity of the moment"; invest based on a clear business plan, and an understanding of the challenges it will present and the resources it will require. Don't skip the due diligence you would conduct back home.

TOOLS FOR SURVIVING THE TOUGH TIMES (*cont'd*)

Survival tool #3: Be adaptable Be humble. Be aware that you don't know everything about the business situation in China.

Survival tool #4: Control your costs and focus on profit Control your expenses and your cash flow. Try to earn a profit within a year of launching your business in China.

ENDGAME

Create an exit strategy, whether you want to remain in China, or prefer instead to sell out and return home after a certain time.

Epilogue

When we authors started working on *China Entrepreneur*, we were not fully aware of the enormous task we were embarking upon. Although we had collaborated on the book *China CEO* (John Wiley, 2006) — which entailed profiling 20 international top executives successfully heading up multinational companies in China — we did not realize how far our new book would take us. Our original plan was to profile 20 expatriates (non-Chinese) entrepreneurs who had successfully launched a business venture in China.

This simple initial goal lead us on an 18-month journey that took us from Shanghai to Beijing to Chengdu and beyond, during which we interviewed not 25 but 52 China-based entrepreneurs, experts, and country representatives. Through a series of in-depth interviews with these veteran China pioneers (captured on video and viewable at www.china-entpreneur.org), we accumulated a vast wealth of first-hand anecdotes, business war stories, success strategies, and tips and techniques for surviving in the world's highest potential — and therefore highest risk — market.

We listened to their stories and learnt from them, then passed them on to our readers. Some of the stories shared with *China Entrepreneur* are painful, others are funny, but all are authentic and real advice from real people. After 18 months of struggling to boil down these stories into 9 easy-to-read chapters, we feel grateful for the opportunity to have met 52 fascinating China hands, and to share their stories with you. We hope you will find their stories as rewarding and useful as we did.

Our greatest hope for *China Entrepreneur* is that the book helps you readers to realize your "China dream" — whether you already operate a business in China, or are planning one day to do business in or with the Middle Kingdom. In case you are still deciding whether to venture into China, we hope *China*

Entrepreneur will convince you to visit and explore this country for yourself. China today must be seen to be believed.

As any true business veteran in this country will tell you, "In China, nothing is easy but anything is possible." You may not end up exactly where you expected to, but in a market as chaotic, dynamic, vast and exciting as China, taking the journey may be even more valuable than reaching the destination.

In closing, we adapt a few lines from the great poem "Ithaca" by K. Kavafis.

> *As you set out for China*
> *may your road be a long one,*
> *full of adventure, full of discovery . . .*

Thank you.
Juan Antonio Fernandez
Laurie Underwood

Appendix
China and Its Trade Partners

This appendix includes interviews with representatives of nine of China's key trade nations or regions. The people interviewed are members of embassies, chamber officials, associations, and trade institutions. Representatives of the following trade partners (countries in alphabetical order) are interviewed:

- Australia
- Brazil
- European Union
- India
- Japan
- Mexico (and Latin America)
- Nigeria
- South Africa
- United States

The countries or regions included were selected on the basis of their trade relationship with China. In total, these nine represent roughly 60% of China's total global trade. All of the interviewees commented on the importance of China for their countries and stressed their interest in expanding the relationship, not only in the trade sphere but also via ties in education, tourism, and investment.

Country Representatives Interviewed (country by alphabetical order)

Name	Country/ Region	Title and Organization	Website
Wright, Christopher	Australia	Senior Trade Commissioner and Australian Deputy Consul General, Shanghai	www.austrade.gov.au
Primo Portugal, Ricardo	Brazil	Deputy Consul General for Brazil (Shanghai Office)	www.brazil.org.cn
Ceballos Baron, Miguel	European Union	Counselor for Trade & Investment, EU (Beijing Office)	www.delchn.ec.europa.eu
Sharma, Madhav	India	Chief Representative, Confederation of Indian Industry	www.ciionline.org
Takahara, Masaki	Japan	Vice President (China), Japanese Economic Trade Organization	www.jetro.go.jp/china/ shanghai/
Valdez Mingramm, Rafael	Mexico (& Latin America)	Co-founder, Latinoamericanos EnChina.com and VP Latin America, ChinaVest	www.chinavest.com www.latinoamericanosenchina.com
Abikoye, Badeji A.	Nigeria	Trade Commissioner, Nigerian Trade Office in Shanghai	www.nigeriaembassy.cn
Khumalo, Vika M.	South Africa	Consul General, South Africa consulate in Shanghai	NA
Foster, Brenda L.	United States	President, American Chamber of Commerce in Shanghai	www.amcham-shanghai.org

China Trade Partner: Australia

Interviewee: Mr. Christopher Wright, Senior Trade Commissioner, Austrade Country Manager for China, Deputy Consul General in Shanghai

Organization: Australian Consulate in Shanghai

Do you think Australians in general have an accurate picture of China?

I think the picture Australians have of China is constantly changing and improving. Australians in general still perceive China through the images portrayed by the national press. They watch television, and read newspapers and magazines. These translate stories about China for ordinary Australians. On a government-to-government basis, Australia has very substantial representation in China in trade, foreign affairs, science and technology, and education. As for the business community, we recently had 600 company directors from Australia visiting Shanghai (in May 2008). The majority of them had never been to China before. They were astounded by what they saw here in Shanghai.

Is China perceived as a threat or an opportunity in the business community in Australia?

I think Australia is quite fortunate in this area. Our economies are very complementary. Australia has what China needs and, at the same time, China offers what Australia wants, especially cheap manufactured goods. If you look at trade, it's fairly balanced. What that means in terms of the individual companies depends on the different industrial sectors. Australia's service sector wasn't affected as directly by the growth of China as was the manufacturing sector. Some manufacturing companies were aware of these changes and made an early decision to transfer elements of their production to China. Others didn't. Australia is seen by OECD and the World Bank as one of the most flexible economies in the world. That means it is able to handle change efficiently. If you look at the current unemployment level, at around 4–5%, talk of loss of jobs seems misplaced. There have certainly been changes in the makeup of employment across industrial sectors, but to characterize these as a "loss of jobs to China" would be misreading the situation.

What can be done to promote a better understanding between the two countries?

I am personally involved in the answer to that question. My particular role is to facilitate export trade out of Australia into China and two-way investment between Australia and China. In order to do that, we need to communicate what China means to the business community in Australia. I recently returned from two weeks in Australia where I spent most of the time meeting with senior decision-makers in the Australian business community, large accounting firms, and the major banks. We held seminars and roundtable discussions about what is happening in China and what that means to our businesses. I also spent some time with the TV networks and newspapers to get those messages out. So, there is a role for the Australian government in increasing understanding in the business community about what is happening in China. What else can be done? Clearly, organizations such as the Australian Chamber of Commerce, Shanghai have a role to play in these efforts to communicate.

What trends are under way in Australia–China trade?

If you look at the figures for 2007, trade between Australia and China totaled A$49.9 billion, making China Australia's largest trading partner ahead of Japan. Around half of this was Australian exports, and around half of that was in resource-related commodities: iron ore, metals, energy, and gas. The rest is in a wide range of services, agribusiness, and industrial and consumer goods. Agricultural business and food have increased dramatically. Wine, of course, is a rapidly growing export to China. In fact, in 2006, of all the Australian wine sold in the Asian region, China bought 35% (bulk and bottled). In 2007, exports of wine to

China doubled! Of bottled wine coming into China, Australia has the second-largest market-share, after France. I expect this will continue to grow. Other products that are coming out of Australia include manufactured products, and tooling and engineering products. Australian construction firms, architecture firms, and building products firms are well represented in China. Another growing area is services—particularly education. There are 90,000 Chinese students studying in Australia, and that number has been growing steadily over the last decade. Financial services will continue to grow. Australia has a number of banks that are already playing in the Chinese market.

In terms of goods out of China to Australia, this includes textiles and manufactured goods. I understand that Chery [Chinese car manufacturer] expects to export vehicles to Australia probably within two years, at a very low price.

What characterizes the flow of investment from Australia to China? And from China to Australia?

Today, the main investment from Australia into China is in building products and financial services. Agricultural business is another area. Australia has a very small automobile industry, and part of its component supply has moved to China. These investments are going to continue.

On the Chinese side, investment into Australia is fairly new. The areas are primarily in agriculture and resources sectors, with more and more Chinese companies looking at investing in mining. China is going to make a big investment in gas. It has already taken very substantial equity in that field. Chinese banks are also setting up in Australia.

What is the general experience of Australian companies in China?

More Australian companies are coming to China, and more companies are doing business in China. What they tell me is that, on balance, the results are good. Does it mean that it's all fantastic? No, of course not. We all know that you have to work hard. There is a famous case of a foreign brewing company that ran into difficulty. They set up a company in Shanghai in 1990, but eventually had to close down all their business here in the beer sector. Some of the reasons for that can be found on the Chinese side, but they can also be found on the company's side in terms of their understanding of what they could achieve in the Chinese market. Today, the company is taking a different strategy. They are still in China, but their new strategy is to focus on wine.

What advice would you give to an Australian entrepreneur thinking of investing in China?

The first thing I would say is to seek advice early and seek it often. China has a lot of peculiarities that you need to understand. In the tax field, in the legal field, in the banking and financial sector, there are things you need to know. If you want to set up a business, you will have to know what legal structure you need to adopt. Do you go as a joint venture? Or, do you go as a wholly foreign-owned enterprise? What are the tax implications of each? I spend a lot of time providing companies with frameworks with which to approach these sorts of problems, so that when they sit down with their banker, accountant, or lawyer, they are sitting down with a fully prepared sheet of questions. They know the questions that they need to address.

Second, there are always a number of general rules. One rule I use is: Whatever you forecast for sales expectations in China, halve it. Whatever your estimates in terms of cost and time, double them. Make sure you have a Plan B and a Plan C. What happens if the tax rate changes? What happens if your relationship with your partner changes? What is it going to cost you? What does it mean in terms of production, time, and distribution networks? Identify the problems in advance, and think about how you are going to address them.

The third point I always make to people doing business and investing in China is: there is no magic involved. It's business. China has some peculiarities, just as you find when doing business in the U.S., or in Latin America, or in any other market. A transaction has to make sense. This means that you should have good commercial sense, good commercial practice, good operational practice, and good market knowledge. It's about marketing, finance, and operations. These are the three fundamental aspects of doing business. If you get these organized, then you've got the main points of doing business in China.

Which sectors or areas are more promising for future development in China?

This is an interesting question. To some extent, there is no answer to it, as the Chinese economy is racing along. Every sector is growing, which means the opportunities within each sector are enormous. As long as the whole cake is growing, everyone is making a profit out of it.

If you look at the Australian economy, it is also growing quickly. Those areas that are growing very rapidly in Australia are probably the most relevant in China. Natural resources are clearly number one, and that will continue to be a high-growth area because China will continue to demand more and more resources. Services will continue to be a very rapidly growing area, because China is still relatively undeveloped in this sector. Tourism is growing in both directions. Visitor numbers from China to Australia will reach 800,000 by the end of the decade. It was 300,000 for last year [2007]. The Australian Tourist Commission is spending a lot of money in China to develop its network of agents.

One area that is growing is energy. Australia has the biggest reserves of uranium in the world, and there is an agreement between China and Australia to explore this resource. For the foreseeable future, though, China will still rely on fossil fuel energy, particularly coal, of which it has very large reserves. Australia and China are cooperating on the development of technology to reduce emissions in this area.

Relevant websites

www.austrade.gov.au
www.dfat.gov.au

China Trade Partner: Brazil

Interviewee: Mr. Ricardo Primo Portugal, Deputy Consul General
Organization: Brazilian Consulate in Shanghai

Do you think Brazilians in general have an accurate picture of China?

The main problem we have is lack of mutual knowledge. Neither Chinese nor Brazilians have a clear picture of each other. In recent years, Brazil has begun to discover China. Three years ago, the biggest Brazilian TV station came to China and made a TV series called *The Rise of the Dragon*. The program had an enormous audience. People were curious, as well as amazed. They could not imagine that China would have a city like Shanghai. Now, they are seeing more and more images of China after economic reform and opening-up. The interest in the Chinese language in Brazil reflects the rapid change. I first came to the Brazilian Embassy in Beijing in 2003. Before coming, I wanted to learn some Chinese in Brazil. I went to the Chinese Embassy and asked them to recommend a Chinese teacher. I got a schoolgirl, 16 years old, whose father owned a Chinese restaurant. She came to teach me Chinese after finishing her own classes. Several years later when I went back to Brazil, I found people learning Chinese everywhere. Universities have set up Chinese departments. Even big enterprises have Chinese lessons for their employees. The discovery of China in Brazil is recent, but it is happening very quickly. Brazilians suddenly woke up and found that China was their third-largest commercial partner. The U.S. is our first trading partner, Argentina is our second, but China is catching up.

How does the Brazilian business community see China—as an opportunity or as a threat?

As both an opportunity and a threat. For some sectors, China and Brazil are competitors; but in most sectors, we are complementary. As bilateral trade relations improve, more people win than lose. Some sectors, such as toys and clothes, are facing strong competition from China. They are complaining and asking for protection.

Basically, though, there are many more opportunities. Brazilian firms are coming to China to sell. There are also initiatives to start joint ventures. Bigger enterprises also have a strong interest in China. For example, CVRD, the biggest mining company in the world, founded a joint venture with Baosteel in Shanghai. They export iron from Brazil and we import steel from Baosteel. They also have an agreement in the transportation sector, and Baosteel has invested in some plants in Brazil.

What are the main areas of trade between Brazil and China?

Raw materials are doing well. What's more promising is the direct investment from China to Brazil, mainly in infrastructure. Brazil is developing its infrastructure and we have a lot of projects. Infrastructure is the only way to develop Brazil and South America. Chinese companies are participating in infrastructure projects and making direct investments. Another example is Huawei, which is investing in high-value goods. There are also Brazilian auto-parts companies coming to Shanghai, Jiangsu, and Zhejiang.

What challenges or problems do Brazilian companies tend to face when operating in China?

Sometimes, there are problems. Two years ago, we established a Forum for Brazilian Entrepreneurs in cooperation with the Embassy in Beijing. In this forum, Brazilian businesspeople meet regularly and share their experiences. There are some problems, such as unclear rules and regulations in China. Sometimes, local governments apply the same regulations in different ways.

What advice would you give to a Brazilian entrepreneur starting a business in China?

The first advice I would give is to make contact with other Brazilians through the Forum for Brazilian Entrepreneurs.

There are a lot of activities organized by the private sector. Representatives from the Brazilian Embassy and Consul-General attend when there is a meeting or forum in Beijing or Shanghai. We give our support when it's needed.

Next, I would also advise them to be patient. Be careful not to trust anyone who comes up to you and says, "I have a lot of *guanxi*." China offers enormous opportunity in the long term, but in the short term, you may lose money. China is risky and complicated. Don't come blindly; come with some connections.

What are some recent trends in the investment flow between the two countries?

Very recently, Brazil began to discover China. The Chinese government had discovered Brazil long ago. They see Brazil as an important gateway to South America. They invest in Brazil, and then reach other South American countries from there.

The Brazilian government is an old friend of China and we have strong relationships in many areas. As more Chinese firms go global, many of them are making direct investments in Brazil. I once attended a seminar in Guangzhou on the invitation of the local chamber of commerce. There were high-tech companies in Guangzhou that are very interested in going to Brazil. Their strategy was to go to Brazil, and then reach the whole South American market. For Chinese companies, Brazil is seen as a platform.

Relevant websites

www.brazil.org.cn
www.braziltradenet.gov.br
www.portalexportador.gov.br
www.apexbrazil.com.br

China Trade Partner: European Union

Interviewee: Mr. Miguel Ceballos Baron, Counselor for Trade & Investment

Organization: Delegation of the European Commission in China

Generally speaking, do Europeans have an accurate picture of China?

There are approximately 500 million people in the European Union, so it's hard to judge how much they know about China. If we look into the business community, I think there is a very good knowledge and understanding of China. They see China as a market in the midst of expansion and offering lots of opportunities. Many European businesspeople have already been here or have included China in their global expansion plans. Of course, China is very big and complex and Europeans often have a limited picture of the country. I wouldn't say that Europeans have a better of worse picture of China than Americans or other foreigners. Certainly, there is significant interest in China among Europeans. There are some surveys available on the perceptions of China in the U.S. and the EU. One interesting conclusion is that many Americans perceive China as a political and economic threat, while Europeans see China mostly as an economic competitor and a business opportunity.

What is the common experience of European businesspeople in China?

The European Chamber of Commerce in China conducts an annual business survey among its members. The main conclusion of the survey is that China remains a good place to do business for European companies. Among the China-based European businesses surveyed in 2007, 73% of the respondents were optimistic about future growth opportunities; 76% were either making a profit or at least breaking even, while 82% of the unprofitable companies expected to make a profit within three years. The profitability of their investment differs from sector to sector, but varies based also on the company's age. The survey explains that the first year in China is difficult and that 50% of newcomers don't make a profit for the first four or five years. After five years in China, a higher percentage of companies start to make a profit. Of course, there are some companies that have been established in China for some time that are yet to make a profit. They stay because they see China as part of their strategy. They keep their operations going, stay in touch with local partners, and develop business networks as they wait for a better business environment.

European investors in general think that China is a good opportunity. China is also a challenging market, with competition growing not only from Chinese companies but also from foreigners. Despite this intense competition, EU businesspeople still believe the market has big potential. It's a good place to do business, due to the excellent infrastructure, advantages such as the low labor cost and large pool of talented people, and the concentration of industrialized production. The main reasons to be in China are, first, to supply and sell in the Chinese market; and second, as part of a global strategy. Very few EU businesses in China claim that they have set up here in order to re-export to Europe. Very few of them come exclusively for the lower labor cost; the competitive advantages lie in other factors, such as infrastructure, stability, the huge labor force and market size, subsidies, and so on.

What can be done to promote mutual understanding between China and the EU?

Some aspects of China's growth and economic success could be better explained, to present Chinese growth as a success story, and not as a worrying phenomenon. Millions of Chinese citizens are rising out of poverty and improving their living standard. The growth of the Chinese economy is benefiting the rest of the world, because it promotes global growth as well. Of course, the media tend to focus on the problems. In such a big market, some problems do exist, and there are concerns in the EU and U.S. What matters is that the Chinese authorities be vigilant in improving the image of Chinese products abroad, and in making every effort to solve consumer problems when they arise.

Intellectual property rights are a big concern, and affect not only European companies but also Chinese ones. In developed economies such as the EU and the U.S., our business competitiveness depends on sound IPR protection to stimulate innovation. We believe very much in this system, and we want the Chinese authorities and Chinese businesses to adhere to it and obtain the same benefits for their economy. IPR protection is a long-term investment—it requires a good legal system, proper enforcement, and the business conviction that R&D and innovation are a better deal over the long term than the shortcut of violating IPR. China has made a lot of effort since joining the World Trade Organization in 2001 and the Intellectual Property Agreement (TRIPS). The Chinese authorities have adopted new legislation and are fighting to ensure proper law enforcement. The EU is helping China in this effort through a technical assistance program worth €15 million. We need more political support, and also a change of mind among many Chinese consumers and businesses.

Given the main trade items between the EU and China, what trends will affect two-way trade in the future?

The pattern of trade flow between China and Europe has been changing in recent years. In general terms, we see a trend where Chinese exports are shifting from low-cost, labor-intensive goods toward high-end, capital-intensive products. This trend is moving very quickly. In terms of trade in 2007, the EU exported to China around €71 billion-worth, a year-on-year increase of 12%. Chinese exports into Europe also grew very fast, to reach €230 billion. That represents an average increase of 21% annually over the last five years, creating a trade deficit of around €159 billion in 2007.

What are the main trade products? China is now the number one exporter into the EU, and 16% of all EU imports come from China. Machinery, electrics, and mechanical equipment are the most-imported items, including transportation equipment and parts for machinery. Textiles are losing weight among Chinese exports to Europe, though they are still significant. The EU has a trade surplus in one particular sector only—transportation equipment—which includes aircraft, cars, and trains.

What is the outlook for the flow of investment from Europe into China—and from China into Europe?

European investment into China is hard to measure, because very often investment transits through other regions, such as Hong Kong and other offshore locations. European investment is very important for China because of its high quality. It is particularly focused on high-tech sectors in manufacturing in-dustries, although in the last two years, we have seen important investments in the financial and services sectors. According to the Ministry of Commerce, the EU invested €8 billion in 2007 in high-tech sectors, which is twice that of the U.S. Japan for the same category was €6 billion. So, we are well ahead of the U.S. and Japan in high-tech investment. Europe is investing a lot in sectors with huge growth potential. It is also a result of the very open system in the EU, with no restrictions on high-tech trans-fers and exports.

Looking from the other direction, Chinese investments in Europe are still symbolic. So far, we have seen China investing in the manufacturing sector by acquiring some EU companies. Chinese investors are attracted by good technology and well-known brands, or both. Some well-known investments have been the acquisition of Thomson by the TV manufacturer TCL, and the acquisition of U.K. carmaker Rover by Nanjing Auto-mobile. In both cases, a well-known brand and the technology were the main reason for acquisition. More recently, we have seen acquisitions of companies and infrastructures linked to Chinese exports. For example, a Chinese company bought an airport in Germany for air cargo, and there have been investments in ports to create maritime hubs for Chinese maritime companies. In recent months, we have seen important investments led by state-owned enterprises and state agencies. The SAFE (State Administration for Foreign Exchange, under the People's Bank of China) acquired shares in TOTAL and British Petroleum, although it has not confirmed this officially. The purchase of a stake in Barclays Bank by China Development Bank (owned by the Chinese government) is the largest Chinese investment in the EU so far. The creation of China Investment Corp (CIC—China's Sovereign Wealth Fund) in the summer of 2007 is the latest important operation in Europe. The European Commission, and in particular EU Trade Commissioner Peter Mandelson, has reiterated the EU's openness to investment and welcomes CIC investing in Europe.

How fast is the growth in number of EU companies in China?

It is very difficult to say. Almost all big EU corporations are present in China. Some have a very strong presence, with factories and thousands of employees; others only have representative offices. There are two European manufacturing companies in China employing 40,000 workers each and producing exclusively for the Chinese market. The European Chamber of Commerce in China currently represents 1,300 members. Many of them are big companies, although around 300 or 400 members are SMEs. Including the national chambers, such as the German, French, Spanish, British, and Italian chambers, the total is maybe around 10,000 members. There are also companies outside of the chambers. But the number of companies isn't so important. What is important is the quality of their presence. Some big European companies have already been in China for more than 25 years. They are well established and conduct very important business in the manufacturing sector. They were the first wave of big investments in the 1980s. In the last five years, we had a second wave, mostly SMEs, attracted by China and also following the big corporations. This is clearly the case in the automobile sector. First, the big carmakers came; and then the SMEs, producing components, followed. It is a similar pattern in other sectors.

What is the general experience of EU companies in China?

The general experience is positive: EU companies have come to China to stay. They are bidding on a long and stable presence in China. What EU businesses would like to see in the future is more transparency and predictability in rule-making, more openness by the authorities to business concerns, and more recognition of the positive role played by foreign companies in China—creating jobs, bringing technology and know-how, and helping to create better respect for the environment and social rules. Sometimes, foreign companies feel that their positive contributions to China are not sufficiently recognized.

Because the rules sometimes apply differently in different provinces of China, the business environment can be difficult to navigate. In particular, big companies that operate all over the country may have to adapt their business operations to the different locations where they have a presence. Companies often complain that there isn't enough clarity in the way the rules are implemented in different parts of the country.

What would you say to a European entrepreneur thinking of starting a business in China?

A European wishing to expand his business into China should first ask himself, "Why come to China?" It is important to understand the purpose of doing business in China. Is it to produce and sell in China? Is it to produce in China for overseas markets or to export to Europe? Sometimes, investors don't think about these basic questions. Do you want to conduct your business alone or with a Chinese partner? If you want a Chinese partner, why, and what do you expect from your partner—that is, what is the added value your partner should bring? In some sectors, it is compulsory to form a joint venture; while in other sectors it is open. It isn't always better to go with a Chinese, and it isn't always better to go alone—it depends on the company, the sector, and the business conditions. The geographic location is important: are you targeting the whole Chinese market or a part of it? China is much bigger than the European Union and conditions differ from province to province. We always advise EU companies to take time to reflect on the best business plan and to prepare it carefully. When planning to produce and sell something that contains high-technology, it is important to ensure the necessary IPR protections. If the company holds patents in Europe, are they registered and protected in China? Do you know how much registration costs, and how long it takes? We strongly recommend getting adequate IPR protection in place before starting a business in China.

I recall one case of a European company that sent a sample of its machine to a potential Chinese buyer. Several weeks later, it found the machine had been copied and was on sale in China. A good engineer had gotten access to the machine, duplicated the parts, produced and assembled the machine, and even registered for a patent in China. Sometimes companies don't pay sufficient attention to registering their products and brands in advance.

Which sectors are most promising for future China–EU business ties?

High-tech in manufacturing still has a promising future, but European companies have even more potential and competitive advantage in the Chinese service sector. The full potential of the service sector is still not developed. In the financial sector — and in particular, insurance — there is huge potential: Chinese consumers need insurance for cars, for businesses, for life, pensions, and so on. Insurance companies in Europe have long experience.

In addition, Europe has a cluster of good construction companies for civil engineering and infrastructure — not only building, but also operating and managing, infrastructure.

Another sector where we Europeans are leaders in the world is environmental protection. This is a promising sector that will develop very rapidly in the coming years between Europe and China. Besides energy-efficient products, there are also services such as water treatment, cleaning, and filtering. The potential for environmental protection products and services is huge.

Relevant website

www.delchn.ec.europa.eu

China Trade Partner: India

Interviewee: Mr. Madhav Sharma, Chief Representative

Organization: Confederation of Indian Industries (CII) in Shanghai

Briefly introduce the presence of Indian companies in China now.

Indian companies in China are quite diversified, actually. There are pharmaceutical companies, electronics, electrical equipment, automotive components, automobiles, steel, rubber, and, of course, IT. There are more than 100 Indian companies already in China and the number is growing rapidly. In the past year (2007 to 2008), 15 to 20 new Indian-invested companies were established in Shanghai alone. Most of these companies had done business with China before and decided it is much better to have a representative based in Shanghai. For example, one of these companies, an auto company, has certain quality standards in India and the suppliers in China were not able to match them. So, the company sent a team here to do sourcing, and at the same time, help the suppliers reach a particular level of standards that could benefit the company in the long run.

What are the main challenges facing Indian companies in China?

Some mention language as one of the main challenges. Documentation and other information is all in Chinese. The interpretation of the legal documents is very difficult. Apart from that, not much.

Which sectors currently represent the best opportunities for Indian companies in China?

The auto industry is one sector, and IT is another. Indian companies are also focusing a great deal on pharmaceuticals, also a very promising sector. India is strong in the healthcare sector and in related services such as clinical research and development. There are some hospitals in China that have approached leading hospitals in India to form partnerships. Food processing is another area of opportunity.

In general, do Indian companies see China as a threat or an opportunity?

Indian companies see China as an opportunity—our types of business complement each other. China is an opportunity for India. People are not talking about India *versus* China, but about India *and* China. When we talk to our China counterpart, we always say "India with China." We have to take advantage of each other's strengths, and that's exactly what's happening.

What lessons can be learned from Indian companies in China? Have any Indian companies failed in China?

Not a single company [has failed in China]. Most Indian companies first establish a representative office here. They want to understand the complexity and the challenges of doing business in China. It's not that they come here, and tomorrow, they set up an office and do business. No, there is a whole learning process.

In terms of investment, Indian companies are investing more money outside the country than India is taking in as FDI. Indian companies have invested aggressively in Europe in the past, and now the same thing is happening in China. Some Indian multi-national companies now have factories in China, Vietnam, Thailand, and Malaysia. For example, one Indian company recently acquired a company in Guangzhou [in China's Guangdong Province]. The whole process took them at least 1.5 years to complete. They brought the board members to China to understand China. There is a proper due diligence, a step-by-step process. They are not coming here for short-term business; they are coming for the long term. Another example is an Indian TV company that is sourcing components in China. It established an office here and has already done US$3 million-worth of business. That's how Indian companies are operating. First, they come and start their rep offices, then they sell their products here, then they say, "OK, it's time to set up operations here." Then they buy the land and set up their factories here. They take a gradual approach.

Are Chinese companies investing in India?

There are only a few sectors. There are a few companies, but they are mostly focused on consumer goods and IT, such as Haier, Huawei, and TCL. Apart from these, there are a few companies that have invested in heavy machinery as well. The Zhejiang provincial government visited India to talk with Indian companies about collaboration. That's exactly what's happening now. One of the largest oil companies in India has already signed a contract with Sinopec to form a JV to invest in a third country.

There is a knowledge gap between our two countries. The CII (Confederation of Indian Industries in Shanghai) is trying to bridge that gap through our newsletters. We've launched a monthly newsletter called *China Pulse* sent to our members by internet. It talks about the Chinese economy, China and the world, China and India, and our activities. We also launched *Market Watch* in China. We identified five sectors—automotive, textile, food processing, pharmaceutical, and energy. These sectors offer tremendous opportunities between the two countries. We try to create awareness among Indian companies to focus on these sectors. In terms of food processing, we are trying to attract suppliers of Indian processed foods, spices, and Indian tea to come here. In term of Indian tea, Tata Tea has established a company in Hangzhou.

What is your advice to Indian companies that want to come to China?

Our response to Indian companies is that, as a newcomer here, they have to do their due diligence. They should be absolutely sure about who they are getting as partners. Similarly, we tell the same to non-Indian companies: do due diligence before forming a partnership with an Indian company.

If you want to find out anything about an Indian company, even if it's a small-scale company in India, you just go to its website and you will find out everything about it, including its audited financial statement. If you want to see its performance for the past five years, you can ask the company and it will send it to you. But it's different in China. That's one of the things we keep hearing, and one of the challenges Indian companies face — how can we conduct due diligence research here? Sometimes, they have to hire a consultant who can do a due diligence on a particular company. That's one of the challenges Indian companies certainly have here.

What trends are shaping the future of Indian business interests in China?

The bilateral trade volume between India and China is now about U$5 billion. If you see the composition of import and export between the two countries, India exports more raw materials as iron ore, cotton, and so on, whereas China is exporting more finished products such as electronics and machinery. The challenge we now face, in order to expand our trade basket, is to see more value-added exports from India to China, to make it more balanced. In terms of investments, Indian companies are growing globally, and they are also looking at China. Some Indian companies are in the process of setting up full-fledged manufacturing operations in China. Another IT company is coming here, which is the fourth or fifth IT company in India. Again, more and more Indian companies will gradually set up operations here. Some Indian banks have already set up offices in Shenzhen and Shanghai.

What is your opinion about China's future? Do you have any concerns about continuing to do business with Chinese companies?

I don't see any issues. If you travel to the interior of China, you generally don't see poverty; if you travel to any city, you will see that every city is developing very rapidly. China has now started to focus on the two critical challenges of IPR protection and environmental protection. The government has invested a huge amount of money in the construction of new airports and the upgrading of existing airports. You see the kind of infrastructure they have and the investment they have made in the energy sector. They are now making strategic investments in overseas markets of US$60 to US$80 billion over the next five years. They are also targeting the right places by focusing on Africa, which is a great opportunity. India is also focusing on Africa. Through *China Pulse*, we tell Indian companies that things are changing in China. China is reinventing itself every day, and every day brings something new. I don't think anything will stop China.

Relevant website

www.ciionline.org

China Trade Partner: Japan

Interviewee: Mr. Masaki Takahara, Vice President

Organization: Japan External Trade Organization in Shanghai

What is the general opinion of the Japanese about doing business in China?

They don't know much about China. They get information from the media, but Japanese TV often broadcasts the bad side of China, such as environmental pollution, forced labor, unsafe food, and so on. Japanese are now paying increasing attention to China, as its economy has been growing for the last 10 years and it is our neighbor.

Does the Japanese business community see China as a threat or an opportunity?

Some people think that Chinese take our jobs, because many plants are transferred to China. But the business community in general views China as a very good opportunity. That's why there are an increasing number of Japanese companies coming to China. Regarding the manufacturing industry, Japanese electronic companies are doing very well in China, and they supply not only to the Chinese market but also export to Southeast Asia and Europe.

What can your association, JETRO, do to promote mutual understanding between the two countries?

By promoting business relations, we enhance mutual understanding. This year, we sponsored the Shanghai International Film Festival, and 13 Japanese films were shown. We want to offer Chinese people a window to see Japanese culture and society, and film festivals offer such an opportunity. There are some Japanese organizations that promote tourism from China to Japan, but it's difficult for Chinese to tour Japan as individuals. Chinese have to join an organized tour, which can be very expensive. The travel-related procedure should be simplified.

What trends are emerging in China–Japan education ties?

There are a lot of Chinese students studying in Japan, and the number is growing. One reason for this could be that the Japanese government gives scholarships to Chinese students, and Japanese universities are willing to accommodate them. Our birthrate is only 1.3 for each couple, and the percentage of old people is increasing, so Japanese universities are competing with each other to get students. Meanwhile, Japan is sending more students to China. Chinese students mostly study in Japan on scholarships, otherwise they face difficulties living in Tokyo, or in other Japanese cities where the cost of living is high. But Japanese students pay for their studies in China. They come to

China to study new areas, which they think will make them more valuable as employees when they return to Japan. They also come to learn the Chinese language. More and more Japanese students are choosing now to stay and work in China. China is a country full of opportunities for Japanese.

What are the main challenges facing Japanese companies operating in China?

One of the biggest issues facing Japanese companies is being paid by Chinese companies. Chinese companies have a habit of delaying payment. Sometimes the Chinese companies disappear. In some areas, Japanese companies need to have a Chinese partner; sometimes, after they invest money, the company is taken over by the Chinese. This is a result of lack of business diligence on the Japanese side. I sometimes meet Japanese businesspeople who come to China after hearing that it is a great place to do business and who think, "Why not go there and make money?" They come to China without doing the due diligence on their partners.

What about protection of intellectual property rights for Japanese companies?

We have two members of our staff in charge of registration of property of Japanese companies. There is also an intellectual property group in Shanghai with more than 150 Japanese companies. We suffer a lot in this area. We have been trying to protect Japanese IP for many years. The best way to protect IP is to train workers, and keep computer security—for example, only allow a few staff access to key data.

What suggestions would you give to Japanese coming to do business in China?

Think it over seriously. Making money in China is not as easy as they think. When they want to have a partnership, they should do enough due diligence about the Chinese partner. Also, the Chinese business culture is different from Japanese culture.

Another issue is human resources; the job turnover rate is very high in China. In Shanghai, after two or three years, employees quit to join another company.

Which sectors are more promising for future development?

China is an ideal country for Japanese manufacturers to set up factories because of its lower labor costs. Japanese companies used to manufacture in China and export back to Japan, or to Southeast Asia and Europe. Now they have discovered the potential of the Chinese market itself. Manufacturers are doing well selling to the Chinese market. This is reflected in the number of Japanese living in China. This year, the registered number of Japanese living in Shanghai is 48,000. We estimate that the real number is more like 100,000.

But the current problem for Japanese in China is that production costs here are rising. It's very costly to have a factory in the coastal areas. Now, they are setting up factories in interior China or Southeast Asia. Japanese companies used to have a lot of investment in Southeast Asia, but after the financial crisis in 1997, investments moved to China. Now, they are thinking about going to second- or third-tier cities in China or back to Southeast Asia. It's hard to say which is a better choice—to set up factories in Chengdu or Chongqing, or in Vietnam or India. The political climate is also important. After the 2005 anti-Japanese demonstrations in China, Japanese manufacturers thought they should avoid the risk of putting all their investment in China. I know one Japanese washing-machine manufacturer that had a production line in China and exported from here to the world market. They wanted to set up a new factory in the interior of China, but after the demonstrations, they built their new production line in Thailand. Also, China's value-added taxes are getting higher.

Relevant website

www.jetro.go.jp/china/shanghai/

China Trade Partner: Mexico & Latin America

Interviewee: Mr. Rafael Valdez Mingramm, Vice President for Latin America

Organization: ChinaVest*

Do you think that Latin Americans generally have an accurate picture of China?

Not really. Even though Latin America has had strong historical ties with China—during the 16th and 17th centuries, trade between Mexico and the East Indies in spices, porcelain, and silver was substantial—it wasn't until recent years that China came to our attention again.

As the Mexican economy is still too closely related to the United States and our cultural heritage links us to Spain and Europe, most Mexicans haven't had a chance to visit, learn about, and understand the positive and negative effects of the Chinese phenomenon. I would say it is a combination of ignorance, uncertainty, and fear that still persists in most cases. For example, in my country, whenever someone doesn't understand something, he or she generally says: "*Esta en Chino!*" ("It's in Chinese!")

This perception is changing, though. Over the last three to five years, the government, private companies, and many individuals living in China have made concerted efforts to strengthen communication and commercial relations.

Is China perceived by the business community in Mexico as a threat or an opportunity?

Unfortunately, most medium-sized companies still perceive China as a major threat. Some industries, such as footwear and textiles, have increasingly suffered tough competition

---

* Rafael Valdez Mingramm is also co-founder of LatinamericanosEnChina.com.

from imported products from China, and therefore are pushing the government to enforce protective measures, review the system of tariffs and quotas in some sectors, and even to consider retreating from the WTO.

Large Mexican corporations and small entrepreneurs, fortunately, see China not so much as a threat and more as a big opportunity, not only to reduce production costs (outsourcing) but also to sell their products to China. In the last three years, companies such as Gruma (Maseca), Grupo Bimbo, and Grupo Alfa (NEMAK), among others, have made major investments in the region. In the same period, hundreds of young Mexican students and entrepreneurs have moved to China.

The online communication and information-sharing platform that we launched in November 2007 (www.latinoamericanosen-china.com) attracted 1,160 registered members within six months, roughly half in China studying or working, and half living abroad but interested in doing business with China.

What can be done to promote mutual understanding between Latin America and China?

First, we need to try to change our mindset and put in place long-term and sustainable solutions, rather than protectionist strategies. Chile took a different approach by signing a free trade agreement with China in 2005 that is having a positive impact on trade and cross-border investments in both directions. I am not necessarily suggesting that Mexico is in a position to follow a similar route, but we definitely need to find a way to avoid competition, specialize in high-tech, value-added products, and look for synergies.

Second, Mexico and China should promote more cultural, technological, and educational exchanges. Even though the governments of both countries have cooperated in these areas for some time, the private sector and civil society need to push in this direction as well. The Instituto Tecnologico de Estudios Superiores de Monterrey (TEC), one of Mexico's leading educational institutions, has taken a leading role by bringing 60 Mexican students every semester to study at different universities in China.

Such initiatives will hopefully incubate more Mexican entrepreneurs interested in doing business in China. Mexico also needs to have more cultural and business exhibitions in China.

What are the trade trends between Mexico and China?

Mexico's total trade is about US$400 billion per year. Ninety percent of this trade is still with the United States, but Mexico's second-largest trading partner is China. Imports from Mexico to China include synthetic fibers, raw cotton, steel, plastics, and electro-mechanical equipment, while China exports mainly household appliances, textiles, and chemical and high-tech products to Mexico.

Whereas other Latin American countries such as Brazil, Argentina, Chile, and Venezuela are increasingly supplying China with commodities such as copper, iron, and soybeans, Mexico and China still compete in a number of manufactured products that can generally be produced at a lower cost here. Again, Mexico needs to scale up in the manufacturing chain and find ways to collaborate and co-invest, benefiting from its unique location to produce and distribute products to the United States and Central America.

What investment trends are taking shape between China and Mexico?

Investment is still very limited, but examples are emerging. Gruma (Maseca) invested US$20 million to install a production facility in Shanghai to sell corn-based products to the Asian market; Grupo Bimbo completed a €9.2 billion acquisition of a baking company in Beijing in 2007; and Alfa's subsidiary, Nemak, acquired two production facilities in Nanjing. There are a number of smaller investments in consumer-related industries: el Fogoncito, a famous restaurant chain, has opened its first branch in Beijing; and Televisa has signed co-production agreements with Hunan TV and Shanghai Media Group to produce and broadcast soap operas in China. Mexican wine companies and tequila producers are finding their way to the Chinese consumer as well.

How about Chinese investment into Mexico?

Even though China's registered investment in Mexico is still very small, it is definitely growing. Lenovo is building a production plant in Monterrey; and the Chinese state-owned FAW Group Corp. and Grupo Elektra, a Mexican retailer and banking chain, both plan to sell Chinese-made cars in Mexico from early 2009. (The agreement calls for producing cars at a US$150 million plant to be built in the state of Michoacan by 2010.)

In other countries in Latin America, we have also witnessed a significant increase in Chinese investments. In Peru, China Aluminum Co. and other Chinese mining companies have acquired and invested in a number of mining assets; Baosteel has started its first overseas investment in a steel plant project in Brazil; and investments in land and agro-business in Brazil, Bolivia, and Argentina are also booming.

How fast is the growth of Mexican companies entering China?

There is no official data on the number of Mexican companies that have invested in China, or on the amount of investment, but it is definitely growing. Most Mexican companies are interested in exporting their products to China and selling through local retailers and distributors. A few companies have small procurement or representative offices in China to source materials to export to Mexico, or to market their products in China. There are still very few Mexican companies that produce in China.

In the last couple of years, a number of state governments have opened representative offices to help local businesspeople to identify business opportunities, find Chinese partners, and encourage Chinese investment abroad.

What generally has been the experience of Mexican companies in China?

Generally, it has been very positive, although it has taken longer for many of them to reach the desired results because adapting to local tastes and preferences, developing relationships with local suppliers, and finding the right employees are challenges that most of us tend to underestimate.

I am sure that there have been bad experiences as well, mainly with companies that didn't take sufficient time to check references and conduct due diligence of their suppliers and business partners.

What would you advise a Mexican entrepreneur who was thinking of investing in China?

I would recommend taking the time to observe and understand business practices in China, developing strong local relationships, and (ideally) partnering with a local. Above all, I would say: "Be patient—doing business in China is much more complicated than it seems." Also, I would advise them to try and pass the two-year learning curve, and to learn the language.

Which sectors are most promising for the future development of China–Mexico business ties?

In Mexico, there are a number of opportunities in tourism, infrastructure, agro-business (farm products), and mining. As the middle-income segment in China continues to grow and more Chinese travel overseas, there is a unique chance to promote tourist spots in Mexico. These might include beach resorts in Baja California, and nearby historical and cultural spots, serviced by direct flights between Shanghai and Tijuana. In the infrastructure sector, there are unique synergies between Chinese and Mexican construction companies for building ports. There are multiple opportunities as well in the automotive and spare parts industries.

Agro-business and mining are promising, as China is becoming a net importer of such commodities. Opportunities in China for Mexican companies and entrepreneurs are mainly in consumer-related products and services.

Relevant websites

www.LatinoamericanosEnChina.com
www.chinavest.com

China Trading Partner: Nigeria

Interviewee: Mr. Badeji A. Abikoye, Trade Commissioner

Organization: Nigerian Trade Office in Shanghai

Do most Nigerians have an accurate view of China?

Yes, I think most Nigerians have an accurate view of China through three sources: (1) the political and economic roles China is playing in Nigeria, and in Africa in general; (2) information from the Chinese agencies in Nigeria, and the Nigerian agencies in Nigeria and China; and (3) the important flow of trade and investment between our two countries. Investment is a powerful tool for knowledge transfer, business creation, and partnership.

Does the Nigerian business community see China as an opportunity or a threat?

In one way, China is considered a good opportunity, while in another way it is considered a threat by some members of the business community—especially those who used to make a good profit from selling cheap products. They lost business when Chinese businessmen came and offered cheaper, more affordable products for the Nigerian market.

What can you do from your position to promote mutual understanding between China and Nigeria?

First of all, there should be more exchange of information. Second, more conferences, seminars, and other political and economic activities should be organized by the two sides. The bilateral relationship between China and Nigeria has been growing dramatically in the last five years. Since 2001, tourism and trade have been boosted. The bilateral trading relationship is in favor of China.

What are the major trading items?

China exports to Nigeria mostly consumer products, light industrial products, machinery, building materials, and motor vehicles—especially motorcycles. Nigeria exports to China mostly crude oil and agricultural products (sesame seed and cocoa products)—mainly raw material products.

In which main sectors and industries do Nigerians invest in China, and vice versa?

China invests mostly in telecommunications and Chinese IT products. Chinese also invest in service industry businesses in Nigeria, such as restaurants. The investment flow from Nigeria to China is still very small—mostly in logistics, warehousing, and shipping.

What future trends do you expect to change the terms of exchanges of goods and investment?

I expect changes in the sectors of petroleum, manufacturing, and tourism. Nigeria allows foreign companies to invest in petroleum instead of merely doing petrol trading. Tourism is another area that can be further developed.

How fast is the influx of Nigerian companies into China?

It's difficult to know. In the city of Guangzhou alone, there are around 20,000 Nigerians working in trading, and the number is growing. We have a steady stream of visitors enquiring about how to open offices and start businesses in China. From these enquiries, I can say that there is substantial interest among Nigerians in investing in China.

What has been the experience of most Nigerian companies in China?

In Guangzhou, we have received some complains against Chinese companies. The main problem is that Chinese companies sometimes don't produce according to the contract.

What advice would you give to Nigerian entrepreneurs coming to China to do business?

First of all, know the rules and regulations and be sure to comply with them. They must know all the government resources and incentives available in order to operate under the most favorable business conditions possible. We ask them which province they want to establish their business in, and to explain their specific area of interest. We normally don't encourage people to set up a business in which they can't expect a quick return on their investment. We also advise them to take part in the China International Fair for Investment and Trade, held every fall in Xiamen. There, Nigerian companies can meet with their Chinese counterparts.

Looking ahead, which business sectors are emerging as the most promising for developing the China–Nigeria business relationship?

The areas of manufacturing, energy, tourism, and infrastructural development. Chinese are doing a lot of work in infrastructure projects in Africa. We also need power generation technology from China, as well as consumer goods. We should encourage increased trade.

Relevant website

www.nigeriaembassy.cn

China Trade Partner: South Africa

Interviewee: Mr. Vika M. Khumalo, Consul General

Organization: South African Consulate in Shanghai

Do you think South Africans have an accurate picture of China? How is their perception changing?

The perception and understanding of China among most African people dates back to the colonial period, during the time when South Africa and most African countries were going through liberation struggles. South Africa sent some of its military people for training to China. There has been a shift, from China being a brother in the liberation struggle, to China becoming a major trading bloc. As one of the developing countries, there is a very strong feeling that China is our friend and equal partner, not a nation that is going to dictate. The trade flow and volume between the two countries has grown exponentially over the past 10 years.

Is China perceived by the business community in South Africa as a threat or an opportunity?

We see China as more of an opportunity. China's economic growth and the Chinese market present South Africa with enormous opportunities—not only for natural resources to enter this market, but also other South African products. Whatever negative perceptions exist, they are overshadowed by the opportunity that doing business with China presents.

What can be done to promote mutual understanding?

There is always room for improvement in any relationship, especially between nations. The best methods we have identified to enhance the relationship are people-to-people connections such as educational exchanges, institutional linkages, and cultural exchanges. That is another area for improvement. We have sent cultural groups to perform in Hong Kong, Macau, Shanghai, and Beijing. And China has also begun to send groups to South Africa. Some of our universities have already entered into some relationships with their counterparts in China. That's a good start. Another avenue is sporting activities. We haven't engaged as much as we should with the Chinese in sports. The other area is to encourage R&D collaboration. There could be more collaboration in R&D because we do have some areas of common interest.

What trends are under way concerning trade between South Africa and China?

South Africa has a huge trade deficit with China, as do many other countries in the world. We are working on that. South Africa has mineral commodities; lots of natural resources. We would like to continue trading these with China. However, we want more value adding to be done in South Africa; this would assist us in creating more jobs, and providing more skills development and technology exchange. For example, South Africa also has a wine industry. Wine consumption in China is growing at 20% every year, which also presents a good opportunity for us to enhance our expertise in the wine sector. We also export citrus fruits and other agricultural products to China. There is a long list of items, but it's not long enough to offset the balance of trade yet.

China exports machinery, textiles, chemicals, and so on to South Africa. It has also now begun to sell cars to us. China hasn't yet begun to assemble and manufacture out of South Africa. The prices of Chinese cars are more competitive.

How would you characterize the flow of investment from South Africa into China, and what changes do you think will occur in the future?

South Africa has invested in a number of sectors in China. For example, SASOL is investing in coal-to-liquids plants; and Miller

SAB, whose roots are South African, now operates a significant number of breweries here. We also have other companies in road construction and media, such as MIH, as well as smaller companies in sectors from manufacturing to services.

And what trends can we expect in terms of Chinese investment into South Africa?

The ICBC (International Chinese Banking Corp.) just invested over US$5 billion in the acquisition of 20% of the shares of one of our largest banks, Standard Bank. There are other investments in other sectors—for example, mining, manufacturing, textiles, of course, as well as in sectors such as electronics, agro-processing, and smaller chemical industries. Chinese are also entering the services sector; we are seeing a growing number of Chinese construction companies. Mining is also growing, especially diamonds, gold, and chrome. We would like to see more investment in agro-processing, the energy sector, and the hospitality industry.

What is the experience of South Africans companies generally in China?

South African companies have generally had very good experiences here, but they have also faced ups and downs and challenges. Some companies have had to deal with IPR issues and bureaucracy . . . the usual problems one sees anywhere in the world.

What would you advise a South African entrepreneur thinking of coming to invest in China?

The first thing I would advise them to do is to find a Chinese partner who has good relationships in business and government, and who is reliable and with a good reputation. You need someone to hold your hand. It could also be a good idea to work through some of the business consulting companies in order to get the best professional assistance. A good partner can give you a competitive edge. Do your research and due diligence before you set up or select your partner. That's critical. Don't pick up a partner from the street. These are some of the things to consider. Also, location is very important.

Which sectors and areas are most promising for future development?

Mining—especially mining coupled with value adding. If you want to do mining in South Africa, we now encourage you to add value to the raw materials before they are exported. There are a number of opportunities in a wide range of sectors, from agro-processing to infrastructure development.

The other area is construction. South Africa is going through a construction boom, and this presents opportunities for a lot of Chinese companies. We are also focused on reducing poverty, so we favor investment in sectors that will benefit everybody and create new jobs. Tourism has huge potential. We would like to attract more than two million tourists from China to South Africa by 2010.

We see ourselves as the gateway to Africa. About 70% of what Africa buys comes from or through South Africa. We do most of our trade with Africa. Currently, South Africa is China's largest African trading partner.

China Trade Partner: United States

Interviewee: Ms. Brenda Lei Foster, President

Organization: American Chamber of Commerce in Shanghai (AmCham Shanghai)

Do you think Americans in general have an accurate picture of China? How has it changed?

I think that most Americans' impressions of China are colored by the media. Many Americans have never had the opportunity to travel to China and their perceptions are based on what they read or see on TV or hear from others. Luckily, there are an increasing number of good books, articles, and films that cover China. We all know how travel broadens the mind, and nothing could be truer of travel between the U.S. and China—with the opportunity it offers to build realistic and informed views of each other's countries. Tourism, educational exchange, and business travel all contribute to the balance of payments in both countries and build cross-cultural awareness and understanding. The more delegations that visit China, the more Americans can learn about China. I actually consider those Americans who visit China as ambassadors who can carry the message back to the U.S. as to what China is really like.

AmCham Shanghai does everything it can to contribute to this understanding through our programs, publications, and briefings in order to provide Americans with an accurate picture of China. Overall, however, Americans need to learn more about China.

Is China perceived as a threat or as an opportunity by the business community in the U.S.?

China is definitely perceived as an opportunity. This year marks the 30th anniversary of normalized U.S.–China trade relations. Over the years, we have established a solid relationship, with trade growing steadily to an all-time high of more than US$350 billion and an unprecedented level of dialogue between our governments. China is now the U.S.'s second-largest trading partner and our third-largest export market. Nearly every state in the U.S. has recorded triple-digit growth in exports to China since 2000, outpacing exports to the rest of the world. In addition, statistics from the U.S. Bureau of Economics in 2006 indicate that U.S. companies in China repatriated profits of US$4.5 billion back to the U.S. If we look at Shanghai alone, in 2007 U.S. companies invested in 4,700 projects which resulted in US$31 billion in trade between the U.S. and Shanghai.

It is also important to note that, based on our research, 75% of American companies that have operations in China are here to serve the Chinese domestic market or other markets abroad. Less than 25% are manufacturing products for export back to the U.S.

Clearly, the U.S.–China relationship is not without its challenges. Unfortunately, in the last year, China has been on top of American minds for a number of less-than-positive reasons, including food and product safety and quality, human rights, security issues, the trade deficit, and IPR. We found on our recent Washington, DC Door Knock that discussion of the trade deficit brought out a protectionist sentiment that is fueled in part by a constituency in the U.S. that is worried about the downstream impact of China's monetary policy on the jobs of U.S. manufacturing and agricultural workers.

But, we have seen this protectionist sentiment on both sides of the Pacific. China's drive to promote "indigenous innovation" is underpinning government policies and standards, government procurement, and other areas that threaten to exclude U.S. business from the Chinese market. AmCham Shanghai's business climate survey found that the drive for domestic innovation has affected U.S. companies somewhat negatively—in particular, policies regarding the import of technical and industrial equipment, as well as M&A policies protecting key enterprises, technologies, and brands.

I personally feel that defending and preserving the openness of the trade relationship should be the core political commitment of both the U.S. and Chinese governments. It is important that the U.S. realize that we are part of an integrated international economy and that this integration benefits the U.S.

What can be done to promote mutual understanding between the two countries?

The Strategic Economic Dialogue (SED) established by President Hu Jintao and President George Bush in 2006 is an example of high-level bilateral dialogue that has focused on transformational issues and changes. It has delivered real achievements, including in food and product safety and an aviation agreement. It provides for multi-agency discussions of the challenges affecting our two economies and seeks input from the business community. The structure itself has been emulated by both the EU and Japan as they develop their own strategic frameworks. Most importantly, the SED has created a culture of cooperation. It has proved to be more productive and positive in addressing concerns than Congressional legislation that might be viewed as being punitive and could elicit protectionist reactions.

Organizations such as AmCham Shanghai are committed to working with the U.S. and the Chinese governments to improve the bilateral business environment and to create opportunities for our member companies. As the oldest frontline organization for U.S. business in China, we act as a bridge between American business interests and the Chinese government on important commercial issues, whether it be at the national, provincial, or municipal levels. Our goal is to foster dialogue and affirmative engagement.

AmCham Shanghai also puts considerable effort into bringing first-hand information to the American business community, through our monthly magazine, *Insight*, our annual *China Business Report*, an annual *White Paper on Doing Business in China* which is done in collaboration with AmCham China and AmCham South China, and our new report on *China's Manufacturing Competitiveness* done with Booz & Company. Our *China Business Report* highlights the challenges and opportunities facing companies doing business in China; the *White Paper*, which represents the interests of more than 9,000 U.S. companies in China, provides recommendations to both the

Chinese and the U.S. governments; and our benchmark man-ufacturing competitiveness study tracks and identifies key trends and challenges that U.S. companies must face in order to stay competitive. In general, this study clearly highlights the need for innovation and the integration of the global supply chain.

Finally, one of the most important areas for increasing mutual understanding between the U.S. and China is in the area of Corporate Social Responsibility (CSR). American companies bring many best practices to their China operations. CSR programs are seen as an integral part of delivering business prosperity and sustainable economic growth. AmCham Shanghai itself supports partnerships between business and the Chinese community through our CSR Program, which has five major focuses: com-munity outreach, philanthropy, environmental stewardship, cor-porate governance, and employee health and safety.

What investment opportunities are there for U.S. companies in China? And, for China in the United States?

With regard to investment opportunities for U.S. companies in China, businesses with extensive expertise and experience in areas that address China's development agenda—such as fi-nancial services, new and high-tech industries, business process outsourcing and logistics, environmental technology, efficient energy and clean-tech technologies, healthcare, edu-cation and technical training, consulting, rural development, and other strategic sectors—will be given tax incentives and commercial opportunities. The service sector, with a target of US$400 billion by 2010, will be an increasingly important driver of GDP production, and one should not overlook the growing consumer demand in China and the opportunities it opens up in the retail sector. The policy shift in China away from high energy and resource-intensive industries toward higher-value-added, high-tech industries also offers opportunities for U.S. companies.

Currently, the top five U.S. exports to China are computers and electronics, transportation equipment, chemicals, waste and scrap metal, and machinery, except electrical.

Regarding investment opportunities for China in the U.S., I would highlight the example of Haier, which is one of China's "national champion" companies and a leading household appliance manufacturer. It entered the U.S. market in 1999 when it invested US$40 million in a 110-acre manufacturing facility in South Carolina employing over 300 people. Haier currently dominates the U.S. mini-refrigerator (dorm room refrigerators) market segment and is targeting the full-size refrigerator segment after the debut of its American-designed full-size model.

There are a growing number of Chinese companies interested in either investing in or sourcing from the U.S. It is important to support and nurture these partnerships to the mutual benefit of both countries. In recent years, China has shifted from being a recipient of foreign investment to being a global investor, investing US$18.7 billion abroad in 2007, including shares in Blackstone and Morgan Stanley. The level of outward FDI is expected to increase significantly in the near future, with predictions of up to US$37 billion as Chinese companies go global, attract international talent, secure resources, acquire technology, and leverage their huge domestic market and strengths in manufacturing.

AmCham Shanghai regards the acquisition of American companies and assets by Chinese corporations as a natural element of China's integration into the global economy and as something that deepens the U.S.–China trade relationship. Chinese FDI brings economic benefits to the U.S. economy, including job creation, promotion of research and development, and enhancement of U.S. exports to China, just as investment from other countries do.

What in your opinion, are the main challenges of doing business in China?

According to our 2007 *China Business Report*, U.S. companies continue to be optimistic about doing business in China and see it as a strong investment destination, with many planning to expand throughout the country. Seventy-five percent of companies view China as a key strategic market in their overall global strategy.

Despite the positive business outlook and improved operating margins, the top five challenges facing U.S. business that were highlighted were human resource constraints, unclear regulations, inconsistent regulatory interpretation, lack of transparency and bureaucracy, and intellectual property rights. The rankings of the major perennial operational challenges have scarcely changed in the last three years and are persistent business challenges dating back to 1999. Several of our businesses also agreed that China is losing its competitive advantage due to rising costs, with the biggest financial impact coming from price pressure from competition and from major customers, salaries and wages, changes in commodities and raw material prices, distribution costs, tax expenses, and real estate cost inflation.

What is your advice for Americans contemplating starting a business in China?

The six Ds: due diligence, due diligence, and due diligence. You need to know the market, the laws, rules and regulations, the culture, and the people. It is important to understand that how you do business at home doesn't necessarily translate to how business is conducted in China. China is an incredible, dynamic, and complex market that requires a fast learning curve and the ability to be flexible. China is also not for everybody. It is still a country in transformation. Someone once said, if you can exist in ambiguity, you will do very well in China. If not, China is not for you.

I encourage everyone to come to China to see for themselves. Come and look at the market—at its benefits, opportunities, and potential—but note that it doesn't come without risk and challenge.

How do you see the future of China in terms of business and trade?

I am very positive about China, but I feel its success will depend to some extent on how it balances its domestic economic and social agendas as it emerges as a global stakeholder. It will need to embrace a mindset that includes a commitment to the WTO principles of transparency, national treatment, non-discrimination, and market access in order to improve the quality of economic growth, while at the same time focusing on an innovative society based on open markets, IPR, the rule of law, and a sound financial infrastructure. Clearly, tackling the challenges articulated by China's leadership of energy efficiency and security, sustainable development, environmental protection, healthcare, and income inequality are issues that need to be resolved. Given China's rapid ascent over the last 30 years since the opening of economic reform, I have no doubts that they are up to the task.

Relevant website

www.amcham-shanghai.org

Index